Naked Eye

By the same author

Hemingway: The Toronto Years (Doubleday, 1994)

Naked Eye

by William Burrill

INSOMNIAC PRESS

Edited by Jenny Anttila
Copy edited by Lloyd Davis & Liz Thorpe
Designed by Mike O'Connor

Canadian Cataloguing in Publication Data

Burrill, William, 1954-
     Naked eye

Collection of columns originally published in eye Weekly.
ISBN 1-895837-31-6

I. Title.

PS8553.U694N34 1998   081   C98-930292-X
PR9199.3.B87N34 1998

The publisher gratefully acknowledges the support of the Ontario Arts Council.

Printed and bound in Canada

Insomniac Press
393 Shaw St.
Toronto, Ontario, Canada, M6J 2X4
www.insomniacpress.com

To Mike Walton and Paul Rimstead — wish you were here.
(And to P.J. O'Rourke for the inspiration, help and the hair-do tips).

Some special people helped to make this book possible — please do not hold it against them! Thanks to Debra Aronson, Bill Reynolds, Donna Lypchuk, Deanna Dunn, Kevan Buss, Stephen Lungley, Greg Boyd and everyone at Eye Weekly except Nathalie Ayotte. Many thanks to John Honderich, Andrew Go, Steve Jarrett and everyone at The Toronto Star who believed in Eye Weekly. Love to Heather for being Heather and being there and for believing my assertion that I am hard at work even when I seem to the untrained eye to be asleep and/or partying till dawn (honest — I do some of my best work when I'm unconscious!). Thanks to my mother Vivienne Trudeau and my late father Scott Burrill for coming up with the original concept of me. Thanks to Ernest Hemingway, P.J. O'Rourke, Hunter S. Thompson, Dave Barry, Kurt Vonnegut, Raymond Chandler, Elmore Leonard, Joey Slinger, The Weekly World News and K-Tel advertising department for helping me mold my writing style. Thanks to William New and the El Mocambo and Richard and the Bamboo for generous use of your stages even when you knew I had a guitar. Thanks to Ziggy Lorenc, Moses Znaimer and CITY-TV/Bravo!, Clifton Joseph, Daniel Richler, Brian Fawcett, Humble Howard Glassman, George Stroumboulopoulos and CFNY, Larry Solway at TALK 640, Jim Richards at CFRB and the boys of 'Game' at the FAN 590. (Sorry it cost you your jobs but I sincerely believe you will work in this town again someday). Thanks to my official 'Naked Eye' and/or 'Burrillapalooza' bands including Art Alexakis & Everclear, Craig Downie, Rodent & Enter the Haggis, Maria Del Mar., Hugh Dillon, The Vox Band, Michelle and Jon of It's Patrick, Megapop, C.J. O'Connor & Mark Holmes, and to Jane Siberry for the neat stuff. Special love to others out there — you know who you are — who I can't name on the grounds that I might incriminate ourselves. Many, many thanks to Mike O'Connor, Jenny Anttila and everyone at Insomniac Press for believing in and publishing this book without revealing that, if people don't buy several thrill-packed copies each, your elderly mom will not be able to afford the life-saving operation and you'll have to sell your sickly child's beloved puppy. Thanks to all you new readers, to whom I say, 'welcome aboard. And hang on tight. And — lastly but most importantly — fondest thanks to all my long-time faithful readers who have stuck with me on this bumpy ride even when I often had one wheel in the ditch. This is all your fault.

— William Burrill
Toronto
April, 1998

table of contents

Preface by Donna Lypchuk 9
The Ballad of William Burrill by Bill Reynolds 11
Putting the Deadbeats to Work 13
A Modest Proposal Concerning the Homeless 15
Jesus Christ Superstar 17
How I Saved Kurt Cobain from Certain Death 19
The Big Bad Sleep 21
My Life as a Dick 24
The Substitute 26
Kids These Days 28
Doin' The Cosmo Hustle 30
Ask Dr. Burrill… 33
The Scum Also Rises 36
All in a Day's Work for the Professional Writer 38
Taking the "High" Out of Hi & Lois 42
Don't Sleep in the Subway, Baby 44
Hey Gen X, "McJobs" Are Not Exclusive To You! 45
Ban These Songs Immediately 48
Homespeak: A Buyer's Guide 50
Biff and Muffy Get Naked! 51
Square Boy Gets No Vinyl 52
Stratford Memories 54
If You Go to San Francisco… 56
Holy Shitimachi, I'm Turning Japanese! 58
Totalled in Tokyo 60
The Long Hot Summer 61
Psych 101 63
Our Man in Cartagena 65
You Just Gotta Laugh 68
City on Fire 70
There Are Some Things You Just Can't Outsmart 71
A Blowhard in the Windy City 73
I'm Bullish on the Power of Bull 76
God's Got the Pioneer Spirit 78
Pro Athletes: It Takes Real Men to Pat Bums 80
A Most Un-Gentlemanly Round of Golf 82
Rockin' by the Seat of His Pants 84
Repent and Save Your Souls!!! 87
A Sloth in Summer 90

Dog Day Afternoons 92
Roughing it in the Bush   93
Have a Horrible Halloween 96
Do the Right Thing 98
The Investment of a Lifetime 99
Read This if You Have No Class 101
Fifteen Easy Steps to Proper Student Nutrition 103
The International Draft Beer Conspiracy 106
Cuba's Hemingway Trail 107
Into the Liver of Darkness 109
You're a Poet, but You Don't Know it 112
Gone with the Broken Wind 113
Insomnia Alert! 115
Here Comes Your 19th Nervous Migraine 117
Seinfeld Prompts Rash of Home Invasions! 120
A (Barely) Living Medical Miracle 122
Toronto Hopeless 125
A Handbook for the Casket 128
Christmas Party Etiquette for the Hopeful Survivor 130
Stop the Insanity of New Year's Resolutions 132
Which Way Ya Goin', Billy? 135
The Agonies of Victory 138
The World of High Finance 140
Four Legs, Hairy Tail, the Whole Bit 142
Beer & Loafing in Las Vegas 145
Hack Like Me 150
The King of Heaven and Earth 153
Weasels Ripped Our Flesh! 155
Career Opportunities 162
Europe on $0 a Day 165
From Here to Paternity 169
How to Get Ahead in Newspapers 171
Street Level 173
Greetings, You Ignorant Savages 176
A Writer's Life 178
Farewell My Belly Rat 179
Zen and the Art of Nose-twisting 180

Preface

William Burrill.

William Burrill is not just the name of a famous writer who writes a column called *Naked eye* for Toronto's popular alternative newspaper *eye*, he is also a sentence (see first sentence). William Burrill deserves to be his own sentence because all you have to do is say the words "William Burrill" to someone and they know exactly what you mean. Then they laugh out loud and order another beer. That is, of course, if they are not mistaking his name with the name of another famous writer whose name is pronounced the same. Then they tend to laugh out loud and do some more heroin.

Like Hunter S. Thompson and P.J. O'Rourke before him, Burrill is a conquistador of this mysterious terrain we call modern, urban living. He can find the Fountain of Youth in a glass of beer, Poetic Justice in the sound of birds splattering droppings on his car, and the Powers of Divination between a pet dog's ears. He has run for Mayor of Toronto and mysteriously. . . lost. He has sat in the same cafes in Toronto as Ernest Hemingway and mysteriously. . . not committed suicide. He has eaten raw death (suffered migraines) and mysteriously. . . written a column at the same time. He has appeared bare nekkid in *eye* and mysteriously. . . not been ashamed. He is also someone who has sacrificed a glamorous, well-paying job as an editor at *eye* (a publication he helped get off the ground) to become a lowly hack like myself, all in the name of entertaining you—the dear reader.

Bill is very dedicated to his craft . . . oops, I mean Kraft dinner, which you will find a step-by-step guide to producing in the following pages.

Aside from being a famous writer, Bill is also a generous philanthropist, great teacher and extremely funny. At one point in my life, when I, Bill's fellow columnist, did not have the money to pay for a root canal, Bill somehow convinced *eye*'s readers to send money to help me out. Although this was extremely embarrassing, I did pay half my dental bill with the generous results of Bill's Donna-A-Thon. (freelance writers don't have dental plans and we have to stick together.)

Bill is also very concerned about the youth of today. In this book you will also find painful step-by step instructions on how to become a famous writer with plenty of free time to sunbathe in cafes and drink away the rest of your days. . . like Bill. Bill has also made the rest of us at *eye* laugh again and again. . . especially when he gets onstage with his electric guitar and sings.

Some of the columns have made me laugh out loud on occasion, too.

People often ask me how it was that I, Donna Lypchuk, came to be a writer at *eye*. Sometimes they even phrase it as a question, as in "Who's the idiot responsible for hiring you at *eye*?"

I look at them straight in the eye and reply with my favourite sentence in the whole world:

William Burrill.

Then they laugh and order another skull-shaped tattoo.

—Donna Lypchuk
March, 1998

The Ballad of William Burrill

Bill Burrill's got horseshoes up his ass. Anyone ever tell you that? It's true. Here's why.

When I first met Bill, he had just left the *Toronto Star* to hang out at the non-union shop, *eye*. But he still had obligations. When he was in special projects at the *Toronto Star*, Bill was tapped to take part in the massive 1892-1992 *Star* centenary project. Bill was assigned the task of writing about one of his heroes, Ernest Hemingway, who had been a *Star* reporter in the 1920s. Okay, Bill probably invented the job for himself, but here's a guy doing his duty, trying to make the *Star*'s anniversary celebration seem as exciting as he can and what does he find? Thirty lost stories by Hemingway. Next thing you know, Boom!! Bill's on every TV and radio station in town, his section's been syndicated around the world, it's a major, major news event, he makes the mothership a pot of cash and he parlays the find into a book deal with Doubleday. Horseshoes.

Yes, Bill was in on the basement floor of *eye*, and was hired to be the paper's first managing editor. Bill wanted to create a sophisticated new weekly newspaper. Initially, he didn't exactly know what he wanted, but he sure knew what he didn't want. He thought a cross between *Lampoon* and *Mad* might work, something as far away from the politically correct mush out there as possible.

Those early days were nothing but a massive cattle call of writers — many bylines did not appear in the paper more than once or twice. As managing editor, Bill didn't really have the heart for cruelly editing other people's work. He would roll his eyes after reading the latest eye-glazing art or dance piece and plead, "I can't do anything with this! The lead's buried! It's as flat as piss on a plate — aaaarggg!" You see, bad writing actually made Bill physically ill. He would lament to no one in particular, "I don't want to be chained to this fuckin' desk any longer!"

But Bill had great plans for *eye*. And he did prod the troops occasionally. The best office gizmo he used, aside from the fake beeper blasts used to disappear from boring meetings, was the gold-ink 100% Pure Bullshit stamp. Bill didn't use it much, but when he did, look out. I got it once. Some huge, shapeless cover story I had to edit about the 1993 Big Bad and Groovy tour, Canada's lame answer to Lollapalooza. I had already toiled for hours when he nailed me with the stamp. Boom!! I had to come in on the weekend, phone the writer, and get more loads of crap to edit. Thanks, Bill. I really learned something after that. Like, you get that stamp out again and I'll stuff you into that desk of yours.

Somewhere around the spring of '93 Bill and I came up with the idea for the *Naked eye* column. I think the first one was about Bill's personal form of fear and loathing at SkyDome, with its endless concrete corridors and its SmokeCave stuck in the most inconvenient spot imaginable and its SkyFoam piss water and its bad Huxlean vibe — here, sit down, have a McDLT, have some pale yellow liquid, marvel at the JumboTron, see spot run, aaaaaaaaaarrrggg!

Bill still files a *Naked eye* column every week . I don't know whether he ever thought it would last as long as it has. He still plays his rock music loud at home, still screens his calls like the credit card goons are coming through the wires any second, and still has his own way of doing things. His version of a laptop computer is an antiquated Macintosh Classic — he unplugs it, carries it under his arm, and brings it into work. "Here's my story." Bill, ever heard of floppy disks? Oh, whatever.

Bill's written about his life, his Toronto, and his craziness over the past five years. Some of these exploits are included here. Of course I recommend this book — I edited most of the columns the first time 'round. But hey, this is a sick, twisted world, and the only sensible remedy is a few laughs from the sick, twisted mind of William Burrill. (Regular readers of *Naked eye*, please note that you are sure to appreciate the satiric mayhem again, especially with anthology editor Jenny Anttila's very fine sequencing.)

Don't think about yourself, think about Bill. You'll be supporting humour in this great land of ours, and Bill'll get paid twice for the same stories.

Like I said, fucking guy's got horseshoes up his ass.

— Bill Reynolds, Editor, *eye Weekly*

Putting the Deadbeats to Work

There are only two certainties in life: death and taxes.

And our short-sighted government is missing the boat on a sure-fire way to cash in on these facts.

Our leaders have been going through the social services and other important public programs with a meat cleaver, all in the name of saving a buck.

What about the poor? "Let them eat Kraft Dinner."

What about the jobless? Their solution to this trifling problem is so simple that it is ingenious: If you don't have a job you should get one. Then you won't be jobless any more!

It's a dirty job, but someone has to use their head around here, and I guess that's me.

This is where my plan comes in about cashing in on death and taxes.

No one can deny that the public has a fascination with death. Have you ever seen the traffic jams — technically called "gawker's blocks" — as people slow down to take a long look at a particularly messy fatal car wreck?

People love staring at corpses.

And with the social spending cuts, we're going to have a surplus of those pretty soon.

With this in mind, I suggest that our leaders take a fact-finding mission to Guanajuato, a town in the mountains of Mexico close to where I used to have a house when I lived for a year in San Miguel de Allende.

In Guanajuato, it's more then just death and taxes: they actually tax the dead.

Once you're buried, your relatives have to pay taxes on your grave, so that's one new source of revenue. But here's the kicker for those who've kicked it in Guanajuato: if the family doesn't cough up the coffin tax — or if there is no next of kin — then the government simply digs up the delinquent corpses and puts them on display in a public museum.

By happy coincidence, the corpses are very well-preserved, because there's something in the soil of Guanajuato that magically turns its dead into mummies, or as they say in Spanish, Las Momias.

So the town has turned its Momias de Guanajuato into a huge profit-making venture: People line up for hours to pay to wander through this dank, dungeon-like maze where you can gawk at the bodies, some naked, some dressed in the clothes they were buried in.

For easy identification, each mummy has a sign to tell his or her name and story: a mother who died in childbirth with a withered baby still attached by the umbilical cord; a hanging victim with the rope still around his neck; a bloated drowning victim; a shrivelled, sadly dressed peasant who was planted in 1959 in what must have been his best shabby suit and blocky black shoes.

What really draws a crowd are the rows and rows of little babies, dressed in sweet frilly baby clothes, like cute little baby apple-dolls. Only they're real human beings.

Or at least were.

There are hundreds of mummies to inspect.

And plenty more where they came from.

Unlike the ho-hum historical detachment of looking at a mummy who is thousands of years old, these are bodies who have only been in the ground for a couple of decades. These are ex-people who probably still have living friends and relatives (albeit relatives who shamefully didn't pay their grave taxes). I've seen some gory sights in my travels but for pure hurl-ability, Las Momias de Guanajuato is easily the most disgusting and unsettling display I have ever stared and stared and stared at. You can't help but stare. You can't help but think... And, guys, as for what happens to your weenie in the Great Beyond, you do not want to know. (I'll never eat one of those Pepperettes again.)

Anyway, I can assure you that the tourists who flock to Guanajuato love it. And when the tourist comes back out of the crypt — if he or she still has an appetite — there are dozens of hawkers and peddlers selling skull- and corpse-shaped candy. Mmmm. And think of the postcard, T-shirt and souvenir revenues.

There's no reason we couldn't do the same thing here.

As for a permanent home for "The Mummies and Pappies," what better spot than the Planetarium?

We could dig up all the welfare bums and put them on display in the newly named Necrotarium.

Of course, people don't naturally mummify in our soil so we may have to cheat a little. I'm sure some kind of freeze-drying gadget could be cheaply concocted. Get the idea boys together and throw money at it. They'll find a way.

It would be a great way to put those who stiff on their taxes to work. Even after they've starved to death on your handy monthly meal plan.

And it's a slam dunk that you could get a baloney or macaroni and cheese company to serve as a major corporate sponsor. You could even come up with a cheap entrance fee and a catchy slogan. Like "They're stiff — but our prices aren't!"

Or simply "Dig it — we did!" The radio commercials could be dubbed over the song "How Dry I Am."

Finally! A sensible and money-making plan to put the "deadbeats" to work.

A Modest Proposal Concerning the Homeless

I have a modest proposal...

It is a sad thing to walk through the icy streets of our city and see the homeless freezing to death on the sidewalk — all the sadder because their refusal to seek shelter makes their inevitable death by exposure not only a waste of human life, but an unsightly eyesore in a city that prides itself on keeping its streets tidy. This is not to mention the added tax burden of a pauper's funeral. Government officials have washed their hands of the case, saying there is simply nothing to do about the sidewalk pauper-sicles we trip over daily. That leaves it to this author to do some swift thinking and come up with said modest proposal to ameliorate this tragic and unsightly situation. Here, dear reader, is my plan, which I am sure you will agree is unusual but extremely practical.

First, I propose that all tragically frozen souls be moved not to the city morgue but the nearest charity food bank. A medical "chop shop" — for lack of a more humanitarian and delicate term — will first strip each John or Jane Doe of any usable parts, thus relieving the shortfall in our strained human organ donor program. Don't expect many useful livers, but you might find a cornea or even a heart that is still recyclable. A street person would die happy knowing that, through their sacrifice, another might live.

Next, the meat of the corpse will be Government Inspected for health reasons and any carcass with a clean bill of health will be set aside for local consumption. Tainted bodies will be ground and canned and donated to the starving hordes of the Third World, who, let's face it, will eat anything. And if the occasional can of tainted meat should cause a Third World death through food poisoning — unfortunate, yes, but call it a form of mercy: The famine-stricken lands will not miss a few hungry mouths. A win-win situation.

As for the frozen street carcasses that pass stringent Grade A meat inspection, volunteer butchers and chefs will combine to create hearty and healthy dishes for the hungry of this city. "A healthy human body could feed a dozen starving people," one chef said. "The human meat — especially from the tender regions of the fore and hind quarters, flank, loin and ribs — can be prepared in any number of delicious ways, with a taste not unlike pork or lean chicken."

Many other usable body parts can be stewed, roasted, baked or boiled —

and the scraps, chefs assure us, can be turned into an exquisite fricassee or ragoût. Homeless wanderers who stray into traffic and have been run over a few times are ready-made, microwaveable and surprisingly tasty "Road Pizza." It is ironic, one might argue, that those who died for lack of dough may end up literally rolling in it.

As for the leftover scraps —known technically as "Whiffle" — these ears, noses, fingers, toes and other bits we shall not discuss will also serve charity by being ground into hot dogs. These will be used to set up conscripts with their own weenie-vending concessions around public gathering spots which — thanks to this proposal — will no longer have to be sold to cut government spending.

"One of the beauties of this plan is that we will not have to build expensive refrigeration units to preserve the meat," said one spokesman. "I mean, they're already frozen solid. We just leave them in the parking lot until we need them. Nature's perfect frozen dinner."

In the spirit of self-sufficiency for the poor, a homeless person who does not technically die, but, say, loses only his or her legs to frostbite can be fed on their own flesh, sparing an additional drain on the food bank and saving even more government money for opera houses and ballets and grants to writers who win prestigious prizes because their books are so brilliantly penned that it takes a month to try to read the first page. "We might even be able to contribute more to NASA," said a federal spokesman. "Did you know that in 1993, NASA lost $537 million just in things that didn't work or blew up? Imagine if we could achieve that status! We'd give an arm and a leg for such honours, so why shouldn't the homeless? At least they would know they were eaten for a good cause."

A government suggestion to flay the carcasses to make winter gloves for the needy was rejected by this author as being in extremely poor taste. "We are not savages," I said in my angry memo to the government. "ARE WE NOT MEN AND/OR WOMEN?"

If there is — as there surely will be under current political conditions — an overstock of homeless meat, a number of community-minded fast food franchises have offered to make sure that none goes to waste and no street person freezes in vain. The names Ham Beggar, McBeggar, Hot Doug, Bob Bits, West Queenie Weenie, Meat Loafer, John Doe-Nuts, Oh Oh Henry!, Scummy Bears and Side Wok have already been copyrighted (as well as the sales pitch, "Will you have FLIES with, um, THAT?"). The revenue from the franchises will bolster the city coffers. The Chilean Soccer Team has already placed a lucrative advance order.

So many other advantages to this cheap, easy and effectual plan can be enumerated that I am confident that it shall be widely embraced: We the citizens may have an overabundance of frozen vagrants but I beg that this fact does not freeze the charitable heart. I seek no personal glory in this venture other than to beseech that, for the good of all, my modest proposal be swiftly adopted into the law of the Frozen North.

Let the sound ring out in every sidewalk heating vent in this fair town: "Drink, Die and Be Merry — For Tomorrow WE may be EATEN!"

Jesus Christ Superstar

With Chanukah tomorrow and Christmas less than three weeks off, the holiday season is upon us and some people are turning their thoughts once more to Jesus Christ. You know, with the beatific smile, the martyr-like pose, the Little Children Come Unto Me open-armed stance, peaceful eyes gazing heavenward, quietly enduring his suffering.

But is that really what The Assistant Big Guy was like? Not according to a story I read in the paper. A new interpretation of the Bible by A Noted Bible Scholar says that, far from his dry, pious image, the real Jesus was a fun-loving guy who loved nothing better than to crack wise and guzzle the wine.

Religious scholar Robert Funk heads a panel called the Jesus Seminar, which is seeking to blow some of the must and dust off the Divine One. Need proof? Check the Bible under Matthew 11, Verse 19: "The Son of man came eating and drinking and they say, 'Look, a glutton and a drunkard!' " Funk also says Jesus was perhaps the world's most famous stand-up comic: "Jesus was very funny. He said things that were sharp and barbed and witty."

This is comforting to hear because at least we can rest assured that, when Christ makes His return to Earth, He'll have a gig lined up for Him as a gag Man.

We take you now to Caesar's Palace in Las Vegas. The marquee outside blazes the words "Christ: The Comeback Performance." But the man in the rhinestone robe who is holding down centre stage really needs no introduction. Here, live from Vegas, we give you... JEEEEEE-sus CHRIST.

CROWD: [Ten-minute standing ovation.]

CHRIST [Modestly waving for silence as he sips on his ninth large grail of wine]: "Thank you, thank you, ladies and Gentiles... It's great to be back. But seriously, folks, being the Son of God isn't all laughs. I mean who else has to go to their Old Man and say, 'Take my life... PLEASE!' " [Ka-boom].

Audience: [Laughter.]

JESUS: "Yeah, My Old Man, He can drive a Guy meshuggah! He's forever kvetching, 'What is it with the wine. All day long, all night long, the wine. People are talking. They're saying take this wine because it is the blood of Jesus — and they ain't kidding.' But I say, 'Dad, YOU were the One who taught me how to make water into wine and to make fish multiply, and, believe Me, when you're out on a date, what do you think works better? An endless bottle of wine or a whole lot of stinky fish?' I mean, I know Mary Magdalen is easy, but even she is always whining, 'Jesus, you smell like a multitude of dead fish. Take a bath, for Christ's sake.' [Ba-boom]. The Old Dad doesn't like Mary much. He's always after Me, saying, 'Jesus, what do You see in her? Don't You know she's a PROSTITUTE?' I said, 'Dad, Dad, what does her religion have to do with it?'"

AUDIENCE: [A smattering of uncomfortable giggles.]

JESUS: "No, but seriously. My Folks don't understand sex. Try asking about the 'birds and the bees' from a mother who's a virgin. [Ba-boom]. And it's tough being an only Child. Oy vey, let me tell ya. My Mother, God love her — and He did, the way the gossip goes — is forever bragging about me. 'My little Jesus. He can walk on water,' she says. 'Show them, Son.' So I walk on the water, sink and almost drown. Ma says, 'What's wrong, Jesus? You could always walk on water before.' I say, 'Yeah Ma, but that was before I had these holes in my feet!' [Ba-ba-boom-bing-bang!] Ma says, 'You never give to the poor any more.' I tell her, 'Ma, I try to beg for alms but the coins keep falling through my palms.'"

AUDIENCE: [Groans.]

JESUS: "Ooooh? My act isn't good enough for ya? I was thinking of bringing out Barry Manilow to warm you up but then I figured, nah, you folks will be in Hell soon enough. Speaking of Hell, say hi to Judas and Hitler while you're down there. Don't worry. Hell ain't so bad. The trouble with eternal damnation is all the waiting around..."

AUDIENCE: [Dead silence.]

JESUS: "You think you're a tough crowd? You don't know from tough crowds. When I used to play the Forum in Rome in the old days, I wasn't the main event. I was the main course. [Ba-boom] But seriously, a lot of people asked why I was crucified instead of hanged. That's because it looks better for your followers to make the Sign of the Cross than to go like THIS! [Feigns his neck snapping, head jerking to one side, eyes and tongue comically bulging.]

AUDIENCE: [Even deader silence.]

JESUS: "Listen, I have the power to bring people back from the dead but in your case I'll make an exception... [Jesus waits for rim-shot but drummer is snoring.] ... Yeah... so... like I was saying... I'm a professional stand-up. But lately I've been losing it. I saw a shrink and said, 'What's wrong with me, doc? Am I nuts?' He said 'No. You're Jesus Christ. No wonder you're feeling hung up.'

AUDIENCE: [Heckling, throwing stuff.]

JESUS: [Picking on hecklers] "Hey lady: Nice high heels! I used to wear shoes like that but now I prefer flats. Those spikes were just killing me... And you, sir. You in the front row. I thought the assholes were supposed to be in the rear... Nice crowd you are. At least Judas kissed me before he turned on me... Do the words 'pillar of salt' mean anything to ya? I could put in one call to the Old Man and He'd make you an offer you can't refuse. Only with a crowd like this, it'd be more like an offer you can't understand... Why doncha all go hit the casino and gamble. Maybe you'll win my robe [Jesus rips off his robe in disgust and tosses it into the fleeing audience. He turns his now-bare ass to the crowd]. KISS MY ASS! And let me turn the other cheek so you can do BOTH sides."

Historical Note: The Jesus Comeback Tour closed after one night but true believers still called it a miracle. It proved beyond a shadow of a doubt that a man can die up on the boards more than once.

.How I Saved Kurt Cobain from Certain Death

My first meeting with Kurt Cobain (in April 1994) came about as a case of mistaken identity — but it was a mistake that would end up saving Cobain's life.

That's right. Kurt is still alive, and I saved him.

It started with a rambling telephone call from a guy who claimed to be Kurt Cobain and who desperately needed to talk to me. Of course, I didn't believe it was Cobain and hung up. But he persisted in calling and I finally had a buddy down at 51 Division trace the calls: It was Cobain all right, direct from his Seattle home.

So, next time he called I said, "What can I do for ya, Kurt?"

"Are you William Burroughs, the writer?"

"No, I'm William Burrill, the writer."

"But you did write a thing called *Naked Lunch*?"

"No, I write a thing called *Naked eye*..."

"Close enough for rock 'n' roll," he slurred. "Be on the next plane to Seattle. And hurry, man. I'm desperate. Here's the address..."

Seattle. No one answered the door at Kurt's Lake Washington Boulevard mansion. I was about to split when I heard a voice from a second-storey window in a greenhouse/garage about a stone's throw from the main house.

"Psssst. William. Up here."

When he answered the door, he was in rough shape, but lucid enough to be careful.

"Are you sure you're William?"

"Yup."

"Funny. You don't look seventy-nine. You could easily pass for like sixty-something. Get in here quick." I entered the 23-by-19-foot room and Kurt bolted the door.

"What's the problem?" I asked.

He pointed to a picture of his wife, Courtney Love. "She's the problem. First the bitch had the cops take all my guns then she sent me to a rubber room in L.A. I escaped. But now I hear she's taken out a contract on me."

"She wants to have you killed?"

"Yeah, before I can divorce her. So she can be the Famous Widow, like that Yoko bimbo. And — get this — the guy's gonna do it for a lousy fifty-thousand bucks."

"What's the grounds for divorce?"

"She's screwing everyone in sight." He tossed me the Seattle phone book. "Pick a name at random."

I riffled the pages and stabbed a name: "Roto-Rooters R Us. Are you saying she screwed a Roto-Rooter?"

He nodded sadly. "Not just one. A whole warehouse-full. And she does-n't even bother to charge any more." He grabbed me by the lapels and fell to his knees, sobbing, "I gotta get out. I want you to make me anonymous, get that bitch off my back, get me out of rock 'n' roll. Set me free. You gotta save me!"

Just then a Bryan Adams song came on the radio. Cobain leapt across the room and smashed the radio with a sledgehammer. "It's guys like that Adams who ruin rock for the rest of us."

That's when the light bulb went off over my head.

"You know, Kurt, you look a little like Adams. You even have the pock-marked face."

He rubbed his rutted cheeks. "Yeah, shotgun accident. But I don't want to be another Bryan Adams. I'll kill myself first."

"That gives me an idea." The more I explained the plan the more Kurt liked it. In fact he was giggling hysterically when I left. "See you tomorrow, Kurt. And don't open the door for anyone but me."

I peeled rubber up to Vancouver and put the grab on Bryan Adams. It was easy. I said, "You wanna meet Kurt Cobain?"

"Would I?" Adams gushed. "I'd die for the chance."

"That's the idea."

"Do you know," Adams said, "that people say we look identical? I'm even growing my hair like his. We could pass for twins."

"Let's hope so," I said.

On the way back to Seattle I stopped at Gus's Guns 'n' Booze and bought a Remington M11 20-gauge shotgun and a fifth of scotch.

It was while Adams was asking why I needed a gun that I sapped him with my blackjack.

Back in the garage we dressed Adams in Kurt's T-shirt, jeans and sneakers and flipped to see who would pull the trigger. I won the toss but Cobain pouted so much that I let him blow off Adams's head.

"Now write a suicide note," I said, giving him some paper and crayons. When he finished he was delighted: "Read this part and its implied follow-line," he said.

I scanned the paragraph. "It's better to burn out than to fade away (Hey Hey My My, Rock And Roll Will Never Die)."

"That's a Neil Young song," I said.

"Don't you get it? If you rearrange the letters you get this: 'Bryan Adams Will Die. Me, Nah!' 'LOVE' to YOU dear. Why? Hee Hee! TA TAAA! Kurt Cobain."

Kurt left his driver's licence beside the stiff to ensure easy identification.

"You're forgetting one thing," I said, flipping him Adams' wallet. "To make the plan stick, you gotta become Bryan Adams."

At first he was horrified. But then he started to like the idea. "I could drive that guy's career into the ground in two years. It's headed that way anyhow. I even got an idea for a career-ending song. I'll call it "18 Till I Die!" This could be fun! Soon I'll be a complete has-been and can do what I like!!!!"

So if you see Adams on Much or MTV and wonder why he looks so much like Kurt, you got your answer, pal.

You're welcome.

The Big Bad Sleep

NEVER-NEVER LAND — Yeah pal, you read the sign right on the frosted glass door of my tacky office. It says: "William Burrill: Fairy Tale Detective."

Wanna make something out of it? So I work the Fairy Tale beat. You think I'm soft? Last guy who called me a "Fairy Dick" is still shittin' out teeth in the parking lot at some joint called Disneyland.

Get the picture? You gotta be hard-boiled to investigate Fairy Tales.

Hard-boiled, unlike a sad case I had to ID last week in the morgue. Buddy of mine named Humpty Dumpty. Took a "bad fall." Yeah, right. Couldn't put the poor bastard back together again even with the "help" of all the King's horses and all the King's men. Humpty and I did two tours of 'Nam before he got shell-shocked. He might have been an egg but he was no chicken and I think he got fried because he found out something the feds didn't want turned over easy. Eggheads know too much for their own good. But I know this much: Humpty didn't fall. He was pushed. He was poached. When a pal like Humpty gets it, you take it personal. But you can't be soft-boiled in this game. When I find the perps I'm gonna scramble their eggs.

Bought myself a shot of rye from the bottle I keep under the couch and tried to think of Humpty when he had the sunny side up. This'll be a hard case to crack. It's a living.

So I'm sitting in the Puss 'n' Boots peeler bar belting back the rye when I get the call. Trouble with a juvie named Little Red Riding Hood. Yeah, I know, she's hooked up with a bike gang and she's knocked over a couple of variety stores in her time, but I got a soft spot for the kid. Claims a wolf has eaten her grandma and is sleeping in the old broad's bed in disguise. Trying to pass himself off as granny. I figured Little Red was back on the stuff but I went out to investigate. It was a wolf all right. Either that or grandma was one of those dames who was meant to be looked at from 100 yards away. I pumped five slugs into him (or her) from my .357 Magnum. Like I say, I'm sweet on Red. She kissed me full on the lips and then said, "My, what a big Private Dick you are. All the better to…"

You can guess the rest.

This ain't kid's work, sleuthing out these Fairy Tales. So OK, a lot of it is routine, like the time I had to evict the old woman who lived in a shoe and had so many children she didn't know what to do. She didn't go easy but I managed to boot her with a right hook. Saved the price of a hollow-point slug.

Had to waste a round on that Troll who lurks under the bridge. Took him out clean. One shot. A Private Fairy Tale Dick doesn't waste ammo.

Routine: Took some old party called Rip Van Winkle to the tank after a serious bender. Took him 100 years to sleep it off. Busted a minor for breaking into the Three Bears' house and stealing their porridge. Also bagged a delirious kid named Jack who claimed he climbed a beanstalk and met a giant. Got him into rehab just in time. Investigated a domestic about some knob trying to climb a tower by grabbing a babe's hair. Turned out there was a wicked witch involved in the scam. Tough broad. Came at me with a broom, so I loaned her three slugs to the head. All in a day's work on the

Fairy Beat. Kissed the babe with the hair hard and took a shot of rye. Then off to bust another Domestic, some guy called Peter Peter Pumpkin Eater. Seems he's got his wife entrapped because he "couldn't feed her." Cheap punk. Fed Peter the Pumpkin Eater a knuckle sandwich, in case he was out of food stamps.

Slopping down a scotch in the Puss when the phone rings. Turns out there's an obvious OD case, some dame named Sleeping Beauty. Found the body, but — to my surprise — this was no DOA. The babe was merely sleeping. And she was a looker all right. I kissed her right on the smacker.

She woke up. I gave her my Number Three smile and said, "Say, Sugar, I could go for a doll like you." She blinked. Looked around, wondering where she was, like when you wake up in a cheap motel with a hangover. Looked me in the eyes. Then she said as follows: "No thanks, I've already had one little prick."

Guess it was around midnight I was off to nab a sweetie named Cinderella, who was obviously stoned. She was missing a shoe and kept babbling about turning into a pumpkin and seeing rats as coachmen. I sparked a Camel and said, "Babe, I could fall hard for you." She looked me right in the bright baby blues and said, "Not until I try you on for size."

And she wasn't talking about my shoes.

Checked out a sad case about a kid named Peter Pan. Thought he could fly. Off to Never-Never Land, he said in his note. Got there too late: the dumb punk was already road pizza: cheese, pepperoni and gravel.

Collared a pathological liar named Pinocchio who claimed that his "nose" gets erect in public. That's not what the kids down at the play-ground told me. Never seen a nose coming out a guy's fly. He's in Diddler's Row under protective custody. Feel sorry for the kid. Just a puppet who can't keep his woody in his pants.

Went back to the Puss 'n' Boots for a triple scotch straight up. Been a long day. I was just cooling out when the bartender passed me the phone. Something about Jack and Jill going up the hill. That's the same hill where Humpty got it. I jumped in my car and raced to the scene.

Too late. My beeper went off. Hansel and Gretel are in the OVEN? I put the pedal to the metal… like I say, this Fairy Tale assignment ain't no child's play.

My Life as a Dick

And speaking of fighting crime — which I know we weren't, but just play along — I have become the Elliot Ness of youth gang busting (provided that the youth gang members are all still in public school. I draw the line at confronting gang members who are not just about the right size for a spanking).

The incident that began my new career was entirely unprovoked. We were proceeding in an easterly direction on Eastern Avenue in a white Nissan Multi van last Sunday night when I noticed a gang of young punks hanging around the corner. As we sped innocently past, a young offender threw a rock at the van, smashing the back passenger window. The explosion of glass nearly caused an accident that would have killed one female (white), three farting dogs (brown and white) and one Juvenile Gang Buster (dashingly handsome).

In doing so, the youth gang in question made the mistake of their lives: they had messed with the Wrong Guy. The kind of Guy who won't take no for an answer. The kind of Guy who can't even remember what the question was.

I leapt out of the car and confronted the thugettes: "OK, which one of you little fucks threw the rock?" They looked at the smashed window and made faces sort of like Macaulay Culkin when he is acting like he's surprised. "Wow? Who did THAT?"

"One of you little shits, is my guess." The biggest little shit, who wasn't all that little, and in fact was almost as big a shit as I am, acted tough: "We didn't see nothin'." He glared around at all the others to make sure they kept their mouths shut.

It was then that this Juvenile Crime Fighter, using detective skills heretofore unknown to him, detected two pairs of feet under the car parked across the street. Criminals evading apprehension! I crossed the street and flushed them out. One alleged perpetrator split west, while the other fled east. I chose the eastbound alleged perpetrator and initiated a foot pursuit. Racing through back alleys at speeds reaching five miles per hour, I kept the perp in sight until he ducked into a laneway. Lost 'im. Damn!

Returning to the scene, I again encountered the bulk of the gang. "OK, who were those guys who ran?"

Big Little Fuck: "We don't know those guys. We never seen 'em before. We don't gotta tell you nothin'."

They smugly strutted off down the alley, walking, as all gangs must, as if they had pencils stuck up their assholes. But a true Juvenile Crime Fighter is not so easily thrown off the scent: I noticed an eyewitness in the form of

a male (white, drinking beer on his porch). "You know any of those guys?"
I asked him.

"Those little bastards?" he said. "They hang out at the schoolyard a couple of streets over. Bruce Public School. They raise all kinds of shit around here. Somebody should kick their ass."

He wasn't volunteering; he was merely making an observation.

"Where is this school?" He told me.

Informed with the information received from my informant I returned to the windowless van and proceeded three blocks east, stealthily pulling up behind Bruce Public School. There they were — the gang and the escaped alleged perpetrators! Before the van skidded to a halt I leapt out like a Super Hero, if you can imagine a Super Hero without the tights and hot pants (actually I was wearing tights and hot pants, but you couldn't notice them under my winter clothes).

Upon observing me, the two perps again fled while the rest of the gang tried to get in my face.

"Get the fuck out of my way," I said. After giving me the Death Stare for a moment the punks realized I was crazier than they were. They got the fuck out of the way. I again initiated foot pursuit but failed to collar the perps.

"OK," I asked three kids in front of the school, "who were they?"

"Who, the two guys you were chasin'?" They looked at each other. "We didn't see no two guys you were chasin'. And anyway, they're way gone by now. You'll never catch them."

The rest of the gang proceeded to verbally compare me to the human anal region from a safe distance across the street.

"You think you're tough," I told them, "but you're just a bunch of little fucks." Upon filing my report with the police, I was told that without a name or address to go on nothing could be done.

Says who? Early the next morning, a shadowy figure in a long trench coat is lurking in the vicinity of Bruce Public School. It is the Juvenile Crime Fighter, burning a little shoe leather in an attempt to crack the case. If he could make one of the perps, he could solve the unsolvable. But upon eyeballing the kids filing into the school, the Juvenile Crime Fighter discovers that they are too young to be among the suspected suspects.

He contacts the principal's office and, working under cover with a member of the school administration, is able to flush out one of the kids who had been hanging around in front of the school while the hot foot pursuit was in progress. Armed with some tips and after ID'ing one of the fugitives from mugshots of thugs who had since graduated from the school, he has a name. And an address. The Juvenile Crime Fighter burns more shoe leather, and knocks on the door. A woman answers.

"Are you Mrs. _____?"

"Yes."

"Are you the mother of J__ _____ (names withheld under the Young Offenders Act)?"

She rolls her eyes. "What has he done now?"

I fill her in and in turn she offers to pay for the window and also tips me off as to the identities of other key gang members, including _____ (alias "Little Big Fuck"). I call 55 Division and tell them to send in some backup.

The case was nailed. The gang was busted. The crime that had baffled an entire Metropolitan Police Force has been solved by one man, one man who was fed up with street crime, one man with the guts to stand up to the human scum that pollutes our streets, one man who is stupid enough to chase punks down dark alleys, one man who will soon be on the wrong side of the sod if he doesn't smarten up. They call that man the Juvenile Crime Fighter. Justice had prevailed.

As a result of this investigation _____ and _____ were apprehended by the police and given a stern caution, which is apparently the Young Offenders Act's equivalent of the electric chair.

The Substitute

I had to take the gun away from Vanilla Ice Tea-Bag. He didn't want to give it up.

"I don't got no steel on me."

"I can see it."

"Why can't I pack no steel?"

"Only the teachers are allowed to pack in class. You know that. It's the rules."

"It be a dumb rule."

"You're a white boy from a rich family. Why do you put on the gangsta pose?"

He blushed and looked around. "Did ya have ta tell the whole class? How I gonna get any booty? Them bitches gonna dis the shit outta me. I said I lived in a cardboard box under an overpass."

"A cardboard box worth maybe a million. Your father is a dentist."

"You just cost me my life, sir."

"Welcome to the world, tooth fairy."

I pretended I didn't see as they stripped him of his dirty, oversized Chicago Bulls jacket and his backwards cap.

I was doing Hall Duty, patrolling the part of the school we affectionately called The Dungeon, when I got paged by the Office.

"What's up, Chief?"

"You gotta take Mr. Leonard's class."

"He call in sick?"

"He called from the airport."

"10-C — you mean the gangsta wannabe Class From Hell bussed in from Rosedale?"

The principal nodded his head. "Aren't they all. What are you packing?"

"I got this .357 Magnum."

He opened a locker and tossed a heavy-duty piece of artillery across to me. "It's an AK-47. All the M-16s are signed out... so are the bazookas."

I gave the weapon a once-over, checked the clip. "This'll do just fine."

I headed for the door.

The principal called after me: "Be careful out there."

I busted down the door to 10-C, did a shoulder roll to my bulletproof desk and answered the hail of gunfire with three quick bursts from the AK-47. That got their attention and quieted them down enough that they took their seats, or at least sat on something.

I'd taught this class before, and they weren't called The Class From Hell for nothing.

"OK, class," I said. "No hats, no colours, no shivs, no guns, no cheap cultural appropriation and no chewing gum. I don't make the rules..."

The first fight was fairly easy to break up. Yolanda called Krista a "Ho" and Krista called Yolanda a "Bitch." I took their knives. No blood. Minor incident.

I could tell that Ice Deadly wasn't paying attention, because he was smoking coke in a tin-foil pipe.

"Mr. Deadly," I said, "would you care to repeat the things we've learned so far about Aristotle for the rest of the class?"

He looked up from his homemade pipe. "Yeah, we be talking 'bout some dead guy who got nothin' to say, him being dead and all." He did elaborate handshakes with everyone he could reach.

I levelled my .357 at him. "Maybe you might understand better if you talked to him in person. Although I doubt he's in Hell. Maybe they have visiting hours."

"Yo, yo, yo — chill! I don't know much but I wanna hear all about this — what's his handle — Ari-Fairy? Peace out, brother."

Some students on a spare were hanging in the window, disrupting the class. I only took out three with the AK-47 but I think I got my point across. Luckily it was a hot day and the windows were open. Didn't break a single pane of glass.

"I'm going through the class suggestion box," I said. "The best idea I've found so far is that I would look good in a body bag. But you didn't specify what colour. Are we ready for the poetry assignment? Why don't you lead off, Ice Dice Knife Slice Heist Vice Yo Mama No YO MAMA — and this is just a suggestion, but couldn't you have thought of a shorter name?"

"All the short names, they be taken."

"All right, Ice Dice, etc. Let's hear your poem."

"I be Ice Dice/ I don't slice nice/ Get in my face/ You better think twice/ I be The King/ And another thing/ You think you got a chance/ Homey you be wishin'/ Stab you in the back/ Bro that ain't my style/ I stab you in the front an' I do it with a smile."

"That's it?"

"I out."

"Well... I liked your sense of chivalry. You won't stab him in the back but in the front. That harkens back to the Knights of the Round Table. Or to legendary heroes — your poem shows that you are a sort of modern day Ivanhoe."

"Hey, who you callin' a ho?"

The firefight only lasted half an hour. I was glad the desk was bulletproof and that the principal had thoughtfully supplied me with plenty of extra clips for the AK-47.

I was very glad when class ended.

Saved by the bell...

Kids These Days

Kids these days. Can't quite figure 'em out.

I mean, when I was sixteen I did normal teen things like getting chased by the cops (they hardly ever caught me), defacing public property, shoplifting from the mall, eating enough acid to earn frequent-flier points on the Space Cadet Express, getting my girlfriend "in trouble" (she didn't look fifteen, honest) and smashing up several cars. (Hardly any innocent victims were injured. Did you know a car can bash right through a brick wall? It wasn't my fault. My view was blocked by my four friends riding on the hood.)

And, of course, like any aspiring writer, getting kicked out of high school. (Not because I was dumb. Principal Bill told me my marks were in the top five per cent in all Ontario, just before he booted me teeth-first off the school property.) Seems I was spending too much time studying anatomy (see "trouble", above) and also the effect of chemicals on the human species.

In other words, just the usual healthy kid stuff of my generation.
But kids these days...

For one thing, in my day we never carried knives. We only shot each other occasionally and usually by sheer accident. Yeah, OK, I almost put a steel-pointed, three-pronged hunting arrow through my boyhood pal Iain The Gas Pipe Weasel's head when we were twelve. But I was shooting from a hundred yards and never dreamed I could actually hit him from that distance. Call it a lucky shot. And I did save his life by yelling "DUCK!"

He did. Just in time. Missed him, as Maxwell Smart used to say, by that much. Sometimes — to this day, since we're still friends — I'm even glad I missed (though it would have been an awesome shot and gotten me big laughs at the Reform School).

But kids these days. I just don't know...

When I was a kid the guys with the brush cuts and the clothes that were way too big for them and walked like they had a pencil up their ass were the ones we used to give "wedgies" to. And any guy who showed up at class with both a beeper and a cell phone on his belt would be labelled the world's biggest nerd. Geek. Loser. Can you spell "Sea Hunt?"

I knew ya could.

I'm a Professional Journalist and I'm not just writing this stuff off the top of my head. I've done my research. When I was a teen I had hair halfway to my ass and lived in ripped-up jeans and a black T-shirt (come to think of it, I still look and dress like that). But according to my latest issue of that Bible of teen-hood, *Seventeen*, THIS is what "cool" teens are wearing these days: bright stripes and plaids together, clash action... wide-leg jeans, platform shoes, flowery pants, overalls, furry coats, butterfly collars, brown lipstick, brown nail polish and (this is the hottest item these days) BROWN CORDUROY. And that's just for the guys.

Like I said, if you showed up for school in that get-up in my day, it'd be Atomic Wedgie Time: you'd soon be wearing the elastic waistband of your underwear over your head.

Another teenie mag called *YM* (Young & Modern) gives handy tips on how you teenie girls can land different types of teenie boys in an article called "Ask Him Out (And Get A YES!)". There are the usual categories of guys to hit on: The Sports Stud, The Scene King, The Shy Guy (I stood behind Shy Guy at a public urinal once and damn near pissed myself waiting for him to tinkle). And then of course there is the "guy" category that I think describes me best: "The Babelicious Brainiac".

According to *YM*, there are some absolute "Do's" and "Don't's" if you want to land a hunk like me. First, you have to make the first move and ask me out. But not just to any old dump: "Ask the Babelicious Brainiac to the planetarium," YM advises the young woman of this era. "It's all dark and starry — way romantic. Plus it'll stimulate his mind (and his interest in you!)." But don't even think of asking a BB to a humongo bash. "You'll both be so busy screaming over the beat you'll miss out on the cool mental bond you could be forming."

Shit. In my day, the best way to "form a bond" with a girl was to "neck" and "pet" while sharing the same plastic bag of airplane glue.

I feel so out of it with all the new music these days. So I turned to the teenie zines for a crash course on what's hot with the kids these days. A reader poll in Seventeen picked the "Most Missed Band" as... The Beatles, narrowly edging out the Grateful Dead and something called Nirvana.

There was also an article in the latest issue of YM called "Get ready to rock!" — "your backstage pass to the hottest music, the hunkiest mega-babes, and the grooviest gals in musicland." It listed ten new 'n' happening acts such as R.E.M. ("awesome"), U2 ("awesome" and "mondo"), Pearl Jam ("can't-miss"), Bjork ("killer songs") and even some completely unknown band called Aerosmith ("killer tunes"). Never heard of any of 'em — but hey, I'm not seventeen any more.

YM even introduced me to a strange new word called "dis." Some unknown named Courtney Love "dissed" another newcomer called Axl Rose of Guns N' Roses, saying: "Axl Rose should leave on the next shuttle to the sun. He shouldn't be on the Earth because he's not good for anything." Maybe Courtney should marry him if she wants to get rid of him. It's worked before, so I'm told.

Kids these days. Guess I'm just too old... and as YM taught me, that's "like, totally freakworthy."

Doin' the Cosmo Hustle

I don't get what all the fuss is about Hustler magazine these days. Of course the skin rag and its publisher, Larry Flynt, have been a hot topic in the press and on talk shows, thanks to the exposure Flynt has received since the release of the flick The People Vs. Larry Flynt, which chronicles the sleazeball's real-life Freedom Of The Press court battle. Flynt freely admits his mag is a piece of trash and that all he is guilty of is bad taste. If you don't want to read it, don't buy it. But don't take away his right to publish.

This has caused a shitstorm of outrage from women's magazine editors, who say Hustler objectifies women and serves no useful purpose (all true, unless slamming the ham is a useful purpose). But what got me was a recent TV debate in which former Cosmopolitan editor Helen Gurley Brown debated Flynt, riding her high horse about how the press has a responsibility to inform and do goodie-goodie things.

So I decided to do a little comparison test: I went to the local variety store and bought both the latest *Hustler* and the current *Cosmo* (now edited by Toronto's own Bonnie Fuller). Here is a report on my findings:

Hustler: Lots of bad jokes, crude cartoons, plenty of pictures of women who seem to think they are visiting their gynecologist and a very few columns with titles like "Asshole Of The Month" and "Farts In The Wind." Just enough words so the average *Hustler* reader will not tire out his or her lips (yes, women read it — 20 per cent of the subscription base is female).

It's trash. Don't buy it. But Flynt already told you that.

Cosmopolitan: Now for a look at the righteous journalism contained in a serious periodical. Here is a sample of the contents:

• Roughly 300 photos of scantily clad, sexy women that you will never look like (if female), and who would never have anything to do with you (if male).

• A "Cosmo Girl" profile of model Charlize Theron: "Kinky sex and a good catfight are the specialty of 21-year-old Charlize Theron." She describes how actor James Spader dampened her fighting spirit by rubbing ice on her breasts in a new movie. She called her mother to tell her there was going to be "a wild fuck scene… she was totally supportive."

• Dating advice from MTV host Carmen Electra: "Wear something hot!"

• Movie capsules of three new flicks: *Female Perversions*, *Bliss* and *Kama Sutra* ("All the places that can be kissed are also the places that can be bitten…").

• A reader's poll called "Is It Okay To Fake An Orgasm?": 56 per cent of the women surveyed said Yes: "Sometimes it's called for when you realize you've made a big mistake and just want to get it over with…"

• Advice on whether a man is worth dating: "I had a crush on this guy for a while, the sex was fine until he stood up in bed stark naked and asked for a blow job. It was kind of like having sex with a gorilla." DUMP HIM! … "I expect [sex] to be good and there's no excuse not to tell him EXACTLY what you want. If it's no good why bother?" DUMP HIM! … "The acid test as to how generous a man is: "I always offer to split the bill on a date out of politeness, but if he accepts on the first few dates it's like a bucket of cold water over my desire." KILL HIM IN THE NAME OF SEXUAL EQUALITY!!!

• There's also plenty of great advice. One woman complains that her boyfriend won't suck her breasts because he doesn't like the taste. The solution offered: "Put whipped cream on your nipples to mask the taste." Or buy some soap.

• There is a three-page spread — "Why High Heels Are Worth It!" —

which actually gives lessons in how to wear you "sex-bomb three-inch heels high and proud and prepare for the chaos ahead." They point to actress Pamela Anderson as the perfect example of how to wear your heels "well-stacked."

• There is a primer entitled "About Down There" which answers such earth-shaking questions as "My boyfriend wants to put food up my vagina. Should I let him?" Expert Answer: Meat should not be shoved up there but "yogurt, which is full of good bacteria that keeps yeast in check, does no harm." Yummy. The primer also advises women to get as much booty as possible: "Staying sexually active keeps vaginal tissue elastic, so it pays to give your vagina a lifetime bedroom workout."

• Who wouldn't want to read the article "Watching the One You Love Make Love to Another"?

• Here is the first bit of sage advice from the article "His and her orgasms: How to slow him down and speed you up!" Tip number one: "Begin without him!" The next tip is "Give yourself a helping hand (i.e., masturbate while you're doing it with him)." Funny. In another advice column in the same issue, a woman writes to complain that her boyfriend likes to play with himself while they are doing it. The Expert Advice: "Your first — and hardest — job will be to get your boyfriend to admit that his behaviour isn't normal." Huh?

• "Cheap Date Strategies" is an extremely relevant pile of piffle about how to get sex with a guy who doesn't have any money (as if any *Cosmo* reader WOULD). Alas. Nonetheless... please do tell: The ideal cheapo date is a pool hall: "Think dark, sexy rooms. Think how he'll be blown away after you blow HIM away!"

• The ads in the back of the book bear titles for non-sexist videos such as Secret Pleasures, Stilettos & Stockings, Knights & Damsels — you can look the rest up yourself in the advertised "Adult Film Catalog."

• There are hard-hitting interviews with someone called David Conrad. *Cosmo* would not dare objectify women, would they? QUESTION: "What part of a woman's body do you find most attractive?" That's Pulitzer stuff. Alright, Bonnie.

• I can't leave without pointing out the piece about what messages you're sending out when you show your cleavage. It seems that going bra-less with six buttons undone is going to prove what we knew all along: that men are pigs.

And all they think about is sex.

At least Larry Flynt knows he's an asshole.

Ask Dr. Burrill...

"Dr. Burrill,"* many of you have been asking me, "how can I have a long and healthy life?"

This is a worthy question, dear reader(s), and requires careful thought and research.

Many of you out there — as trend-pundits like Faith Popcorn have recorded — are at a stage in life where you are overwhelmed by the feeling that nothing is safe, that all is toxic or poison or somehow deadly. Sex. Air. Sun. Water. Drano.

And in these frightening plague years, many of you are demanding more control over your own well-being. Doctors are fine, but we must also take an active role in unlocking for ourselves the secrets that keep us alive and well.

To aid in this quest, I have enlisted the use of a powerful computer database that contains real, actual, not-even-made-up newspaper stories that have appeared over the last eight years.

After years (well OK, minutes) of research, I have custom-designed Dr. Burrill's Ten Step Program For A Long Happy Life. This unique program is totally unscientific, yet at the same time, completely worthless. But hey, it works for me.

1. DON'T GROW TOO TALL

Short people outlive tall people, according to a study reported in *Men's Health* magazine. Men under five-foot-eight lived to an average age of eighty-three, the study found, while men over six feet tall tended to check out at seventy-three. In other words, every extra inch in height knocks 1.2 years off your average life span. A growth-stunting regimen of heavy masturbation and cigar-smoking is the only known cure for this health hazard.

2. HAVE A COUPLE OF BELTS A DAY

Those who have a couple of alcoholic drinks a day live longer than tee-totallers, according to studies conducted by Harvard University and several other institutions. Moderate drinking — two to four snorts per day — greatly lowers the risk of stroke and North America's number one killer: heart disease of all kinds.

The trick, of course, is to keep your drinking moderate and not spend every night yodelling into the porcelain canyon.

3. DON'T DRINK MILK — EVER

You've probably seen those TV ads where impossibly cheesy girls and guys are running everywhere after drinking milk. They run to school. They run home. They run out on dates after school. The milk marketing board would like you to think these people are running because they are just, like, totally bursting with energy. But now the truth can be told: these people are running because they have the shits.

At least 20 per cent of all Canadians suffer from lactose intolerance (which basically means Bossy's milk makes their bowels moooooo-ve). Another 10 per cent are allergic to milk, perhaps without knowing it. "Milk," a report by the Physicians Committee for Responsible Medicine says, "is overrated as a source of calcium [and] is often contaminated with antibiotics (fed to cows and passed on in their milk)."

Among other maladies linked to milk in studies: gastro-intestinal diseases, allergy attacks, juvenile diabetes, hyperactivity, migraines, post-nasal drip, middle-ear infections, asthma, blue circles under eyes, behavioural difficulties... Even famed baby doctor Benjamin Spock has changed his views and now says babies should be breast-fed only, and weaned off milk completely by age two.

Milk: it's udder bullshit. Don't be cowed by pressure groups. Just say "beer."

4. WALK, DON'T RUN

Health nuts who jog in the city are not only blowing out their knees and ankles, but also deep-sucking enough smog and pollution to equal a couple of decks of Export A Plains a day, according to an Environment Ontario study. All that running's also hard on your ticker. Just ask the late jogging enthusiast James Fixx, who claimed we'd all live to 100 if we'd only get out and run for our lives. Fixx keeled over at fifty-two (while jogging).

You want exercise? Take a good, brisk walk (but you don't have to be obnoxious about it — like these wiggle-bum-elbow-swinging jerks who are taking over the city. While not hard on the heart, this kind of ostentatious speed-walking greatly increases the chances of random and unprovoked gunshot wounds).

5. TAKE ASPIRIN

There's mounting evidence that a single buffered ASA tablet every other day not only prevents stroke but cuts the risk of having that first heart attack by 44 per cent for men. More stunning is the recent news (The *Toronto Star*, March 15, 1993) that simple ASA wards off and inhibits stomach, esophagus, colon and rectal cancers.

6. IMITATE THE FRENCH

The French smoke like chimneys, guzzle wine with every meal (even breakfast), and basically spend all day sitting in the sun, being rude to tourists. They never run anywhere (unless they see the German army coming). They eschew all the puritanical rules foisted on Canadians by assorted pressure groups.

And yet:

• The French have a longer average life expectancy than health-obsessed Canadians (77.6 years on average, compared to 77.3).

• The French heart attack rate is less than half what Canadians suffer (69.8 French per 100,000 die of heart attacks per year, compared to 188.1 Canucks per 100,000 and 193.4 Yankees per 100 grand).

• The chain-smoking French use much more (and much stronger) tobacco than we do. And yet they have a much lower lung cancer rate than smoke-free Canada (33.7 per 100,000 compared to our 52.2 per 100,000).

Why? Some say it's the magic of red wine. Some say it's the relative lack of stress. And yet others point to the typically French trait of being great big meanies ("Meanies better at recovering from heart attacks than softies," TheToronto Star, May 6, 1992).

7. DON'T BE RELIGIOUS

Preaching is not good for the health. Just look at what happened to Jesus. And just look at how many people have died fighting in the name of God (Allah, Buddha, Koresh, Manitou, Quetzalcoatl, whoever). The respected New England Journal of Medicine has even identified a new and extremely painful malady called "Prayer's Knee." Better for all if we chill out and strictly adhere to Rule 2.

8. DON'T BOWL

Bob Nittner of Taylor, Mich., bowled his first perfect game after 31 years of trying, then dropped dead of a heart attack as his cheering friends mobbed him (*Associated Press*).

9. FIGHT STRESS, BE HAPPY

Learn to laugh. Don't let your job get you down. Don't — whatever you do — bottle up stress. It's far better to break a beer bottle over your boss's head than eat his niggling bullshit. You may lose your job, but working in an office building isn't healthy anyway (See "Sick Building Syndrome").

10. STOP HAVING BIRTHDAYS

Men have a 21 per cent higher risk of popping the big aorta on their birthday than any other day, a study by the Robert Wood Johnson Medical School found (the risk to women rises 9 per cent). The only problem with this plan is that the only sure-fire way to stop having birthdays is to kick the bucket.

So there you have it. But — you ask — does this program work?

Celebrity testimonial: "Hi, I'm Winston Churchill. I was mean as hell. I fought them on the beaches. I fought them in the alley. I fought them behind the pub. I never jogged. I drank a bottle of brandy a day (which ensured that I also took lots of Aspirin). I never bowled. I crushed bossy, stress-inducing dictators. I never got religious. I smoked like a tire fire (which ensured I never grew too tall). I went to France. I sure as hell never drank milk. And yes, I eventually stopped having birthdays. But not until I'd already had ninety-one of them.

"And I owe it all to Dr. Burrill's Ten Step Program..."

While Dr. Burrill is not technically a real medical physician, he is a practising hypochondriac, has taken lots of pills, and spent many years playing doctor as a child.

The Scum Also Rises

I like hanging around in outdoor cafés as much as the next guy. Better than the next guy, because the next guy is drinking gassy French water and I've had three beers.

Me, I never drink gassy French water and it's not because the entire world supply was recalled a few years ago when it turned out it was benzene that was giving it that distinctively funny taste. I don't drink the stuff because it's my theory that the "natural bubbles" are the result of guppy farts. Guppies aren't too fussy about what they eat and it has to be hard on their guts. (Note: The most prolific bubble-producing fish is not the guppy but the aptly named smelt, which is used to carbonate American beer. Dutch beer, by contrast, is carbonated by submerging an angry skunk in a vat of water, hops and barley.)

Zut alors.

I am sitting in an outdoor café drinking Canadian beer (carbonated by placing a mouse in each individual bottle). One thing I like about sitting in cafés is it makes you feel so damn literary. Just look around. I'm not the only one here feeling damn literary. There's a woman with bright orange hair that reminds one of a Fuller Brush 100-per cent synthetic mop head. She has round red granny glasses and a big thick book by somebody like Proust or maybe Joyce. (James, not Brothers).

At the next table is a woman all in black. She has black leggings and a black dress and a black coat and a black hat and black eyeliner and a black cigarette. She's reading Sylvia Plath (who was always good for a few laughs).

Beside her is a Mr. T. clone wearing army boots, sweat socks, jeans with the knees and ass ripped out of them. A knife, shotgun shell, hook, spoon and various other items dangle from a chain around his neck, like an exploded K-Tel Pocket Fisherman. Beside him is a Kate Bush lookalike, who seems to be ready to do an interpretive dance at the drop of a hat. She is drinking something bright red. She has an open notebook. The page is blank but she is so damn literary that she could make a poem appear on that page just by giving it a hard stare.

Zut alors.

You Generation ZZZZ slackers may not remember this, but this simple act of sitting in the sun and drinking a cold beer and thinking warm, fuzzy,

100 per cent fact-free thoughts was actually banned here in Toronto the Goody-Goody until just over a decade ago. Even in very recent years, any place where you might drink alcohol in T.O. had to be suitably dark, dank, airless and subterranean to hammer home the message that you were committing the blackest of sins. God forbid — and for years He did — that you should actually be able to do all this hellbound stuff right out in the open sunlight where decent citizens might see you.

Zut alors.

The book I am reading as I sit here in the sun is *A Moveable Feast*, Ernie Hemingway's posthumous memoir of his life in Paris of the '20s (not Hemingway's best book but pretty good when you consider he was already dead when he wrote it). *A Moveable Feast* always makes me feel like sitting in a café and being damn literary. But what is little known is that Hemingway actually wrote a chapter of *A Moveable Feast* about his four-year association with Toronto (1920 -24). The lost chapter was recently discovered by this reporter among Hemingway's papers at the JFK Library in Boston. A sample:

Then the warm weather came and I would sit at a table outside the Selby Hotel and let the good and true whisky warm my body and my spirit. I was writing that day about Paris and how Scott Fitzgerald got drunk and dropped his trousers around his ankles and how Gertrude Stein used this as the plot of her next three novels. The words came truly and a man can always write what he knows truly as long as he is not lying nor fibbing nor making things up. I put down the pencil and ordered a cold beer and the lunch special and picked up the fork and went across the liver and into the peas. It was warm in the sun and it was good for I knew what would happen next in the story about Scott and his trousers and I was only slightly angry when Morley Callaghan came by and interrupted my thoughts. Morley was drunk as we all were in those days and he had bottles in all his pockets and made a clattering sound as he walked.

"How are you?" Morley said.

"That is a good question."

"Isn't it."

"Yes it is."

"It's a hell of a question."

"It's awfully good."

"It drives me crazy."

"You had better have a drink."

"I had one."

"Have another."

"That is a good idea."

"Yes it is."

We had a drink and then Morley knocked me cold and I lay under the table and did not speak nor talk nor say anything. I would often lie under the table in the Selby Hotel café in those days and so no one noticed that anything was odd. I ordered a brandy and soda and the waiter passed it under the table and it was good and I had another and it was better and it was only much later that night that I found out the Selby was a gay bar.

Zut alors.

I opened my notebook and tried to write a poem of my own but could not. You can't write poetry while drinking beer. Beer makes you write crap like this. The trick to writing poetry is to drink a whole lot of cough medicine. I had the flu last week and drank a whole lot of cough medicine and the poems were just bursting out of me. Of course this cough medicine was wimpy stuff compared to what they used to give the Romantic Poets, who all claimed to have consumption just to get their hands on the stuff. One gulp of that stuff and stand back! The diarrhea medicine was pretty good in those days too. Just ask old Samuel "Trots" Coleridge. His outhouse was called Kubla's Can. Did you know that? Neither did I.

Zut alors.

The waiter came by and I grabbed my throat and stuck out my tongue and made loud gurgling noises, which is international café sign language for "Another beer, please. And hurry." I like cafés. The beer came and I drank it and sat in the sun, wondering in a warm fuzzy way just what the hell "Zut alors" means, anyway?

All in a Day's Work for the Professional Writer

I was sitting around all day drinking beer, as always, when the most incredible idea occurred to me. I just figured out — completely out of the blue — how to solve some of the most serious problems facing our society, all with one deft but simple action.

Here are the problems I'm talking about:

- The spiralling cost of health care.
- The high price of seizing smuggled drugs.
- The threat of terrorism to every innocent traveller.
- The fact that fully qualified doctors cannot find work in the Metro Toronto area and are being forced against their will to relocate in the hin-

terlands of Ontario.

And here is my beautifully simple but highly effective solution.

We simply employ all the out-of-work doctors as airport security officers, since they already know how to read X-rays.

Rather than simply putting a passenger's luggage through the high-powered X-ray machines at airport security checks, from now on the passengers themselves will lie down and be fed through the machine. In this way, the doctors can simultaneously check for terrorists' weapons and smuggled items while providing an inexpensive physical check-up. "Your suitcase looks fine, Mr. Burrill," the security doc will say, "but I don't like the looks of your gall bladder."

Meanwhile, when asked at the arrival customs checkpoints if he or she has "anything to declare," the traveller can answer, "Yeah, I declare that my piles are killing me." The travellers will then be shown into a private room for a thorough strip search and physical examination: "OK, open your suitcase...take off your clothes...empty your pockets...turn your head and cough...fine, fine...bend over...now let's just snap on this rubber glove here and check for smuggled heroin and a healthy prostate..."

The plan is perfect. It could really work. Think about it!

And although it will doubtless save countless lives and billions of tax dollars, I want no special thanks or humanitarian awards.

It's all in a day's work for a Professional Writer.

I get a lot of calls from students who are considering a career in journalism and want to question me about the mysterious and romantic life of being a weekly columnist.

That's not exactly how the students phrase their inquiries, mind you. What they usually say is something closer to this: "Hey, is it true that you writer guys get paid for, like, drinking beer in bars all day and making up bullshit and stuff? And, if so, how can I get into the profession?"

This is, of course, merely the romanticized image of a writer's life. In reality, no true writer would spend all day drinking in a bar. It's ridiculous. For one thing, most true writers are asleep most of the day. They don't start hanging around the bars and drinking until well after noon.

And writers certainly don't drink beer in bars every day. On warm sunny days, like this one, they sometimes drink beer outside bars.

I am, of course, only too pleased to help out these students in any way I can. Consider it a public service. Here are a few of the most frequent queries from brown-nosing little keeners who want to make their mark in journalism:

Question 1: You suck.
Answer: That's not a question. Remember: It has to be in the form of a question. Try again.

Question 2: Do you know something? You suck.
Answer: That's better. But you see, you asked and answered your own question. That's poor interviewing form. Let the subject do the talking.

Question 3: Are foreign languages helpful to a writer?
Answer: You should know at least the key words in Spanish, French and German.

Spanish:
A. "Otra cervaza, por favor, muy frio." ("Gimme another beer and make it a cold one.")
B. "Dos cervezas mas, tonto." ("Two more beers, foolish person.")
C. "¡Rapido!!! ¿Donde esta el bano?" ("Quick! Where's the can?")

French:
A. "Qui a coupé le fromage?" ("Who cut the cheese?")
B. "Quel bozo!" ("Where is the train station?")
C. "Mangez la merde, garçon." ("What is good on the menu?")

German:
A. "Achtung! Halt Amerikana!" ("Please carry my luggage.")
B. "Schnell, sweinhund." ("Thank you very much.")
C. "Rat-a-tat-tat-tat-tat." ("Hello, excuse me, I read too many war comic books as a child,")

Question 4: Do you have prejudices? Do you think some people are third-class citizens based on where they come from?
Answer: Of course not. Some of my best friends come from Calgary.

Question 5: Do you believe in gratuitious use of profanity in the media?
Answer: Fuck, no.

Question 6: How do you get good ideas for your columns?
Answer: I'll let you know… if it ever happens.

But don't be fooled by the apparent lack of work ethic displayed by such writers. They are working very hard on their story ideas. Top-notch writing requires a gestation period during which the subconscious mind wrestles and grapples with the highly complex ideas that will soon be honed into diamond-hard prose on the page. A writer can be creating the most beautiful prose when — to the untrained eye — it looks for all the world as if he is merely lying in the ditch with his pants around his ankles.

As Ernest Hemingway put it, "in the newspaper business... it is such an important part of the ethics that you should never seem to be working."

I've learned a lot about the craft of writing from Hemingway. Unfortunately, there is a false perception that Hemingway was the very writer who started the sit-around-and-drink-beer-all-day school of writing. This is patently false, the ignorant babblings of new-age weenies who have never actually even read a Hemingway book. Any true "buff" knows that Papa Hemingway was extremely dedicated to the craft of writing. He rose every day before dawn and carefully sharpened five pencils with a penknife and then proceeded to sit around all day and drink whisky and soda. Or maybe gin. Possibly rum. But never beer. He hated beer.

By carefully employing this discipline, Hemingway literally revolutionized fiction writing. He did this by using short, lean sentences. Like this. Or that. Really tiny ones. Short. As. Possible. Scholars agree that Hemingway favored short sentences because by the time he was ready to put pen to paper, he was far too drunk to write a long sentence. Instead, Hemingway would find one true word, the truest word he knew, *le mot juste*. Then he would write this word.

Then he would take a nap.

Here, in his own words, is the most valuable piece of writing advice that a beginner can glean from Hemingway: "You always stop when you know what is going to happen next. You write until you come to a place where you still have your juice and know what will happen next and then you stop and try to live through to the next day and hit it again."

By always stopping when you know what will happen next, a writer can never become stalled or stuck. As long as the juice is in mid-flow, you can always return to the story the next day. Or the next week. Or even several months later. It is through this technique that Hemingway was able to write absolutely nothing — not a single book — from 1939 to 1950 and still not develop writer's block.

A writer also needs a keen eye for detail. Little things that might entirely escape the untrained eye. You must always carry a notebook and write down your observations while they are still fresh.

For example, the other day I went to the dry cleaner to pick up my dry cleaning. And the barely perceivable thing that I picked up on right away was that the dry cleaner was gone. The shop was empty. No dry cleaners working away inside. And more importantly, no dry cleaning hanging inside. And no note or sign indicating where they had vanished to. Most people would not think twice about such a mundane thing. But, as a trained writer, I noticed that it was "odd." It set off an internal alarm bell, and my writer's "sixth sense" told me to take out my notebook and write down not only my acute observations, but also the sense of mystery that they evoke:

1. The dry cleaners is gone without a trace.
2. Where did it go?
3. And where the fuck is my suede vest?

I'm thinking of turning it into a novel.

Taking the "High" Out of Hi & Lois

When Abbie Hoffman mounted the stage to spout off a political rant at The Who's Woodstock gig back in 1969, Peter Townshend knew exactly what to do.

He clubbed Hoffman with his guitar.

Take that, and THAT, you fucking git!

Those were the days when rock music was sheer, vacuous entertainment and not a medium for politically correct thought.

But now we're mired in a neo-moralistic period in which art, books, music and even television shows are expected to carry some redeeming, weightier-than-thou message.

It's getting so artists are starting to second-guess themselves if they don't produce something that simply oozes of political meaning. "Sure, I like it," they tell themselves, "but is it relevant? What's its message?" Then they've got to jump though all the PC hoops to make sure the thing — a dumb rock song — doesn't offend anybody.

Social pressure groups have learned the power of forceful lobbying and have been frighteningly successful in squeezing out every potentially harmful or offensive image from advertising and entertainment media. No one smokes on TV anymore, unless they later die of cancer. No one gets hammered — or if he does, it isn't fun. Oh, commercials do their best to portray a party atmosphere, but no one's actually quaffing.

A recent David Letterman Top Ten list of TV movies we're not likely to see included *The Really Popular Boy Who Smoked and Drank Too Much.*

What's scary is that when you see a black-and-white sitcom from the staid, repressive, right-wing, moralistic '50s, there's good ol' Mom working away in the kitchen, smoking a butt. In those days there was always one character who was a lovable drunk, the type who'd guzzle twenty martinis and then park his car on your front shrub. That always got big laughs. Not anymore. Dean Martin wouldn't have much of a career today. Neither would Foster Brooks. Remember the old colour comics? Hi and Lois's next door neighbour, Thirsty, was always smashed on beer (hence his name). Not anymore. Now he's just the lazy guy next door. Same with Stan in The Better Half. When was the last time you saw him with that formerly hilarious morning-after ice-bag on his head, as his wife recapped all the horrible things he'd done and said? Kinda scary when you think that we're more heavily censored and thought-manipulated now than in the '50s!

And where has all the media violence gone?

Sure, people still get shot up and punched out. But when I was a kid, the body count in a single cartoon would make Gettysburg look like a skirmish. And the Three Stooges entertained kids by bonking each other on the head with hammers, twisting noses, poking eyes and ripping out tufts of hair. These days, the Saturday morning cartoons are so sanitized that it's not surprising kids have to form street gangs in order to vent the aggression they used to be able to purge vicariously through Moe's well executed double-slap of Curly and Larry's faces. Whack-whap!

This is the era of thought police, of fundamentalists who want to suck every supposedly free-thinking person into their own tunnel vision of morals and mores. You can't see what you want. And you sure as fuck better not say what you think. Writers are at special risk because, in order to write, you have to have an opinion. And having an opinion is against the law these days. Legions of pressure groups are lying in ambush, ready to pounce on any statement, however offhand, that trips one of the countless mines of politically correct no-nos.

"Dear Editor, I was shocked and disgusted to read your story which said 'Barry Manilow is a mincing, half-assed old fart.' This is sexist (it should say 'Personilow'), ageist (what's wrong with being old?), racist (Barry's Jewish, I think, or maybe Italian), homophobic (so what if he minces?) and also belittles the handicapped (can Barry help it if he's born with half an ass?). How dare you publish something that I don't agree with?"

It's scary how successful these picketing, protesting, letter-writing lobbyists have been. They've managed to whip the government and the media into one cowering, cringing corner, fumbling to comply with a code of correctness that's as ever-changing as it is arbitrary.

And the songs or books or TV shows that pander most to political pressure are the ones that become quickly dated. Beatle songs of the '60s sound much fresher today than John Lennon's string of cliché political slogans that passed for tunes in the '70s. At some point (you hope, if you still have a shred of faith) the people will rise as one and say, "Shut the fuck up!" when the PC thought cops come whimpering to our doors.

Then we'll poke 'em in the eye and hit 'em on the head with a hammer.

Don't Sleep in the Subway, Baby

People could use some basic rules for living in the Big City.

We're all concerned about rising violence. But I'm sure there would be far fewer casualties if we would all live by these obvious but often ignored rules for urban living:

1. Do not drive at ten miles an hour below the speed limit in the left hand passing lane on the expressway. If you wanna drive slow, haul your dragging ass over to the right-hand turtle lanes.

2. Don't ride your bicycle at high speed on the sidewalks — especially if you're one of those whip-in-and-out couriers. You're supposed to be riding on the road, where it's easier for cars to kill you.

3. Don't take fifty items through the "eight items or less" express checkout at the supermarket. For some reason, the cashiers never do anything about this, but Type A shoppers with stun-guns just might.

4. How many times have you tried to run up an escalator at rush hour, when you're hurrying to get to work or a meeting or something, only to find both sides of the stairway blocked by two oblivious fatties in lime-green stretch pants? It's the same rules as the highway: slow-poke lard-asses should stand to the right, leaving a clear passing lane for those in a hurry.

5. Don't talk in the movie theatre. Shut up already. And quit rattling that cellophane candy bag or I'm coming over there with a can of mace.

6. Don't pay off fifty bills at an ATM when there are a dozen people lined up behind you. And quit checking your balance after every transaction. After you're finished, don't study your transaction slip while blocking access to the machine. Move your ass and do it somewhere else.

7. Don't stick your boogers on the wall in the washroom above the urinal. You may be proud of them, but nobody else wants to look at them, no matter how colourful they may be.

8. When you're at the ball game, don't keep getting up for beer while the game's in progress. Wait until the end of the inning. Same rule for coming back to your seat. Wait at the top of the stairs and come back to your seat when the play has stopped. Goof.

9. On a crowded bus, streetcar or subway, don't sit in the seat near the aisle, blocking the window seat so that no one else can sit down. Shove over, ya jerk.

10. Don't take up two parking spaces with your goddamn car.

11. Don't fart in a crowded elevator and then shoot dirty looks at someone else.

12. If your dog shits on the sidewalk or in a public park, scoop it up with a plastic bag and throw it away. And you! The guy who's always letting your

dog shit on my front lawn and then leaving it there. I don't want your dog's shit. It doesn't smell good and — as you're gonna find out next time — it doesn't taste very good either.

13. You. In the BMW. The guy who just cut me off without looking and then flashed me his Toby Tall when I blasted my horn. Take that cellular phone and ram it up your Hershey Highway.

14. Don't hork greeners on the sidewalk. And if you must, be sure to suck them back up. No one else wants them. Trust me on this one.

15. Don't bring extremely loud and squeally infants into nice, intimate restaurants where others are trying to have a nice, romantic time. You may think Junior's howls are adorable, but you are alone on that one. Get a babysitter, ya cheap bastard. Or go to Chuck E. Cheese.

16. Some rules of urban life have to be improvised on the spot. For example, if you enter an ATM booth — as my friend Iain the Gas Pipe Weasel did the other day — and see a big fat bare bum going up and down, up and down, up and down on the floor, over some splayed bare legs, amid the obvious sounds of romantic rapture, have some decency! Go away and come back later. This is basic ATM etiquette: it is not polite to watch too closely or crowd the space when another customer is making a deposit and a withdrawal.

Hey Gen X, "McJobs" Are Not Exclusive To You!

The air is so heavy and dirty that you could shovel it. All the highways have been shut down for construction (except for the one that was shut down by a berserk, bennie-crazed tractor-trailer driver who found out that it is not a good idea to drive a 100-foot-long, 18-wheel rig at 120 miles an hour around a hairpin curve. Who knew? Only a few people were actually killed).

The Leafs have fallen and the streets are alive with the shrieks of Blue Jay "fans" who are doing their annual early-season header off the bandwagon. There is nothing on TV but reruns. People who should not be caught dead wearing tank tops and shortie-shorts are. Except, sadly, they are not dead. You can tell by the way they jiggle. And, as the school year screeches to a close, students everywhere are throwing away their math and English Lit notes and preparing to get on with a few, hot, sweaty months of life's real lessons (including how to drink beer while you are projectile vomiting).

All the signs point to one thing.
Hot town, summer in the city.

The only drawback to summer is that — if you're a student — you may actually have to go out and get a McJob.

One of the most important factors in choosing your summer employment is to get a job that actually pays some money. This is the key. Trust me. I learned the hard way one summer when I was a kid. It was when I took a job as a Fuller Brush Man. This is a true story.

As a Fuller Brush Man I had to go door-to-door with a heavy sample case of cleaning shit. I also carried catalogues with pictures of mops and ironing board covers. And a plastic bag full of free samples, which were mainly two-cent plastic combs and shoehorns. We had to take a training course, which explained how to respond during any Fuller Brush Man emergency. A manual contained scripts of every possible scenario or situation. For instance:

Fuller Brush Man: Hello, Madam, I'm your friendly Fuller Brush Man and I am here to show you some really cheap crap that you would never buy in a million years unless you had the brains of a piece of gravel. And to give you a free shoehorn.

Lady of the House: Hello! I'd love to buy many things so that you will make yet another huge commission, but this is a bad time. Just now my elderly mother is upstairs dying of a heart attack.

Fuller Brush Man: That's OK. I can wait in the living room until she's done.

Lady of the House: [Cheerfully] Please do come in. Can I get you some pie?

The only trouble was that the real life encounters never quite seemed to follow the prepared script.

Fuller Brush Man: Hello, Madam, I'm your friendly Fuller Bru—

Lady of the House: Fuck off!

Fuller Brush Man: But I—

Door: Slam!

Fuller Brush Man: —have a free plastic shoehorn for you...

Lady of the House: [from inside] Bruno! Come quick! And bring your belt!

It was about 100 degrees my first day on the job, and I was wearing these gleaming white pants. The first house I approached, some little kid ran down the path to greet me. She was eating a melting, dripping chocolate ice cream cone. She was exactly crotch-high. I know this because she ran directly into my crotch and smeared the entire crotch area of the white pants with melted, poo-brown ice cream.

There is something — as I found out that first day — that sparks distrust in a person as they peek out of their window and see a long-haired weasel creeping up the pathway with brown stains all over the crotch of his white pants. Shouldn't the brown stains be on the back of the pants? the householder was wondering as she ran to bolt the door, sic the pitbull and load the shotgun.

There was no salary involved in being a Fuller Brush Man. I worked on a straight commission, which meant I earned a whopping ten per cent on everything I sold. The only slight drawback to this scheme was that, after almost a month on the job, I had not sold a single item. Not one single mop. Nothing. Nada. And 10 per cent of nada works out to nada.

Not everyone slammed the door in my face. Some people actually let me in the house. But these people broke down into three basic sorts:

1. People who wanted to buy something on the spot, but balked when I explained that they couldn't buy the samples. They had to place an order and wait several weeks for delivery.

2. Very lonely old people who wanted to talk for an hour (but not actually buy anything). Their houses smelled funny.

3. Very lonely perverts who actually understood how you could get brown stains all over the crotch of your pants. They smelled funny.

On the day I decided to quit, I sold all the samples for a very reasonable rate and gave the entire bag of shoehorns to a couple of little kids (who are no doubt now multi-billionaire shoehorn tycoons). I made just enough to cover the dry-cleaning bills for my white pants. The dry cleaning weasel looked at me very strangely. I did not bother to try to explain.

I ended up getting another summer McJob as a bag boy at Safeway. One dollar and thirty-five cents for every single hour I worked. The only catch was that, to earn this highly lucrative salary, they wanted me to cut off all my hair.

I compromised by wetting my head and smearing on an entire bottle of Dippity-Doo. This had the effect of hardening my hair into a two-foot-high pompadour that could deflect anti-aircraft missiles. The Safeway brass were not as impressed by the results as I was.

The trouble was, as the shift progressed, hard sticky clumps of hair would fall down into my face. They hung down about a foot and were so hard they could be snapped off like icicles. A few weeks into my bag-boy career, one of the Bobs — there were four "Bobs" working in Safeway management; it seemed to be a prerequisite that your name be "Bob" if you wanted to become a fully grown man working in a supermarket for minimum wage. Anyway, one of the Bobs pulled me aside as I showed up for work and said, "OK, Ringo. You're fired."

But I still had to finish my bag-boy shift before I could collect my highly lucrative final paycheque.

That last day, I put the eggs on the bottom and the cans and bottles on top.

Ban These Songs Immediately

Should songs by recording artists with criminal records — or songs that promote and glorify unlawful acts — be banned from the airwaves and rock video TV shows?

That was the question I found myself kicking around last week when I took part in a panel discussion on MuchMusic called Too Much For Much.

If you've never seen the show, the premise is simple: you pose a Serious Artistic Issue, gather together a bunch of people who don't have a clue what they're talking about, and let them scream at each other for an hour or so. So, naturally, I was a perfect choice as one of the panelists.

I tried to voice my opinion that Art Is Art and Censorship Is Bad and who cares if Snoop offed a few guys and, as for Tupac Shakur, any man who can take two bullets in the head and still be walking around is not going to get any arguments from me.

But the trouble was, I was seated right next to a woman from one of those lobby groups, you know, with a name something like Association of Ranting Strident Hissy-fitters Objecting Loudly to Evil Songs (ARSHOLES). And she kept interrupting and shouting down everyone else, insisting that rap and rock lyrics are corrupting innocent children and must be banned. She was very convincing — so convincing, in fact, I confess she made me see the error of my ways. Because the more I think about it, there are some songs that should be banned.

Of course, we can't ban every single tune that is by a criminal or promotes criminal acts or radio stations would be left with a very short playlist. Gangsta rap songs about offing cops or torching variety stores are fine because people are simply missing the subtle meaning of the lyrics. But other songs have clearly crossed the line of common decency.

So, as a free public service to radio and video programmers, I have drawn up a "Dirty Dozen" list of the worst offenders. Ban them now. Ban them often.

1. "Feelings" by Morris Albert: This song clearly promotes unlawful sexual fondling and groping.

2. (Tie) "Bang Bang (My Baby Shot Me Down)" by Sonny & Cher and "Johnny Get Angry" by Joanie Sommers: Both songs advocate domestic violence by losers with names like Sonny and Johnny and bad hairdos by women with names like Cher and Joanie.

3. "You Light Up My Life" by Debbie Boone: What exactly are you lighting up there, Debbie? A crack pipe? Or are you simply advocating wanton arson? Either way, ban it.

4. "Sometimes When We Touch" by Dan Hill: Hasn't our own Danny Boy

learned to keep his filthy hands to himself, especially in crowded elevators or subway cars? School kids are hearing this trash.

5. "A Horse With No Name" by America: This "song" is a two-time loser. Besides its guilt as an obvious Neil Young rip-off, it plainly suggests cruelty to animals. "I've been through the desert on a horse with no name." Think about it. This bozo has been through the entire desert on a horse and has not even bothered to think up a lousy name for it. If that's the case, what are the chances he's going to water and feed the poor nag? Get a camel, ya lazy bastard. And name the fucking thing. Call it, oh... Gus. There, was that so hard? (I hope Gus bites your fat ass.)

6. "Baby I'm-A Want You" by Bread: Another double offender. This little number promotes both cradle robbing and bad grammar.

7. "Rocky Mountain High" by John Denver: Rocky Mountain High? C'mon, Johnny, who do ya think you're fooling? We know what you're talking about and it has nothing to do with topography or altitude, ya pot-sucking, child-corrupting geek. And another thing. Lose that fucking 'do. Haven't you ever looked in a mirror, for gawd's sake? You look like you got plastered — or was it "high"??? — and attacked yourself with a bowl and a Hair Whiz™.

8. "Young Girl" by Gary Puckett & The Union Gap: "Young Girl, get out of my mind/ My love for you is way out of line/ Better run, girl/ You're much too young, girl." What? A song about some perv chasing minors around with his pickle poking out of his pants? Ban it! And send this guy to Diddler's Row.

9. "Escape (The Piña Colada Song)" by Some Dink Whose Name I Forget: This song blatantly promotes consumption of cutesy, sugary drinks with tiny parasols and pink flamingos in them. Get a life, creep. And a beer.

10. "Take The Money And Run" by Steve Miller: This little ditty should be banned, not because it advocates knocking over gas stations, which is just good clean fun, but because it attempts to rhyme "Texas" and "facts is" and also "hassle" and "gas hole." Asshole. Hey — that rhymes too!

11. "Yummy Yummy (I Got Love in My Tummy)" by the Ohio Express: Promotes unsafe sex, unprotected blowjobs and the possibility of a cover version by Rod "Stomach Pump" Stewart.

12. "Honey" by Bobby Goldsboro: OK, "Bobby," if that's your real name — freeze. You've made it very clear that Honey is dead but you've failed to explain one tiny little detail: What exactly happened to her? Eh? Answer the fucking question, slimeball. Somebody get a warrant and check this creep's freezer.

Homespeak: A Buyer's Guide

The real estate market is one of those rare opportunities in which even a mere neophyte can invest $200,000 and quickly parlay it into $100,000. But the real trick for first-time homehunters is to crack the arcane code of real estate agents. Here, then, is a primer to compare what real estate agents and ads say (and what they really mean).

Real fixer-upper, a handyman's delight. (Falling apart.)

Century Home with loads of historic charm. (Condemned.)

Roughed-in fireplace and intercoms. (Many large holes in the wall.)

Vendors are very motivated to sell. (You would be too if you lived in this shithole.)

Shows to perfection. (Vendors have neat furniture, which they'll take with them.)

English cottage with rustic charm. (Weird, unidentifiable fungi and weeds growing out of crumbling walls and holes in roof.)

Good starter home. (Grungy shoebox.)

Unique. (Hideous.)

Affordable home for first-time buyer. (Trailer.)

Peaceful setting. (500 miles from the city.)

Convenient to subway/train. (Tracks run through your backyard.)

Good investment property. (You wouldn't dream of living in this pit yourself.)

Unique reno. (You won't believe what the asshole did to this dump.)

Neighbour's garden is very lush. (They haven't cut the grass in ten years.)

Show and sell. This won't last long, so call today. (This dump has been on the market for eight months without a nibble.)

Lake view. (If you stand on the roof on a clear day with a telescope, you might make out a tiny band of blue waaaaaaaay over there.)

Inquire about price. (We don't dare actually publish the price in the ad or you'd shit yourself laughing.)

Executive home. (Ridiculously overpriced.)

Reflects price of ownership. (Tacky Italianate mirrors on all the walls and ceilings.)

Hot! Hot! (No air-conditioning.)

Cozy neighbourhood. (Houses two feet apart.)

Open concept. (Termites in all the walls.)

Wide-open spaces. (No fences. The neighbours share your backyard.)

Fully air-conditioned with built-in sprinkler systems. (Holes in roof.)

Close to nature. (Raccoon in attic, mice in cupboards.)

Junior executive. (Big enough for anyone under five feet.)

Very clean. (That's the only good thing we can think of to say about this hole.)

Drastically reduced in price. (We've knocked a few thou off after tripling the original buying price.)

In-law suite. (Large closet in basement.)

Calling all yuppies. (Here's another slum you can renovate.)

Private sale. (Real estate agents have given up trying to unload this turkey.)

Sacrifice sale. (We're making only 800 per cent profit.)

Perfect for two-car family. (Vendor has paved the backyard.)

Must be seen in person. (We wouldn't dare show you a picture.)

Biff and Muffy Get Naked!

Life is one continual laff-riot around the old Burrill homestead, thanks to the rascally but lovable antics of my two youngsters, Biff and Muffy. Biff, who's in Grade 8, is the real "egghead" of the family. He's getting straight A's in science class and is forever up in his room, conducting some kind of experiment. Old Dad is not really sure what the young Einstein is up to. Something to do with little weight scales and Bunsen burners and some kind of white chemical compound. But the boy must be smart because his "chums" come over at all hours of the night and actually pay him money for samples of his chemistry experiments.

They say kids are lazy these days but not my Biff. Chipper? Why he can go two or three days straight without even sleeping! And talk? The kid's a regular little motormouth. It's like "Hi-Dad-how-are-you-gotta-go-bye-Dad-gotta-go." I'm telling you. He keeps us all in "stitches" around here!

But it's Muffy who's the little "prankster" of the family. She's in Grade 9 and you know how kids are at that age. She and her group of young people are forever up to some mischief or other. Like the time they "knocked over" the variety store on the corner. Or the time they "rolled" old Mr. Beasley down the street! Boy was he grumpy about that! But I gave him back the $12.75 they "scored" off him and a little extra to cover the medical bills for his "ruptured scrotum" and then pistol-whipped him until he finally agreed not to press charges. Ha ha ha! They're just a little too "spunky" for their own good sometimes!

But sometimes, to be honest, I kinda worry about the younger generation. I mean, take Biff, for example. Biff is a great one for making airplane models, just like his old dad used to do when he was a kid. And yet, for such a bright kid, to be painfully honest Biff is just not very good at airplane modelling. Lord knows the little nipper tries his best. He goes through six, seven, maybe eight tubes of airplane glue for a single Hawker Hurricane but just ends up lying on the floor with the little plastic flaps and landing gear bits stuck to his face. He's been working on the same model for over a year now, and, frankly, it's starting to look like a bit of a mess.

(*OK, Burrill. Enough already. You don't have any rascally but lovable kids. You're just bullshitting again to fill up space. — Ed.*).

Hey! How the hell am I supposed to write a column week in and week out without any rascally but lovable kids to drone on and on about?

It's not fair. I mean, we male WASP Boomer columnists don't have much else to talk about. Columnists like Michele Landsberg have it made. She never has any trouble coming up with column ideas:

1. Men suck.
2. Men bite.
3. Men are weasels.
4. Men are pigs.
5. Men: Dirtbags or merely scumballs?
6. Repeat cycle.

So that subject is pretty well covered, is what I'm saying. In other words, if I decide to sit down and write a column about what a bunch of weasels men are, I'll just get accused of being derivative, if not an outright plagiarist. I hate all kinds of men. Scads of them. But can I write columns about it every week? Noooooooooooooo. It makes it tough to come up with new material.

Luckily, we True Professionals can always come up with an entire column without having to rely on things like "facts" or "ideas."

Sort of like this crap.

Square Boy Gets No Vinyl

The Partridge Family is on while I'm writing this. And you know what? This may come as a shock. But I've just figured it out.

Danny Partridge isn't really playing his bass. The little fucker is faking it.

I can't even write about music any more. After about fifteen years or so, there are only so many euphemisms you can come up with for "loud and really shitty."

Not that I get a chance anyway. Around the old *eye* newsroom, all those damn Generation X dudes steal the good stuff that I really want, like the new Bubba & The Shrieking Cellmates box set. All Greg the Music Editor gives me to review is stuff like the new Linda McCartney solo album. I know, I know. I oughtta beat him senseless with a chair. Except he's a lot bigger than me. And he has this way of looking at you that makes you feel like you've just been offered a blindfold and a last butt. All this guy needs is a monocle and a cigarette holder. Here's my review:

LINDA McCARTNEY
My Daddy's Rich (So Piss Off)
Eastman Kodak Records

Linda McCartney has surrounded herself with musicians with whom she feels a common bond in the recording of this, her brilliant first solo album. The twelve-song compilation of goth-like tunery features scorching backing vocals by Rob and Fab of Milli Vanilli, who, using their real voices, sound eerily like an off-key Colonel Klink and Sgt. Schultz. In the rocking and raucous title tune, Peter Tork's searing lead riffery is ploddingly counter-pointed by the now-infamous "Hands of Stone" rhythm section from the Jeff Healey Band, which kicks up a sound that brings to mind a Tin Man being bludgeoned to death with a lead pipe while frantically trying to signal an S.O.S. on a foghorn. (Axeman Healey did not take part in the session as he was back in Toronto, mixing his latest album, *Hot Cheating Little Bitch I'm Tailing You*.)

On such cuts as "Jam'n'Tarts," Linda not only handles her customary keyboards but also jams on maracas, triangle and, in what has to be a world's first, even chips in with an eight-minute tambourine solo. Yoko Ono makes a guest appearance, bleating like a tortured sheep throughout the rousing, 20-minute "Town Pump." Linda's original tunes are assured but show a hint of husband Paul's influence on "I Wuv You Wittle Winky Woooo": "I went out to tea with my old auntie/Lovely fairy cakes and a poof through her panties/I wuv you wittle winky/I wuv you winky wooooooooooooooooo." And so on.

It sucks donkeys.

When I was a kid, Lik-M-Aid cost one cent. Used to buy it all the time on my way to school.

Purely on impulse, I bought some the other day on my way to "work." And you know what? Now it costs 25 cents. If I had only stockpiled, say, $10,000 worth of Lik-M-Aid when I was eight years old, it would now be worth a quarter-of-a-million bucks! Think about it. But that's not the scary thing. The scary thing is this: now Lik-M-Aid comes with instructions written on the package. To tell you how to eat it.

When I was a boy, we didn't need any instructions. We just figured it out for ourselves. No wonder the world is going to hell. Oh well. Guess I'll just tootle on up and see how Biff is doing with his science project. And maybe see if I can get the plastic Zero fuselage off his upper lip.

Kids these days.

Stratford Memories

So I went to Stratford the other night to see the new production of Shakespeare's *Macbeth*. It's the tragic story of a royal guy who is murdered, and then another royal guy kills a bunch of people, sees ghosts, goes nuts, has a lover who also goes bonkers and kills herself, and a final scene in which the hero kicks the bucket in a sword battle.

You might argue that this plot is not unlike Shakespeare's *Hamlet*, which is the tragic story of a royal guy who gets murdered, and another royal guy who sees ghosts, goes nuts, has a lover who also goes bonkers and kills herself, and a final scene in which the hero kicks the bucket in a sword fight.

But — as usual — Shakespeare's work has been sadly misinterpreted. The important and obvious difference between *Macbeth* and *Hamlet* is that Hamlet procrastinates before killing a bunch of people while Macbeth just gets right to the hacking, slashing, dicing and slicing without wasting time.

Likewise, many of the most famous lines of Willy the Shake's work have been grossly misunderstood. For example, in Macbeth, Lady Macbeth rises in the middle of the night and says, "Out, damned Spot!" Some scholars have read this as a reference to the fact that she cannot wash the blood of her dirty deeds off her hands. (This was in pre-O.J. times, when people did not wear gloves when they bumped people off.) But what Lady Macbeth actually meant when she said, "Out, damned Spot!" was that she had just noticed that the damn dog (cleverly named "Spot") had pissed on the carpet and would have to go "Out" to spend the night in the backyard. Thus: "Out, damned Spot!" (You would have thought that a writer of Shakespeare's genius would have come up with a more original name for a dog than Spot, but he was under a serious deadline that day and had a hangover you could take a picture of.)

It's the same deal with the famous line, "To be or not to be, that is the question," from *Hamlet*. Many scholars claim that this was a plaintive cry in which Hamlet was trying to decide whether or not to kill himself (which would be an understandable act if your parents named you "Hamlet." Imagine all the rumbles Hamlet must have got into in the school yard at recess over a handle like that? "Hey, Piglet! Oink oink! Nah nah! Boink. OUCH!"

(In truth, the reason the hero was named Hamlet was a cryptic message proving the persistent theory that the play was actually written, not by Shakespeare, but by Sir Francis Bacon, who got into a lot of recess punch-ups over both his first and last name. Hamlet. Bacon. I rest my case.)

But back to the key textual misinterpretation. The original folio of *Hamlet* indicates that the famous "To be or not to be" scene was actually set in a medieval underground parking lot, in which the hero is going slowly and tragically mad because he cannot remember where he parked his car.

In that first version, the lines read: "2B or not 2B, that is the question." You could look it up.

I once knew a Heavy Metal butthead, and we were watching TV and some old codger quoted Shakespeare's line, "All the world's a stage."

Heavy Metal Butthead: Like wow, man. Can ya believe an old bastard like that would be a Rush fan?

But I can understand the ignorance of youth. When I was in high school, my drama class made a field trip to Stratford to see the famed Shakespearean ham William Hutt star in a production of *King Lear*.

My friends and I, serious students of the arts all, waited until the lights went down and then crawled up the aisle under cover of darkness, snuck out and found the nearest pub, which turned out to be several blocks away. We had a couple of pitchers and then raced back in a torrential thunderstorm in time to mingle with the crowd during the intermission break.

We tried to look very innocent about the whole thing but our drama teacher cornered us, wanting to know how, during the first half of the play, we all mysteriously: a) got stinking drunk; b) became soaking wet; and c) were trying not to giggle but finally letting out a laugh like a suppressed fart every time we caught each other's eye.

But we weren't the only ones. That audience for that entire matinee performance of *Lear* was comprised of high school day-trippers and at least half of them were making noise and giggling all through what is not noted as one of Shakey's lighter knee-slappers. One guy from our school — his name was Mike, and he was famous for being suspended from every hockey league in my area due to his propensity for beating the crap out of people — became annoyed because a kid from another school kept putting his feet up on the back of Mike's chair.

Mike acted as any normal theatre-goer would do in such an impolite situation. It happened as William Hutt was in the middle of a moaning soliloquy in which he was holding one of his dead daughters in his arms on a stage littered with the bodies of many Slain Guys. The knob in the row behind put his feet on Mike's chair yet again (despite a previous warning). Mike reached behind him, grabbed Mr. Footsie by the throat and proceeded to beat the shit out of him.

King Lear: Oh! Oohh! Ohhh!

Mike: [Punching out perpetrator's lights] Take that and that and that ya fucking asshole.

Punchee: OW! OH. OUCH!!!

King Lear: [Peering into the seats with obvious annoyance] Oh! Ohhh! OH AND IF YOU DON'T STOP THAT RIGHT NOW I'M LEAVING.

Since Mike did not stop that, and since the crowd seemed more interested in Mike's act than William Hutt's, Hutt unceremoniously dropped his dead daughter on the stage and stormed off in the middle of the act.

Since Stratford's Festival Theatre has a thrust stage, there are no curtains to draw. So the other actors, all currently playing corpses, lay there for an uncomfortable minute or so and then — when it became obvious that Hutt was not coming back — rose from the dead as one and shuffled off the stage to an ovation of giggling and snorting.

End of show.

On the bus ride home our drama teacher said she had never been so humiliated in her life and we would never ever get to go on another field trip. But she later relented and took us to see a production of some play — it might have been *The Three Sisters* — at the O'Keefe Centre.

This time we did not sneak out and sneak back in at intermission. We snuck out and did not come back at all.

If I have to play theatre critic and compare sneaking out of *King Lear* to sneaking out of *The Three Sisters*, I would have to go with the latter. The O'Keefe Centre aisles are wider and better suited for crawling up in the dark. There are several pubs right down the street.

And it didn't even rain.

If You Go to San Francisco...

Just got back from California and, as always, going to California brings back a lot of memories, both bad and really gruesome. The first time I went out to California I was nineteen. I drove west in my '66 MGB, which I'd been able to afford by working in a factory making electronic comb brackets from midnight to 7 every night for nine months. Yep, I reckon I made more comb brackets than any man-jack or woman-jack of you lot. So there. I made millions of them. The fact that I never figured out what a comb bracket was for is not the point. The point is I never bothered to ask. I was that good.

Once winter came I quit my comb bracket career and bought the MGB and took off for California. I think I got the idea from a Led Zeppelin song when I was stoned on Toad Blotter. Sounded like a good idea at the time.

This was 1974, when we were in the grips of the Oil Crisis. You young-sters won't remember those days, but it was a time when the Big Multinational Fossil Fuel-Spewing Giants banded together and pretended they were running dry of oil. (Just for a laugh. They were really hoarding the stuff and snickering about how much they could jack up the price once we all got sucked in.) During the Oil Crisis, drivers were only allowed to buy gas every second day, depending on whether your licence plate ended in an even or odd number (this is in the days before people had vanity licence plates that spell out cute things like "FUCKU"). You had to be lined up at the pumps by 7 a.m. or the day's ration would run out before you got yours. Often gas-crazed drivers tried to cut into the line, which resulted in many comical scenes involving complete strangers beating the shit out of one another with baseball bats. It passed the time.

The MGB had a fuel range of about 300 miles (a whole bunch of kilome-tres) so I had to take the trip west slowly, staying for two days at a time in places like Des Moines, Iowa; Kearny, Nebraska; Cheyenne, Wyoming; Salt Lake City, Utah, and who could forget Elko, Nevada? I made the best of the experience by spending a lot of thoughtful hours drinking beer in cheap bars with the "locals," who usually had maybe two teeth and one brain cell among them.

Anyway. Got to California and did the cool hippie thing — rented a dive in Berkeley, just outside San Francisco and Haight-Ashbury, where my fel-low hippies had flowers in their hair. Not stuck in their hair — growing right out of their filthy skulls (you could also grow vegetables in your hair if you went without washing long enough). My first day in the City of Love, a crazed, acid-baked woman tried to stab me to death in a pizza joint. I did the brave thing. I ran around the restaurant screaming with the psycho in hot pursuit until she was tackled and disarmed by a black marine sergeant. I bought him a beer.

Next day my flophouse neighbour, some guy named J.D., came over to my room for a social call. I should have guessed something was odd when J.D. took off his shirt, put on my leather jacket and kept stroking the leather sleeves while he played my Ziggy Stardust album over and over. But I was a rookie in the City of Love and I just thought he was weird, like everyone else I'd met. I went to the corner for a six-pack and when I returned J.D. was lying on my bed with his pants off and his hard on. Two days in town and already I'd had two dangerous weapons pointed at me. I tried to kick him out but he refused to believe I was serious until I pulled out my .22-calibre gas-powered Luger-replica pellet gun and told him "Beat it!"

Bad choice of words...

At the Berkeley campus I met a pretty flower child named Poppy who was playing guitar. I introduced myself and soon we were trading songs. She would play "You Are My Sunshine" and then I would play, say, "Why Don't We Get Drunk And Screw?" You know. Love songs.

Poppy invited me to a "big party" at her place that night and I drove out there. To my surprise she lived in a huge, spooky mansion. Poppy answered the door, told me to take off my shoes, leave the beer in the car and put out the cigarette. She introduced me to a room full of zombies as "Brother Bill" and soon I was surrounded by people who were making intense eye contact and rubbing my shoulders and praising every dumb thing I said. We sat down at a long, Last Supper-like table that had no legs and ate a meal of some kind of slop that contained nothing edible and certainly no protein. No one was drinking, smoking or doing drugs. As for sex, when I took Poppy's hand and, you know, suggested we lose these clowns, she started to cry.

When I went outside for a butt I was closely tailed by a Chinese guy. He even followed me into the can. The dinner ended when some old short-hair in a bad Nehru shirt and huge medallion made a speech about one world, one people all living in peace and then invited me to join them "on the bus" for a trip to their private camp near Mendocino. Everyone else oohed and ahhhed and said "Yes! Please come on the bus, Brother Bill." Then they actually presented a slide show of shiny happy people prancing blissfully around the camp. By now I had pretty much clued in to the fact that I was dealing with a room full of Moonies. So I pretended I was thrilled at the idea and even offered to give them my car and money. Which is what they seemed to be hinting at. I bullshitted them into trusting me and then — when my minder let down his guard — I bolted shoeless for the door and jumped into my MGB. It was blocked in by other cars but I got the engine fired up fast and burned sod while tearing across the front yard with several Brothers and Sisters in chase.

I wasn't ready to become a brainwashed Moonie. Not unless they served free beer. I hate grape Kool-Aid.

I didn't stop driving until I reached Los Angeles.

Holy Shitimachi, I'm Turning Japanese!

TOKYO — The Japanese have to be the friendliest people on this planet. I was only "in country" for five minutes before I found myself in a small, well-lighted place, buck naked and surrounded by four complete (but very good looking, I might add, in case they are reading this dispatch) strangers. Unfortunately, they were:

a) All men
b) Had uniforms
c) Had guns
d) Had a keen interest in my prostate gland.

This "friendliness thing" comes as somewhat of a shock. I mean, I guess it's a local custom, since these men identified themselves as "customs officers." Maybe I'm not clued in to the "ways of the world," but in Canada even my very best friends do not tend to shove their fingers up my ass — at least not until after maybe ten beers. The probe team found a light bulb, a coke bottle and that "Dinky toy" I've been missing since I was 5. I had wondered what happened to that. It's a really cool Jaguar (white). But — and this seemed to come as a great disappointment to my new pals — they did not find whatever they were poking around for. They also closely inspected my bag (and also my luggage). Must be something about my manly, rugged good looks that allows me to make intimate friends so closely and easily.

Finally they said goodbye — a little grudgingly, I thought — but they didn't even kiss me. I think next time I want to play "poker" I'll go to Vegas. (By the way, my prostate was just fine.)

Japan is actually a very cool place. For one thing, even in business meetings, the Japanese love to drink. Here's an actual quote from my Lonely Planet Travel Survival Kit book on Japanese culture:

"Japanese culture features a serious interest in drinking and, unlike most other Asian countries, drinking is a popular pastime for both sexes. It is routinely taken to excess, presumably as a release from the straitjacket of proper conduct at work... By 11 p.m. in most Japanese cities, it can seem that everyone on the streets is in various stages of inebriation. Fortunately, the Japanese are fairly good-natured drunks. Drunkenness is readily tolerated as an excuse for bad behaviour."

In general, the Japanese let it all hang out. My guidebook notes, "It is quite common to see men urinating in public — typically in the evening in the bar district." Go for it, is my way of looking at it. Or at least go...

I'm trying to take a crash course in the Japanese language and here are some actual, not even made-up Japanese words you might be wise to commit to memory. Class, be seated.

Mibun — 'Social rank,' also of extreme interest to Tokyo customs officers.
Ofuku — 'Return ticket,' in case you choose to make a side trip to such Japanese exotic spots as Fukui, Fukuyama, Fukuoka, Fukuda, Fukue-Jima, or who could pass up on an excursion to Shitamachi? Not this boy.

Other words of interest and extreme importance include:
Wafuku — Japanese-style clothing.
Yofuku — Western-style clothing.
Shitimachi — As previously noted, this word designates the low-lying, less affluent part of Tokyo.
Daifuku — Literally, 'great happiness' — and I guess if you are getting fucked every day it would bring a smile to your face.
New Humans — This is the Japanese term for, and I quote, "The younger generation, brought up in more affluent times than their parents, who consequently are less respectful of the frugal values of the post-war generation."
Kachi-Gumi — "The victory group." They refuse to believe Japan lost World War II. Just because they own America, what would give them that idea?
Sayonara.

Totalled in Tokyo

Kino O nomisugimashita.

That's the key phrase to memorize here in Japan. It means "Yesterday I drank too much." That's why the phrase ends with "shita," as in "feel like..."

But you have to take the lows if you want the highs. You've gotta pay if you want to play and — believe me — there are plenty of places to play in this city of twelve million people. There are bars everywhere and even beer vending machines on every street corner. Of course, I'm here strictly on business and what that entails is none of your business.

The trouble with doing business in Tokyo is that you have to speak through an interpreter and you can never be sure the interpreter is translating your speech accurately. Take this anecdote from *Uncle John's Bathroom Reader*. An American businessman started a speech with a joke and not only got a huge laugh from the Japanese audience, but even — to his surprise — a standing ovation. He thanked the translator and said: "I've been telling that joke in Japan for years and that's the first time I got a laugh. You sure know how to deliver a joke."

It was only later that someone tipped him off that what the translator had actually said in Japanese was as follows: "American businessman is starting speech with joke... I don't know why American businessman thinks he needs to tell a joke... he thinks I am telling the joke right now... I won't even bother to translate it because you won't understand it... The polite thing to do when he finishes joke is to laugh [pause]... he is almost finished joke [pause]... OK... now... laugh."

The Japanese are extremely polite, even if they privately think you are a wombat's asshole.

Good thing, too, about them beer-vending machines, because it's been over 100°F and so humid you might as well be in a sauna. So the routine I've discovered is: Walk a block, drink a beer, walk a block, drink a beer, repeat process. (It is vital in this heat to keep your fluid level topped up, simply for medicinal reasons, you understand.) And when you take your sneakers off in a typical Japanese restaurant, as is the custom, it is amusing to watch the locals keel over. Then you can steal their beer, which is also a good thing, because everything here costs roughly 100 times what it goes for in Canada.

There are more than 2,000 McDonald's in Tokyo. The Japanese sure love their Big Macs. In fact, a Japanese teacher I met said he took his students on a trip to the United States and they were shocked to find out that they actually had McDonald's in the U.S., too. Of course, here in Tokyo, a Big Mac costs roughly the same price as a small house in Toronto. The Japanese wouldn't even stoop to pick up a Canadian $100 bill unless they were short of bum wad (which I found is in short supply here in the land of the Rising Thumb). My hotel minibar tab alone was $35,000 yen (more than $350 U.S.).

I hung out with some of the NFL San Diego Chargers in the hotel bar. They were in town to play an exhibition game called the "Tokyo Bowl" against the Pittsburgh Steelers. Now these guys, at six-foot-eight, 350 pounds, weren't hard to spot in the tiny Japanese crowd (unless we're talking about a crowd of sumo wrestlers — nice buns on them boys!). "You guys players?" I asked a couple of hulks in the bar. They were dressed in cut-off jeans and ripped T-shirts. "Yeah," a Charger offensive lineman said. "How could you tell — because we're so well dressed?" Several beers ensued, which accounts for the fact that the Chargers stomped the Steelers 20-10 the next day, all thanks to me. Beer: breakfast of champions.

I'm not religious, but I visited a Shinto temple because this is a faith I can get behind. It has a) no founder, b) no ordained preachers, c) no written scriptures, and d) you can choose to worship whatever you please — for example, a tree, an eye columnist — mmmmm, maybe even a beer bottle...

The Long Hot Summer

How I spent my summer vacation...

I guess one way that I could put it is: If you are going to fuck up, you might as well throw your whole heart into it.

You can tell you're screwing up when you actually start winning trophies, medals and other awards for Sheer Ineptitude. Call it The Summer of Living Stupidly. I have the proof right here (and a few scars).

ITEM: On a trip to San Francisco I entered a bowling tourney as captain of a team called The Three Dirty Dwarves. The fact that none of us had ever bowled 10-pin didn't alter our decision to compete: It seemed like a good idea at the time, is what I'm saying.

To say we stunk is about the equivalent of saying Saddam Hussein is nuts. In others words, the obvious. Walking halfway up the alley tossing the ball between your legs while facing backwards. That sort of talent. Even then my shot ended up in the gutter.

After the tournament I was having a beer and a guy came up and said, "Step outside. I have something to give you." Now where I come from, the only thing people give you when you're asked to step outside a bar is a severe shit-kicking.

"What did I do?" I asked. "I got no problem with you."

"Just step outside." So I did. And it turned out that "outside" was another room in which they were handing out the bowling awards. And it shocked the shit out of me to hear them calling my name for an award: a lovely trophy for "Most Spirited Team" (read: Drunkest Team) and a special mention for the captain personally (me) for scoring the most gutter balls. It is one of those beautiful trophies that your wife says will look just fine in the furnace room.

It could have been worse, I suppose. I could have been GOOD at bowling. Now that would have been frightening...

ITEM: On a trip to Tokyo I played one of those laser war games. The battle was tight until I decided to lead a charge. In the end, for my extreme bravery, I ended up with a fake Congressional Medal of Honor medal and an award for the Person Who Got Blown to Bits the Most Times (not to mention the minor concussion). I ended up with a score of negative 2,300. If war really breaks out in Iraq again and I'm drafted — as a (very) last resort — I predict my lifespan will be approximately three seconds. Operation Desert Dweeb.

ITEM: So then it's sixteen hours on a plane back to San Francisco, complete with jet-lag, head wound and more than a few beers. What a good idea, thought I, it would be to call up my ex-girlfriend whom I had not seen in thirteen years. She's now a partner in a San Francisco law firm. My advice to any of you guys considering such a move: Don't.

Actually she was very understanding: I didn't win any trophies but I did get a free couch and a delicious breakfast. In the morning I said, "This wasn't a very good idea." For some reason, she agreed.

ITEM: My good pal and editor Wolfgang D. (not his real name to protect his loved ones) gave me a Serious Talking To before he passed out in the outhouse up at our cottage.

So I'm starting clean this fall. New attitude. New work ethic. I even went on the wagon for a century or so (well, OK, it was only two days but it seemed like a looong time). I also kicked my heroin habit (actually, I've never had a heroin habit but it sounds trendy to say you've kicked one).

Fall. Time to get busy. Gotta put my nose to the ol' grindstone — which would hurt like hell, as much as I can figure. I mean, how are you gonna work with your nose ground off? But if that's what it takes, by god, I'll DO IT.

Got books to write. Got books to promote (*Hemingway: The Toronto Years*, published by Doubleday, now available in beautiful trade paperback in fine stores everywhere).

Even the Hemingway book gets me in shit. My friend Brian Fawcett the Actual Writer sent me an email that someone named Debbie had for some reason sent to him. It was entitled: "burrill, one lucky dude" and it went on for two pages and you could tell that Debbie and her friends must be really poetic garret dwellers because the whole thing was written in lower case.

It was a story about how she and her two male friends Vern (nice handle) and somebody else were getting hammered and pouring beer on their own heads and they decided that they were "living in a Hemingway story." Then they started talking about me and my book and — although she freely admits that none of them had actually read it — they collectively decided to find me and "kick the shit out of [me]."

Luckily, they somehow ended up pissed out of their minds instead. How Hemingwayesque. Anyway, to Debbie and friends I say: meet me at midnight Friday. You'll get your butt kicked. Not by me, of course. I'm not going anywhere at that hour. But hey — Hemingway would. Don't be a suckhole. Besides it's FUN riding in a meat wagon.

I'm going to shave off the beard I grew. Maybe that's why people want to pound on me. There's something about looking like a biker from hell that makes people aggressive toward you.

Maybe I'll get a bikini wax at the same time... Hemingway did.

Psych 101

New Year's Day. Time to reflect on things past. All those who feel guilty about things they have done in the last year, please rise and come over to my house for a beer. All those with a totally clear conscience, get the fuck outta here. What planet are you living on?

It is a scientifically proven fact — especially if you are a magazine columnist — that you have to be a jerk now and then or you will end up with nothing to write about but your house in the suburbs and your witty neighbours and the cute thing that your wife/kids/dog did at the mall.

My feeling, after several seconds of deep thought, is that if you do not feel at least slightly bad about the way you've acted in the last year, it's time to see how far you can fly off the nearest bridge. You're not living your life anyway, so why take up space?

As a minor example, I got a call from a friend the other day who said I was using "low- grade psychology" on her to make her feel guilty. We are sort of phone pals because at least half of us is nuts. I promptly apologized. But then I got to thinking: Was it really Low-Grade Psychology? When I was in university I majored in English and Psych and my best marks by far came in the psychology courses. Beowulf can fuck himself. I remember one course — "Bird Psych 303," I believe it was called — in which I attained a 90 per cent grade without attending a single class. My college girlfriend was in the same class and would rise at 7 in the morning and actually go to the campus. I would sleep until noonish and when she came home I would ask her what the prof had prattled on about. And then I did the important thing: I read the textbooks the night before the final exam (bennies aren't just for truck drivers, you know). When the results came in, I had 90 per cent and she had 74. She was, to put it politely, fucking pissed off at me.

Low Grade Psychology? Hardly. I have the marks to prove it.

I could tell you all about passive/aggressive cognitive dissonance etc., etc., etc. I could claim to be an existentialist, a nihilist, a Dadaist. Or I could simply say that sometimes I'm an asshole.

That's life...

I did ONE good thing this year: I brought the freezing spider on the outside window inside for the winter. Friends say that's crazy because spiders are supposed to die in winter. But I say "Sez who?" I find dead bugs for her (I'm assuming it is a "she," but who can tell? Where do you look?) and she is still alive and well as of January; she hangs out in the corner of my living room. If anyone knows how to feed a spider, get in touch... Or just mail me your dead bug.

You know, the light you see from the distant stars is actually something like six million years old. It takes that long to get to us. And maybe a reflection of everything we did in our life will reach some distant galaxy in another six million years. Bore them shitless.

If we could travel faster than the speed of light we might even be able to look back at our own past. Or else we could just fry our eyes out with red-hot pokers. Besides, I have a feeling that if you were travelling faster than the speed of light you would be too G-force air-sick to deeply regret the time you did You Know What I'm Talking About.

Forget about sweating about it at 4 in the morning. That's for amateurs.

As I stated: If you are guilty, the beer's on me (just as long as you keep your beer — semi-digested or otherwise — OFF me).

Puritans need not apply.

When I was a kid and my dad died and my stepdad kicked the shit outta me daily, I was hanging with a My Three Sons/Brady Bunch friend who showed me a model airplane his father had made for him. Not a plastic pre-fab. Out of real wood. Struts and all. He left it with me when he went to lunch. I smashed it with a large rock. Why? Can't really say. When he came back he cried and then ran for his older brother and I said two Big Kids did it and they went that-away down the railroad track. And — to my surprise — Big Brother actually sprinted down the tracks and found two Big Kids who matched my imaginary description to the letter. But, to my dwindling credit, I said, "No, it wasn't them. It was me."

Why? Did I say I didn't know? I lied. I know why.

Low-grade psychology.

I guess we use it on each other all the time, even if we don't know how to spell it. I've had my share of deeply psychological experiences in the last twelve months. I think I told you earlier about how I visited my ex-girl-friend in San Francisco on the flip side of a trip to Japan. That was weird. It was like a Seinfeld episode except we didn't drink coffee and talk about Absolutely Nothing. And Kramer never did skid through the door.

Anyway, somehow — like a symbol — I got back from Tokyo to find an airline safety vest in my carry-on bag when I got home. How it got there... one never knows, does one? It's hanging on the wall in my office, you know — just in case.

I guess what I'm hinting at is that I'm not the perfect Shiny Happy Person. But if I were — and students, please take note of the use of future conditional tense — then I would have nothing to write about.

Except maybe my house in Riverdale and my witty neighbours and the cute thing that my wife/kids (if any can prove it in court)/dogs did at the mall. I might even sink so low as to talk about my pet spider...

Our Man in Cartagena

CARTAGENA, COLOMBIA — The streets are only wide enough for a horse cart to pass. Balconies hang overhead, spilling over with the kind of beautiful flowers that spill over balconies in South America. Church domes rise over shady squares. Five-hundred-year-old walls surround the city, with their cannon still pointed expectantly out at the Caribbean Sea. It makes a pretty picture, especially after three beers. But few know of the horrors that lurk in Cartagena's dark past.

Off the Plaza de Bolivar is a three-storey colonial building with a mas-sive baroque stone entrance. This is the Palacio de la Inquisicion. This imposing structure was, for more than 200 years, the seat of the dreaded Spanish Inquisition. No one knows how many innocent souls were dragged before the Grand Inquisitor and then burned at the stake just for laughs. Even to this day, a room in the Palace is filled with a rack, stocks, hangy-up thingies and other gruesome reminders of man's inhumanity to man. And what is most horrifying to some visitors is this medieval burning, flailing, impaling and scrotum-stretching was supposedly only abolished in 1811.

I say supposedly because, after one week in Colombia, I can now reveal this shocking news: the unspeakable tortures have not ended. The only difference is they no longer call the hellish torment an "Inquisition." Now they call it a "one-week, all-inclusive package tour."

Last week I was crowing about spending a week in sun-soaked Colombia at a resort whose biggest selling point was that it offered unlimited free food and booze to its residents. I thought that this would be a pretty nice way to spend a week. And don't get me wrong: I had a great time in Colombia. Loved the old city of Cartagena, loved the beach, loved the Colombians (except the ones who kept trying to braid my hair). Even the coke dealers were very friendly, as far as hardened, crazed, potentially very dangerous hombres go.

But that hotel. Man, I gotta tell you. Never, ever again. The joint had five restaurants and as many bars, all operating at full tilt from dawn 'til 2 in the morning or so. But I quickly noticed that I was one of the very few packaged turistas there who weighed in at 145 pounds soaking wet.

I now have intimate knowledge of from whence the expression "to belly up to the bar" came. I mean, these people were huge, mean, ugly and all elbows.

Sure, I was able to get my share of free booze by crawling on all fours between the thickets of blubbering thighs and popping up at the front of the bar like a crotch-kicking jack-in-the-box with a stun gun and a can of mace. But it was work. And work is what you're trying to avoid on a one-week vacation.

But, ah yes, the tortures. You want to know about the horrible tortures I was forced to endure until I almost CRACKED!

Our room was right over the hotel pool and sound stage. From 8 or so in the morning, when the aerobics weasels started mincing around, until well past midnight, when the last Karaoke Klown had sputtered out, we were assaulted by the inhumane sound of non-stop disco.

The thing about disco that makes it an effective torture tool is that all the songs sound exactly the same from a distance. That's because all you can hear is the bass.

BUMPA-BOOMPA-BUMPA-BOOMPA.
Get down, fat turista!
BUMPA-BOOMPA-BUMPA-BOOMPA.
You bloated clown, fat turista!
BUMPA-BOOMPA-BUMPA-BOOMPA.
You made me spew, fat turista!
BUMPA-BOOMPA-BUMPA-BOOMPA.
It looks like stew, fat turista!
BUMPA-BOOMPA-BUMPA-BOOMPA.

Layered over the sound of the continuous disco was the nonstop babble of the Impossibly Cheezy Hotel Activities Co-Ordinator. Everyone onstage for the Miss Bikini Contest! Everyone in the pool for the Balloon Relay Race! Line up for the Man With the Best Legs Who Sounds Sort of Like Elvis (But Not Much) Contest!

All this gibberish was hurled non-stop at members of a poolside crowd who were mostly interested in the How Much Free Food Can I Stuff Myself with Before My Guts Actually Shoot Out My Asshole Contest, or the Boy Don't I Look Just Like a Beached and Boiled Beluga Pageant. Or, in my case, the Crazed Sniper on the Balcony Shoot-a-Thon!

We interrupt this torture for another important disco ditty:
BUMPA-BOOMPA-BUMPA-BOOMPA.
Drink booze, fat turista!
BUMPA-BOOMPA-BUMPA-BOOMPA.
Get stewed, fat turista!
BUMPA-BOOMPA-BUMPA-BOOMPA.
Get fried, fat turista!
BUMPA-BOOMPA-BUMPA-BOOMPA.
Pie-eyed, fat turista!
BUMPA-BOOMPA-BUMPA-BOOMPA.

One of the cruellest torments of the Spanish Inquisition was to force the poor victim to continually drink water until he or she actually burst. This was thought to have been abolished centuries ago but actually it was only slightly modified. Now, with the All You Can Gargle at the Free Bar Torture, modern-day victims eschew water for watery, pissed-in rum punch drinks that have unsuspecting turistas exploding left, right and centre, like a Fourth of July fireworks display. Oooooooo. Did you see that one? Ahhhhhhhh! He blew up real good! So, as you can clearly see, the Torture continues. The only difference is that the victims of the Spanish Inquisition were innocent.

But today, hell, we deserve whatever we get.

As I fled the compound, running for my very life to a nice, quiet bar where they actually made you pay for your beer in exchange for some peace and quiet, I could still hear that horrible sound ringing in my ears.

BUMPA-BOOMPA-BUMPA-BOOMPA.

BUMPA-BOOMPA-BUMPA-BOOMPA.

BUMPA-BOOMPA-BUMPA-BOOMPA.

AIIEEEEEEEEEEEEEEEEEEE!!!!!

The horror.

The horror!

You Just Gotta Laugh

LOS ANGELES — I guess the first clue that things were getting a trifle out of hand was when I found myself chasing a midget down a dark alley in the bad part of south L.A.

It happened like this: This midget comes up to me and tries to sell me a genuine Italian 14-karat gold neck chain. Only, like, a hundred bucks. He even burned it with a lighter to show it was real, although I have no idea what burning genuine 14-karat Italian gold with a lighter proves. I told him I wasn't interested. He said OK, name your price. I said I have no U.S. cash. I even showed him my wallet — which I'd forgotten held a U.S. $50 bill. I got distracted by a hooker who was trying to hit on me and, as I was losing her, I realized the midget had dropped the chain in my hand and grabbed the fifty bones from my wallet and was running like hell down the alley. Now, midgets are not famous for their sprinting ability, but I must admit this guy could motor. And he had a good headstart. I lost him in the alley and came across a bunch of dudes who were smoking something (ten guesses). I said, did you just see a guy run past here? They looked at me with wired eyes and said, "Yo man, we see a lotta dudes run past here."

I said: "This one is easy to pick out. He's three feet tall, give or take, he's black, and he's got my fifty bucks." They all just looked at each other and shrugged. Pissed me off for a while but then I developed a new philosophy: "You just gotta laugh."

Stayed at the Hyatt. Saw some bands, hit some clubs. Did some actual work. I even — I don't want to disillusion anyone out there — used the weight room and Jacuzzi each morning. Found out I can lift 185. Not very far, weighing only 140 myself, but definitely in the air. Now I know why they say body builder weasels are "ripped," although I suspect the bit that I ripped was not what they had in mind. Also found out I could drop a 25-pound hand weight on my right big toe (which is now way bigger). Just call me Gimpy.

The last day my buddy Tom and I were sunning on Venice Beach and drinking a few Cream Sodas (or something — I can only attest to the fact that whatever we were drinking was cold and wet). Up on the beachside path a blond rollerblading surfer dude with gravel for brains ran over the little dog of a strolling black guy. Words were exchanged and the next thing I knew they were lying on the sidewalk pounding the shit out of each other. I'd had just enough cream sodas to decide it was a good idea to race up and break up the fight, especially since the surfer dude was clearly winning. And so I did (I've got the bruises to prove it).

I finally got between them like a boxing referee and held them apart with my arms. "Are you cool?" I asked the black guy, who had blood all over his nose and teeth. He said, "Yeah, I'm OK. But he hit my dog." Then I turned to surfer boy and said, "Cool out. Break it up."

He grinned a smug surfer boy grin and said, "OK, man. I'm chilled. But I still wouldn't mind taking another punch at the nigger."

Where are all the 1,000,000-volt stun guns when you need them? Eat tasty death, surfer boy. Anyway, I got them apart. And, by the way, the dog was OK. Thank god for cream soda.

Downtown Los Angeles is like a ghost town. There's nothing there. It's like walking through a skyscraper canyon. To get to any place where the action is you need a car or a $40 cab ride (each way). I know some 900,000 Canadians live in L.A. (making it, like, the third-largest Canadian city in the world) but for my money I'll take a little town by the lake that they call Toronto.

But any time you're down in La-la-land give me a call and Dusty and Warren and Jack and I will get together and do lunch and blue-sky some projects and then talk package.

On the plane I had a roughly 900-pound guy in the seat in front of me. He had his seat all the way back and was crushing me. He had headphones on even though he was asleep. And he farted up a major storm.

You could get a trifle pissed off.

Or you could just laugh.

City on Fire

LOS ANGELES — The first thing I did when I met Michael Jackson face to "face" at a Tinseltown party was to say something extremely witty, as only we razor-sharp columnist types are capable of on the spur of the moment.

I had bullshitted my way into the "VIP" lounge of the Sony-owned Columbia Pictures lot when there he was, the gloved one himself, right in front of me. I said — this was clever — "Oh, Michael Jackson! Hi."

He smiled a Mikey-like smile and extended his hand to shake. Not exactly a Chuck Norris grip, but a handshake all the same. And — this was the scary part — he did it without a glove. I am not sure if he immediately ran off and dunked his hand into a huge vat of industrial-strength germicide … but I know I did.

Next we hit the Glam Slam club, owned by His Purpleness, the Man Who Was Once Known As Prince.

There was a huge lineup on the street outside and — as usual for a trendy L.A. club — everybody was either a "VIP" or "on the list." But nobody was getting past the extremely beefy Door Monster. A scout with a clipboard was cruising the lines and tapping people at random. You can go in. You can't. And most couldn't, not even John Wayne Bobbitt, who — I am not making this up — barged to the front of the mob with his usual entourage of losers. Leave it to a Bobbitt to try to take a shortcut. The door monster told him to get lost.

Once I had weaseled my way inside, the Ramones were just finishing a wild all-out set and then two never-heard-of-'em bands played and then it was like 2 in the morning and then — nothing. Prince (dare I breathe his name aloud) was supposed to come on but he was a no-show. I even sneaked backstage and knocked on his dressing-room door. I'd had just enough cocktails to make this seem like a good idea. Did the guy think we had all night to hang around? In short: yes. While we waited, I chatted at the bar with Hall of Fame pitcher Rollie Fingers.

Me: Oh hi. You're Rollie Fingers.

Fingers: Grunt.

Finally I asked Rollie where the men's can was. I had to pee and if anyone would know where the men's can would be, it would be a Hall of Fame reliever named "Fingers." Either him or Jim Palmer.

His Purple Majesty took the stage after 4 a.m. He had sparkly things in his hair and either a "Prince" symbol on his face or someone had been playing tic-tac-toe on his right cheek to pass the time.

By the time he finished an arrogant set of jamming around on a bass guitar with his back to the crowd, it was daylight and there weren't enough hangers-on left in the club to lay a proper beating on a mime. (Note: under U.S. federal law, a mob of no less than 100 is required to lay a proper beating on a mime.) Prince, viewed from ten feet away, is maybe four feet tall in platform heels.

Just about the right size for a spanking.

Next night I hit Johnny Depp's club, the Viper Room. Same huge mob of "VIP"s and "on the list"s who were "not getting in." I used my usual method — sheer gall — to get past the doorman but then he noticed I was toting a bulky backpack.

"Hey. No bags."

"Why not?"

"You might be bringing stuff in."

"I might be bringing stuff in my pockets. I don't need a bag to do that."

No matter. I had to find a parking lot on Laribie Street and — this is a first — park my knapsack in a car lot. It cost me ten bucks — real bucks, not the Monopoly money they hand out around here.

The Viper Room is a small black smoky box designed to encourage suicide. I was at the bar for at least ten full seconds before someone tried to sell me drugs. It was, he assured me, "most cool." Meet him in the can. But the prospect of doing drugs in the same black dingy crapper where River Phoenix OD'd somehow gave me the creeps. And besides, Johnny Depp was watching our every move from his own private booth with the one-way mirror, in case we tried to buy Kate Moss a square meal. So I stuck to the usual until I finally stumbled out on to Sunset Boulevard late into the night. I would have stayed all night but — hey? — my backpack was double-parked.

There Are Some Things You Just Can't Outsmart

SAN FRANCISCO — I once left my heart (and other bits) in this city. It was eleven years ago. We had an apartment over at Franklin and Lombard, a short walk from Fisherman's Wharf. We used to go out to the pier and have dinner, a few drinks. On the day it all blew to hell I packed my bags and walked out to the end of the pier to look at the bay. Alcatraz and the Golden Gate and the white rubberneck boats. The water was very blue. I grabbed a cab and took off for the airport but when the driver asked me where I was going I had to admit I had no idea.

It turned out to be Mexico.

I found my heart again in a place called San Miguel. It was sitting in a cantina, guzzling tequila with the town drunk, Pancho Pemex, so named because he could produce more natural gas than many Third World nations combined. (Sorry for all the cheesy Tony Bennett references. Did I tell you that Tony is a close friend of mine? Years back, I wrote something snotty about him in *The Toronto Star*, when he was over at the Imperial Room. Next day a delivery guy came into the newsroom and handed me a bouquet of thirteen roses and a card from Tony. I was flattered until the mob reporter told me what it means when somebody sends you thirteen roses. Tone, if you're reading this, I want to assure you that I have nothing but the highest regard for you and your work. May I call you "Mister"?)

In Mexico I went to bullfights. To see what they were like. The bulls died and were tied to horses and dragged out of the ring, leaving a trail of blood in the sand. I didn't like to see the bulls die but there are some things you can't do anything about.

I like Hemingway but I have never understood why he liked to see animals die. His argument was that he killed animals to keep from killing himself. This is not a good system. Eventually you run out of animals.

Anyway, there I was, back in San Francisco. After a very long day of being a Professional Journalist I went out to the wharf and walked out to the end of the pier. It was midnight and everything was closed. The place was deserted. A searchlight swooped around from the watchtower on Alcatraz. The Golden Gate Bridge was lit up and stretched off into the night, disappearing into the fog. I thought of the time I came out here to say goodbye to the city. You always wish you could do these things the way Humphrey Bogart would do it. Saying goodbye.

But I've never been very good at these things.

On the way back to the hotel I paused to watch them making a movie at Post and Hyde. It was a disaster movie. A whole corner of the block had blown to hell and firemen and cops and ambulances were everywhere, the red and amber lights swinging around in the night. Cameras were rolling.

The next morning on the plane I read the paper and found out that the disaster had been no movie. A building had blown to hell. Two dead so far, many others in bad shape. An eyewitness, quoted in the *Chronicle*, described the explosion as follows: "It was like a really big boom."

I turned the page and there was another headline that read, "Suicide Shocks Half Moon High School Students." It made me wonder why the other half had been so heartless.

Trixie was our second oldest dog. Eleven years old. Seventy-seven in dog years. She was more intelligent than many humans I know. She was old and had a bad heart and we knew it was coming but didn't want to.

It was a Sunday morning not long ago. She came in from the backyard and it happened. I was in the bedroom but knew it was bad by the way my wife called my name. I tried to hold Trixie up, tried whatever I could think of. Trixie wasn't giving up easy, fighting for it. But there are some things you can't outsmart.

My wife tried artificial respiration. She took her to the vet's in the van. I threw on some clothes and followed in my car. Trying to hurry but held up by some Sunday driver who took perverse pleasure in blocking the road, giving the finger when you honked to get out of the way. I swung around to the wrong side of the road and ran a red light.

All the vet could do was be sympathetic and offer a reasonable rate to "dispose" of the body. But there are some things that you simply do not throw away.

I carried her out and put her in the car. Curled up in the front seat, she was still warm when I patted her and she looked like she was sleeping. If there's a dog heaven, you can bet that Trixie's already found out where they keep the food.

It was a sunny day, but for some reason it was hard to see the road.

Frisco was our other old dog. Twelve years old, eighty-four in dog years. He had been a kennel dog in England for the first year or so of his life and someone must have been mean to him because he barked at everyone and especially distrusted men. It took a year before he trusted me but once he did, he decided he was my dog.

When he wasn't lying in his favourite spot — behind the toilet — he followed me everywhere, to the point where I suddenly understood what it meant to be "dogged" by someone. He lay by my desk when I wrote, or out on the deck, keeping an eye on the world in case there was something that needed emergency barking at. Even after he got old and sick, he still tried to tootle after me wherever I went, wagging his tail. But he was very sick and the vet said nothing could be done.

I got back from San Francisco just in time to say goodbye to Frisco.

I'm still not very good at these things.

A Blowhard in the Windy City

CHICAGO — I was in my usual suite with my size 10s up on the windowsill, tickling my tonsils with scotch and looking down on the Chicago River as it slopped past the old Wrigley skyscraper. I was in town to do a job. In my racket you have to stay ahead of the game if you want to keep calling yourself a two-fisted, hard-boiled Video Game Columnist. And a little bird told me there was some action shaking down over at the convention centre on the waterfront. I bought myself another belt from the desk mickey and then it was time to go out and burn some shoe leather.

I flagged a hack outside the hotel and told the cabbie to step on it. We took Wacker Drive past the Loop and down to the lakeshore and followed the water past the museum and Soldier Field and pulled up by the McCormick Center. It was three storeys of only the best concrete and glass, big and sprawling but no larger than the state of Nevada. I headed for the entrance but a sour-looking gunslinger dressed up in a security guard's costume blocked my path.

"Where's your badge?"

I flashed him my badge. He looked at it then looked at me and knew he was looking at a real Video Game Columnist. This was just the sort of gunslinger who was smart enough to step aside before I had to slug him.

I cased the joint, gave it the quick once-over. There were video games in there all right, just as I suspected. Thousands of them. And it was all being kept under wraps. The public had a right to know but they never would unless someone blew the whistle. That's where I come in.

I'm a Video Game Columnist.

It's my job.

I was making a beeline for the taxi stand when I noticed the *Penthouse* booth. Yeah, *Penthouse*. The girly mag. The one I keep in the top drawer along with my Smith & Wesson and my pint of scotch. I investigated the scene and found out that *Penthouse* had got itself mixed up in the video game racket. They were showing off this new CD-ROM game that lets you use your mouse to point and click on the Penthouse Pets and make them do rude things. This was definitely not a game for little shavers, unless what they're shaving is their palms. I wondered what *Penthouse* was doing here in Chicago until I remembered that one of the main streets is called Wacker. The game should be called "Are You a Man or a Mouse" but it wasn't.

One of the Penthouse Pets was there in person, getting slobbered over by a bunch of knobs. She took one look at me and I could tell she'd fallen for me hard and who could blame her? There's something about being a hard-nosed, two-fisted Video Game Columnist that drives the women wild. It goes with the territory.

She was a tall, slim, self-satisfied little number named Tiffany. She wore nothing but a short, tight, sleeveless, backless, lowcut gown that showed off a pair of breasts that were just like any other pair of breasts, only more so. Her brunette hair had shades of red and was slicked back in a high part that was wide enough to have made Moses proud.

"What's your name?" she asked. It was a loaded question and I gave the answer I always give when I'm doing dangerous work, whether it's smuggling drugs out of Colombia or running guns in Africa or talking to a bimbo in Chi-town.

"Anderson," I said. "Jason Anderson."

"That sounds like a made-up name," she said.

"That hurts," I said, "coming from you."

"You mean you're named for a mythical character and a guy who writes fairy tales?"

I gave her a slow, easy grin. "It sort of fits."

"So, in other words, you're full of shit."

"If we have to use other words, sweetheart, those ones will do."

She made a fast move and I thought she was going for her gat but instead she whipped out a pen and scribbled a love note on a glossy photo of herself. It read: "Jason, XOXOX." She signed it "Tiff." The poor kid. She had it bad.

I shoved the photo in my pocket. Then I broke it to her gently. There was no point in us seeing each other any more. I'm a Video Game Columnist. And I had a job to do.

That night I cruised over to a bar on the North Pier to have a few belts with the usual suspects. And then, of all the gin joints in the Windy City, who should happen to walk into mine? My brother-in-law from Toronto. T.L. is his handle but he's also known to the authorities under his street name, "Lang." He's part of the Moffat gang who used to run stoves out of Weston until they went legit. He was in town on business and our meeting was pure chance. It was lucky I'd given Miss July the brush-off or I might have had some fast talking to do back home.

"Lang" used to call Chicago home for a couple of years and he knew the turf. We grabbed a cab and headed for a blues club on the west side. This joint was hotter than a machine-gun barrel on Valentine's Day. The locals were chugging with both hands and you could cut the cigarette smoke with a machete. There were bullet holes in the ceiling and cracked cement on the floor. Above the stage was a hand-lettered sign that looked like it had been scribbled in extreme anger. It read: "NO CLOVE CIGARETTE SMOKING! AND NO PIPES!" Yeah, this was the place all right. The house band had maybe five teeth between them and they were playing the kind of blues that made you feel like your whole life had been wasted until this moment. Then an old sax player took the stage. He was no older than God. He wore a jewelled belt and weird pants and a ruffled shirt and showed us a lot of bad dental work. His name was A.C. Reed and he was full of shit. I knew this for a fact because a huge sign on his amplifier said: "A.C. REED THE MAN THAT FULL OF SHIT."

When he started to play, this creaky old junk jewellry geezer did nothing more than turn the dump upside down. He didn't just play the blues. He was the blues. He was also full of shit, a point he stressed early and often.

"I full of shit coz I hate playing music," he howled at us. "And you full of shit coz you hate your job." Then he swung around and looked right at me, where I stood beside the stage. He pointed a bony finger right at my heart. "YOU full of shit coz you ain't got no job." Then he turned on "Lang" (alias "T.L.") who was standing beside me. "Now I gonna shove the blues right up YOUR ASS."

He showed us that upper plate, the one that looked like a row of gleaming Chiclets. Then he shoved the blues right up our ass.

Coming back across the border, the Customs Bozo eyed me with the usual suspicion. I'd had a late night and my eyes looked like two pissholes in the snow.

"OK, mister," he said. "Who exactly are you?"

I gave him my Number Three smile.

"Anderson," I said. "Jason Anderson."

"Occupation?"

"The man that full of shit — in training."

I'm Bullish on the Power of Bull

"You're bursting with bullshit."

That's the sort of thing that people say or write to me all the time. And my response is: "I thank you for the compliment." Because to be considered a Master of Bullshit is a great honor indeed. Bullshit is one of the strongest forces in the universe, a power to be harnessed and used with respect. For as Darwin said, life itself comes down to "survival of the bullshittiest."

From the earliest times, the human race has revered and even worshipped the sheer power of bullshit. Almost 5,000 years ago (60,000 months ago in Celsius) the great Minoan civilization of Crete was kept in line by the Minotaur, a creature that was half man and half bull (a model that is still used today when electing prime ministers). In King Minos's palace of Knossos, citizens were forced to wander through an endless maze, or labyrinth, and — just when they thought that they were totally lost and confused and would never get out alive — the Minotaur would pounce on them and basically rip them into very small bits, eat them and then go have a long dump. And through this, the model for modern bureaucracy was born.

My point is; living in a world full of bull-roaring blowhards is hardly a new situation for the human race. Even in Biblical times, the average citizen could barely step out the door without having to put up with bull from all sides:

Many bulls have compassed me; strong bulls of Bashan have beset me round. They gaped upon me with their mouths, as a ravening or roaring lion. (Psalm 22: 12-13) Thus, from the scriptures, came the expression "to roar like a bull."

With the rise of organized religion, it was the church itself that often dished up the loudest and longest bull roar. The Pope would frequently come up with this or that weighty pronouncement in which he first claimed to be a humble "servant of servants," before using his complete authority to enact some really nit-picky little rule, like "Thou shalt not get shit-faced on the Sabbath and lie in the ditch with thy pantaloons around thine ankles."

Whenever the Pope started spewing out these little wet-blanket decrees, the people would groan and whisper, "Oh, shit. Here comes some more bull from the Pope." From that day forth, any official order from the Vatican has been known as a "Papal Bull." The expression soon spread to include government pronouncements, such as the "Golden Bull" issued at Nuremberg by Emperor Charles IV in 1356. To this very day, all such freedom-squelching pronouncements from rulers and leaders are known as "Official Bulletins."

Through the ages, in times of war, generals and admirals quickly learned that pure bullshit could be a highly effective military strategy. One need only look to that fateful day on June 25, 1876, was when a General George Custer encountered a small band of Indians at Little Big Horn, Montana. The handful of braves feigned an attack on Custer's superior force of 200 U.S. Cavalry troops, only to quickly turn and run for a narrow pass between two hills. Duped into sensing an easy victory, Custer's riders gave chase. But once trapped in the pass by the diversionary force, Custer found himself surrounded by more then 2,000 native warriors charging down the hills from all sides. As Custer drew his pistol, he turned to his doomed force and calmly pronounced his now immortal last words: "Oh shit! We're really fucked now!" To pay homage to this brilliant bullshit-powered military strategy of sitting in ambush of Custer's troops, the Indian chief who led the attack was dubbed Chief Sitting Bull.

By the 1920s, it was stockbrokers who wielded all the power over an easily bullshitted public. With stock prices soaring to ever-higher heights with each passing day, investors all over the world were easily persuaded to pour their life savings into stocks bought on margins of as little as 5 or 10 per cent. After that black day in October 1929, when the stock market crashed and the world was plunged into a decade-long depression, those brokers who did not leap to their deaths voluntarily were rounded up by angry mobs to be summarily shot and pissed on (and not necessarily in that order). That explains why, to this day, brokers who try to entice buyers into the stock market are said to be "bullish" or calling for a "bull market."

Bullshit is now everywhere in society, piled layer upon layer as an electronic superhighway links the world, allowing those in even the most far-flung hell holes, such as Calgary, to become global village idiots. And with the rise of mass communications, the purveyors of politically correct thinking have discovered that — by making up new rules every day — they can not only force their views on everyone else, but actively suppress all dissenting views by "bullying" others into silence.

Now we're mired in a neo-moralistic period in which there is almost nothing the average person can do, say or even think without running afoul of hundreds of pressure groups who feel that their way is best for everybody. Even the most commonplace pursuits — drinking a beer, eating meat, smoking in public or, God forbid, using the English language as it appears in the dictionary — are now bound to spark a shit-storm from some faction or other. The Age of Bullshit has reached its zenith. And you had better be up to your ears in it yourself if you hope to survive. Because the bullies are everywhere and the bullies think they are very brainy. But, as Plato once quipped, "Bullshit beats brains every time."

Sheer unadulterated bullshit. It is the highest power known to man. Don't leave home without it.

God's Got the Pioneer Spirit

SOMEWHERE IN THE MUSKOKAS — It was a dark and stormy night. In fact, it was dark and stormy several nights in a row. We were just sitting there minding our beer cooler when — BANG! — we got whacked by the wrath of God.

Not the New Testament God. I'm talking the Old Testament God. The One who was always turning people into pillars of salt and causing floods and famines and plagues and clouds of locusts.

Ever wonder why the Old Testament God got sacked and replaced by the New Testament God? I think it was the clouds of locusts that showed He was losing it. Locusts are just sort of like grasshoppers with wings. You spray a bit of Raid on them and that's that. A really fearful Lord would send maybe clouds of rabid flying rats or snakes or ABBA fans. Something to make you piss yourself at the very thought. But locusts? I don't think so.

Not that I'm arguing with the Old Guy. Like an aging but wily pitcher, He still has a lot of junk in his arsenal even after He's lost his fastball. Like tornadoes.

That's the wicked screwball He hurled our way last week.

Tornadoes are scary. They have only one purpose: To wipe out trailer camps, which is perfectly understandable. But, like an assassin who hits innocent bystanders with stray shots, a tornado has a way of taking out random targets that just happen to get in the way.

Luckily no one was carried off to a land full of midgets, wicked witches and flying monkeys. But houses and cottages were totaled. In the aftermath, it was something awesome — in the pre-Beavis & Butthead meaning of the word — to behold the power a tornado can let rip, how it can tear a swath right through a stand of century-old trees. Or literally blow the roof off the joint. Hydro poles were flying like... well... like flying hydro poles. Thus pulling the plug on the juice of a large chunk of cottage country. Our power was out for only three days, but others will wait a month to get the juice back. You can't watch the TV when the damn thing won't work. It's torture.

Back to the Dark Ages. No light or water, every store sold out of ice, candles and flashlight batteries. Warm beer. Makes you appreciate the hardships our pioneer forefathers and foremothers endured.

Pioneers were strong folk. Never showered. Never shaved. Never brushed their teeth (if they had any). Never shampooed. Never used deodorant. They slept in their clothes for months at a time and slapped bear grease over any exposed skin to ward off black flies and skeeters. If they had to take a dump, they didn't run to some fancy modern washroom. They just dumped away (sometimes they'd even lower their breeches first).

Your typical pioneer had body odour that could knock a buzzard off a shit truck at a hundred yards. But they didn't mind. Because so did everybody else.

And they'd never whine about some minor inconvenience, like a tornado. They'd simply wait it out while playing quaint pioneer games. Like Nude Twister. (That's when they really needed the bear grease).

Everyone has a Tornado Yarn to spin after an event like this. This guy in a Huntsville bar told me he'd just opened a beer and put it on the table and went out to the woods to take a leak when the tornado scored a direct hit.

"This big twister comes out of nowhere — bouncing off everything it hit — then it smacks my place, tears the roof right off, sucks out all the insulation, chairs and papers and shit flying everywhere. I go back inside, the whole place is totalled. Except for the bottle of beer. It's still standing there on the table. It hasn't moved an inch. It's a miracle!"

The Lord works in strange and mysterious ways. And likes beer.

When I was a kid we had a cottage in a town on a lake just down the road from my wife's family cottage, where we now go. Which is bizarre, since we met in a small Mexican town and didn't even know we were both from Canada, let alone Toronto, when we first started talking. After a year in Mexico (three for her), we came home. Turned out her cottage was only about two miles from where the Burrill cottage used to be. It also turned out her cousin was boinking my cousin. Strange and mysterious ways.

I say where the Burrill cottage "used to be" because it burned to the ground when I was a kid. The only thing left standing, oddly enough, was the fireplace. The lodge next door bought our family lot and expanded onto it. This has always pissed me off. I still can't drive past that lodge without cursing it, thinking that's our land. That's where our cottage should be, but for an Act of God. A curse upon thee.

The Old Testament God must have been listening because guess which place really got whacked by the tornado: the lodge that usurped our former land. No casualties, but the place took hits from about fifteen flying trees. We're not talking saplings. This is Up North, where trees are trees and gerbils are gerbils. I tried to go and have a look at the damage, maybe take a picture, maybe have it framed. But the cops had a roadblock to keep rubberneckers away from the scene.

"That used to be my cottage," I explained to the cop.

"Well, it used to be a lodge, but you still can't go look."

I guess it's just as well I wasn't allowed to visit the cursed site. First fire. Then a tornado.

If I'd stopped to look, I'd probably have been turned into a pillar of salt. Or maybe get swarmed by really nasty locusts. With huge teeth.

Better to go home. And play some Nude Twister.

Pro Athletes: It Takes Real Men to Pat Bums

A new millennium is dawning and all over the world a new breed of man is emerging.

Men everywhere are forsaking their macho, unfeeling, heartless personas to evolve into a kinder and gentler Liberated Male. Just go check out any place where there's a woods or wilderness and you'll observe disciples of this so-called Men's Movement bonding together into one weeping, emoting, touchy-feely pile of raw sensitivity. This is where men go to run in packs, dance naked by the firelight, beat drums, eat mud, howl like wolves and make up Indian-sounding names for each other, like Broken Wind or Floating Log. This is where men get in touch with their primal beings, shedding the thick skin of their insensitive past incarnations.

This is where men truly evolve.

Unfortunately, it is this very same new breed of Sensitive Male who will probably tell you he would never be caught dead sitting in front of a boob tube or in a stadium swilling cans of beer while watching pro football, baseball or hockey players do their caveman routine. Pro sports, the New Male will argue, is nothing but a primitive throwback to the Bad Old Days when men were expected to keep a stiff upper lip (and other bits) and be macho at all costs.

Pro sports players get a bad rap from the touchy-feely crowd. And that's really too bad. Because if you take a closer look at any group of professional jocks, what do you see?

You will see that it is these very men who are breaking down the barriers, smashing through the stigmas, and unleashing the Truly Liberated Male all over the Earth's all-too-thick crust.

Let's take baseball, for starters. What do you notice when a bunch of baseball players are standing around their pitcher, waiting for him to unleash a ninety-mile-an-hour fireball?

They are not just standing there.

On closer inspection, you will find that they are quietly, sensitively offering encouragement: "Hey babe. Hey babe. Hum babe! Hey babe! Hey-babe-hey-babe-hey-HEY-BABE!!!!"

Then, after the pitcher retires the side, what do the other men on the field do? Do they coldly ignore their fellow male's achievement? They do not. They:

• Gather around him in a close, nurturing, hugging, circle of affirmation.

• They pat his (and everybody else's) bum.

• They all go off together, screaming, hugging and touching.

• They take off their clothes and continue the bum-patting in the communal shower.

Is this common male behaviour? As a sociology experiment, try walking into any biker bar you know of and calling some vicious Unliberated Male "babe." Then try to pat his bum. Suggest that you shower together. Observe his responses. Take notes. I theorize that you'll discover that not every male is comfortable with the close, bonding behaviour exhibited on any given night by pro athletes.

Where else but in pro sports do you see males doing any of these things in public:

• Crying: Pro athletes often weep after the Big Loss — or even the Big Win. Other pros will move in to coddle and comfort the tearful one(s).

• Discovering the Child Within. One need only watch such players as John McEnroe, Derek Bell or Vince Coleman to see that a Real Pro is not afraid to revert to a childlike, infantile state in front of thousands of witnesses.

• Deep Professions of Faith and Communal Love. Where else but in pro sports do you see so many males openly and gushily profess their over-powering love and gratitude for God and their fellow males?

• Standing Around for Hours, in Front of Lots and Lots of People, with Your Hands Between Another Man's Legs. If one male stood around on Yonge Street with his fists jammed between the legs of another bent-over male, the grannies would faint and the vice squad would haul them off for Public Perversity. But no one thinks there is anything twisted or weird about the bond between a pro quarterback and his centre lineman during any given football game.

• Pet Names. In the Real Macho World, men tend to call each other things like "Spike" or "Killer" or "Snake." But in the Big Leagues, men openly refer to their fellow males as "Sweetness" or "Babe" or (nudge, nudge) "The Pocket Rocket."

• Kissing. Just watch any soccer game and you will see that men are not afraid to kiss other men. I mean, yuck, right on the lips, in front on millions of viewers worldwide.

Don't give this stuff a bum rap. This is healthy. This breaks down more barriers and stereotypes than all the Iron John drum-pounding in all the mock-primal tribes in all the forests in all the world.

Pro sports.

Real life.

Real drama.

Really sensitive guys.

A Most Un-Gentlemanly Round of Golf

Last week I played a round of golf.

Golf! You know, the game with the sticks and the funny clothes and the TV announcers who whisper in British accents while describing the "action"?

First hushed British announcer: He's using his mashie for the approach and — by Jove — he's sliced it into the pasture and the ball's stuck right up a sheep's ass! I don't think that was the shot he was planning.

Second hushed British announcer: Aye, Nigel. But rules are rules. The bloke will have to play it where it lays. His caddie's handing him an Ass Wedge… the gallery is hushed…

That kind of golf.

Except that — mercifully — there were no hushed British announcers or hushed gallery of spectators watching me. Just my friend Iain The Gas Pipe Weasel, and he didn't actually laugh out loud. But he smirked very noisily. And beat me by nineteen strokes. The good news is I broke 100, carding a

95. The bad news is I was on one of those "pitch 'n' putt" courses that consists entirely of par threes, the type of course that professional golfers with names like Arnie or Chi Chi or Fuzzy would play entirely with their chipper and putter.

I don't play much golf because, although I kind of like the game, I always mentally associate it with Creeping Old Age and Really Funny Pants, not to mention those shoes. Taking up golf is just another reminder that you're getting old and that you're one step closer to kicking the Big Bucket. While I was duffing my way around the course, I tried to figure out what it is that makes older men so attracted to this sport. And I think I've figured it out: Golf is a metaphor for sex.

I mean, just think how most old golfers dress — those lime-green shirts and plaid pants and white belts with matching wing-tipped shoes. With threads like that, they're never going to get laid in the real sense of the word. So, with actual sex out of the question, golf has become a subliminal substitute. That explains why the game is so popular with creaky old-timers. It's the only way they will ever rack up a score.

I'm not just puttering around with this theory. I am serious. It's disgusting and a trifle disturbing, but sadly true. And I think some scientific foundation should give me an award (and a huge research grant) for stumbling upon this shocking psychological behavioural breakthrough. Because if you just take the time to stop and think of all the similarities between golf and sex, you can't deny the connections. In both sex and golf, the object is to fondle your stiff shaft, take a lot of "strokes" and try to "get it in the hole."

Golfers are advised to "play it safe" and frequently wash their balls, keep their heads clean and their putter straight. The smart golfers buy protective covers to put over the heads of their clubs. Golfers frequently "play a round" with the intention of getting a "good score" and avoiding the many "hazards." Many pay pros to improve their stroke, or buy manuals, glossy magazines and instructive videos to learn how to do it better.

Being honest and staying faithful to the rules is the ideal. But cheating is frequent. And "bad breaks" are a costly part of the game. All too often these cootish stickmen who are dressed up like pimps find themselves "swinging" with a "hooker" that leaves them "caught in a trap" that produces some very "bad lies" (if only Hugh Grant had paid a golf pro instead of the other kind of pro to help him with his club head, the penalty strokes would not have been so costly).

Codgers love golf because the object is to get it over with as quickly as possible, to move fast and "hole out" with as few strokes as possible. If you can get the job done with a single stroke, you're applauded, not labelled a "premature ejaculator." You're supposed to yell "fore" before you play, but for many, "fore-play" is ignored. And if you can't get it up with a woodie, you simply switch to a nine-iron.

Sex and golf. Golf and sex.

After the final hole, male golfers are prone to hanging out in bars with their buddies, chugging frosties while bragging about (and exaggerating) their latest scores. The talk usually moves on to a boastful discussion of whose equipment and bags are the biggest and best.

Like sex, golf can be a group activity.

You can do it with a partner (even a threesome or foursome), which accounts for the fact that one of the best golfers in the world is Fred Couples. Not Couple, you notice. But "Couples." Plural. It's the only activity where swinging in groups is still considered normal these days. But, as with sex, if you can't find a willing group to swing with, you can play with yourself. That's why "placement of hands" and finding "the proper grip" are topics that are so important to golfers. And this clearly explains why perhaps the most famous golfer in history is named "Palmer." (If golf star Fuzzy Zoeller's daughter married Arnold Palmer's son, and they had a male baby, would the "little shaver" be named "Fuzzy Palmer"? Just wondering.)

Anyway. There you have it. I've joined the ranks of the golfing set. Hand me my white belt and matching shoes. And my Ass Wedge.

(Note: Hardly any sheep were injured the last time I played a round. But that cow — that was purely an accident. I swear.)

Rockin' by the Seat of His Pants

I always wondered why they called Maple Leaf Gardens a "garden" because that's usually a place where you grow flowers and things. But then I realized a garden is also a place where you dump a lot of fertilizer.

And a lot of shit has gone down in the Gardens over the years. I went to a concert at the Gardens recently and I thought the show sucked because the sound in that hockey palace is so awful. I hadn't been to a Gardens show for years and it got me thinking. There was a time in my youth when I thought rock shows in that acoustical mecca of musical mush sounded just great! It's not that the sound has gotten any better over the years. It's just that, as a sixteen-year-old youth, I knew how to properly prepare for a Gardens concert.

Preparation was an art. First you had to warm up with some good acid, mushrooms, speed, horse tranquilizers, hash brownies, snow-cone doobs and a couple of bottles of Four Aces Port or Old Sailor Sherry, both surprisingly affordable at eighty cents a bottle. (That was in the good old days before Four Aces skyrocketed to $1.05 a bottle.)

The trick to drinking Old Sailor was to swallow about half the bottle in the first chug. This was vital. There was no sipping anything as vile as Old Sailor. You chugged and then hoped for the best. There could be only two results. You'd either immediately spew you lower intestinal tract across the room, and pass out cold. Or you'd somehow manage to keep it down. If you could keep down that first chug, the rest of the evening was clear sailing, matey! Harrr. (Note: I looked the other day and the LCBO has for some reason taken both Four Aces and Old Sailor off the market. Must have had something to do with all those complaints from customers who had gone blind.)

Once the warm-up exercises were complete, the next trick was to smuggle sufficient supplies into the actual Gardens itself in order to keep the buzz going for the duration of the show (and some of these concerts — like the marathon festivals they used to have on New Year's Eve — went on for a couple of days).

Of course, Gardens security would frisk you at the door but the trick I always found to be a surefire success — and I hope I'm not giving away a trick that some of you are still using — was to stuff whatever I was smuggling down the back of my pants, into the waistband of my gauchies.

The door Nazis would pat-check your knapsack, frisk your pockets and legs and underarms and hats and boots and even pat your crotch. But they never seemed to get around to frisking your ass. At least not mine. I don't know if I should take this as an insult or not, but the fact remains.

Then, you see, you could take your seat and listen to the awful, mushy, echoing sound blasting out of the amps of Alice Cooper or the Stones or Humble Pie or Black Sabbath or whoever the hell that was way down there on the stage and you'd somehow know the sound was awful. But, due to proper preparation, you just did not care!!!

Ah yes, the good old days.

I remember with particular fondness one concert I attended with a girl I was going out with for the first time. You know, First Impressions and all that. So important to handle the situation with cool charm.

I remember it was the dead of winter and when I picked her up it turned out that she had decided to bring five of her friends along — all female.

So there we were waaaay up in the nosebleed seats right by the rail and a long drop to the floor. Six rock babes and me.

The show was kind of hard to concentrate on for a couple of reasons. First of all, a bunch of greaseballs had taken up the seats in the row behind us and were constantly pestering the women who, in turn, were all looking to me for protection. I issued a stern warning and the greaseballs responded by putting their feet up on my head, using it as sort of a footrest.

I had — and God knows why because these days I wouldn't even use this stuff to kill rats — smuggled in a bottle of Southern Comfort which I was passing around. One of the greasers snatched it and started inhaling it and when I demanded he give it back, he did so promptly — by driving it at my head. I ducked and managed to get a cat-quick, Felix Potvin-esque hand in front of the bottle, catching it just as it hit the rail and shattered.

So now I was covered in: a) Southern Comfort and b) blood spouting from a major artery in my wrist area.

That was exactly the moment when the girl to my right — a little bopper weenie who was not part of my entourage — decided to freak out on whatever she'd ingested and try to jump over the rail to her doom (and the doom of all those she would land on below — it was quite a drop). I grabbed her, pulled her back, put my arms around her, comforted her and talked her down. Slowly she calmed and cooled out and then passed out with her head in my crotch.

I thought I had been fairly heroic but for some reason my date du jour did not seem all too pleased that I was sitting there with my arms around a teenie-bopper who had her snout between my legs. I was trying to defend the virtue of my situation when my passed-out teenie suddenly woke up long enough to barf all over my crotch. I mean, she really let it fly! You see *The Exorcist*? Then you'll have some idea what she did to my lap.

Luckily, not a drop stained the Gardens, concrete floor. My jeans soaked up every last chunk. So now I was covered in: a) Southern Comfort; b) blood spouting from a major artery in my wrist area and c) bopper chunks.

It was a chilly walk home not only because my date suddenly, for some reason, seemed to be trying to keep her distance from me, but because — this being the coldest day of the year — the assorted fluids that had accumulated on my crotch had frozen solid. It's hard to walk with a frozen Popsicle between your legs. She didn't even invite me upstairs…

I flagged a cab and the driver gave me funny looks in the rear-view mirror as I thawed in the back seat. But he was just jealous. He had to work. And I had been out at a Gardens rock concert, having ***fun***!

The good old days. Gone forever, alas.

The cab driver rolled down the window as we made an illegal turn onto Yonge Street.

Repent and Save Your Souls!!!

Being a citizen of Canada's number-one city can be a heavy burden to bear after awhile. So much is expected of you from all the jealousy-crazed provincial truckstops that blight the rest of our nation's bleak tundra.

When you travel across Canada you quickly learn that Toronto-bashing is a national obsession in our far-flung regions.

What's the very first thing that you'll notice when you set foot in one of those amusingly-named frontier towns like Calgary or Moose Jaw? Well, OK, the very first thing you'll notice is that you've got a cowpie on your shoe. But the second thing you'll notice is that everybody spends their days dumping on Toronto.

Same thing if you visit one of those quaint little fishing villages like Vancouver or Halifax. "I wouldn't live in Toronto for all the money in the world," the quaintly-dressed locals will tell you (almost as if you'd actually asked them for their quaint opinions).

This can be amusing at first, in the same way watching Hee Haw is amusing.

But it grows old fast.

Even right here in Ontario, you get people from a little bureaucrat-infested town called Ottawa claiming that their little hamlet is really Canada's top city. As "evidence," they point out that Ottawa — not Toronto — is Canada's capital.

These poor misguided souls don't seem to realize that Toronto was once Canada's capital but, because Toronto is such a neat place, the Americans kept pouring over the border trying to capture it. Torontonians were so busy kicking Yankee butt that nobody had time to make up new laws or pass bills or decree anything.

It would be nice, thought our forefathers and foremothers, if we could move the capital to a place so desolate, so Godforsaken, that no Yankee would ever bother trying to invade it.

Just then, a little pisshole in the snow called Bytown was discovered by some drunken *coureur-de-bois-sans-pantalons*, who had made a wrong turn (*coureur-de-bois-sans-pantalons*, if you remember your history lessons, is French for "runners in the woods with no pants on").

"Whoa," said one *coureur-de-bois*. "Get a load of this dump."

"*Sacré bleu*," said the other *coureur-de-bois*, scratching at a nasty deerfly bite on his butt. "No American would ever attack a festering pit like this."

And so the Canadian government moved there, built some Parliament buildings, and renamed the joint "Only Town That Americans Won't Attack," which was later shortened to the less unwieldy acronym of O.T.T.A.W.A.

Still, strange as it may seem, it's people from just such fly-blown places as Ottawa who are the most likely to froth at the mouth about what a dive Toronto is.

It's sad really.

But you have to understand that it is only the result of a deep inferiority complex. The only thing you can do with such people is be patient, nod and grin a lot when they speak, and wait for them to go away.

It's not their fault. Be nice. There's no point in arguing with them. Maybe even lend them some pants. It's all part of the intrinsic burden of nobility that every Torontonian must bear.

Still, it can get tiresome.

Luckily, when it all gets to be too much, there is one surefire cure. Just as famous movie stars must sometimes escape to places where nobody will recognize them, so Torontonians must occasionally seek refuge in a place where the very name Toronto won't evoke a spray of curses and spittle.

That place is just across the border, in the United States.

The charming and refreshing thing about Americans is that most of them have no idea that any places exist outside of U.S. borders. To suppress the memory of so many painful butt-kickings at the hands of the Torontonians, they have mentally blocked the entire city out of their collective "minds."

Just last week I met a guy in Chicago, and when he found out I was from Toronto, he said, "Oh yeah. Toronto, Ohio. That's near Stuebenville."

(I knew about Toronto, Ohio, because I once went down there to write a story about the place. It's the Sewer Pipe Capital of the World. Honest!)

Another time, on the Spanish isle of Ibiza, this American navy guy asked where I was from. I said Toronto.

"No shit," the guy says. "You speak real good American for an Italian."

You see? This is the beauty of it all. Not only do Americans have no clue about Toronto, they've never even heard of Ontario.

One time I drove down to California in my old MGB. Guy sees my Ontario licence plates and goes, "Are those special plates for the speedway?"

"What speedway?"

"Ontario Speedway. The racing track."

I said, nope, I'm actually from Toronto.

"Oh yeah," the guy says, "I know Trona. It's up towards Death Valley."

I later looked this up in an atlas and damned if the guy wasn't right. Right there near Ontario, California, is Trona, California.

Now, as a handy guide for your relaxing escape into anonymity south of the border, I've compiled the definitive Top Ten list of real and actual places Americans will think you're from if you say you're from Toronto.

1. Toronto, OHIO
2. Toronto, KANSAS
3. Toronto, SOUTH DAKOTA
4. Taranto, ITALY
5. Trona, CALIFORNIA
6. Toronto, IOWA
7. Trento, ITALY
8. Trani, ITALY
9. Tran Ninh, LAOS
10. Tomato, ARKANSAS

Don't think you can avoid confusing an American by explaining that you're from Toronto, Ontario.

This will only confuse him, her or it all the more. Here, at no extra cost, are the Top Ten Ontarios that Americans will think you're talking about if you mention Toronto is in Ontario.

1. Ontario SPEEDWAY
2. Ontario, INDIANA
3. Ontario, OHIO
4. Ontario, OREGON
5. Ontario, CALIFORNIA
6. Ontario, VIRGINIA
7. Ontario, NEW YORK
8. Ontario, WISCONSIN
9. Antero, COLORADO
10. Ongonhororusumu, CHINA

After a few weeks — or even a few days — of drinking from these deep and refreshing wells of total ignorance south of the border, you'll come back home to Canada's greatest city with your batteries recharged.

You'll be ready, once again, to take up that heavy burden that every true Torontonian must shoulder.

You'll be ready, as Torontonians, to once again suffer the slings and arrows of outrageous fortune that those at the pinnacle must endure.

You'll be ready to march bravely, head held high, through that shit-rain of rural resentment that will forever fester in every hamlet and hamburg of this great nation we were chosen by the gods to rule.

In short: you'll be ready to really piss off people from Calgary. (Bastard city-boy! — Calgarian editorial staff.)

A Sloth in Summer

It's summer time — party time — and you better enjoy it as fast as possible because this is Canada. Before you know it you'll be freezing your ass off in a ten-foot snowdrift yet again. And again.

It's time at last to take a little holiday. We deserve it. "If all the year were playing holidays," William Shakespeare once muttered, "To sport would be as tedious as to work."

Which shows how full of shit Willy the Shake was. Me, I could take a holiday in the sunshine twelve months a year. I didn't ask to be a Canadian. I was just born that way. I keep swimming across the river into Mexico but they keep sending me back. And as for work, if I'm a workaholic, I've been on the wagon for years.

There are some things that just aren't good for you.

That's why I'm here to guide you through the summer months in the best way possible — by doing absolutely fuck all.

Listen carefully. You might want to take notes.

• Exercise and Health. It is essential to stay in shape during the hot weather and, of course, it is vital to drink plenty of fluids to avoid dehydration. So here's a simple exercise that has always worked for me. Find a sunny spot and bring along a two-four of beer. Now, carrying the case of beer in itself is exercise, but we're not finished yet. I want you to firmly grip a cold beer in your hand and, with the other hand, twist off the top. You can feel you triceps working already, can't you? Now liiiiiiift the beer to your mouth and take a long swallow. Repeat. One more. Two more. Three more. And rest. Now do it all over again. Repeat the exercise until the case is empty. You won't be in any better shape. But believe me, you won't care.

• Grease Is Your Friend. Make sure that everything you eat during the summer months is smeared with grease. Excess grease can also be used to style your hair and makes an excellent skin cream. While on the job in the city, make sure you eat nothing but those sidewalk "Smog Dogs" the hot dog vendors sell. Not only will you be getting a healthy diet of ground-up pig's assholes and mad cow noses but you can rest assured that your meal is smoked in only the finest car exhaust fumes. Kind of makes my mouth water just to think about it.

• Get as Much Sun as Possible. You want to be tanned to a crisp so work on it now before the hole in the ozone layer disappears. And remember: sun block is for wimps. If anything, use grease (see above). It makes an ideal suntan lotion and dogs will actually like you.

• Go Camping. Yes, there is nothing finer to do in the summer than to hit the wilderness with nothing but a tent and a few cases of beer and, of course, a lot of grease. You'll feel just like the First Nations did before we came over the Big Pond and fucked up their land. Drink that beer. Smear on that grease. Beat a drum. Dance naked by the bonfire.

• Work on Your Self-Esteem. If you're feeling like you're not performing well at work or in your life in general, simply go to a baseball game and watch millionaires screw up big-time. Even the best batter on the team is bound to fuck up seven out of ten times. There. Don't you feel better already?

• Have Fun With No Pants On. Go to the beach. Take a picnic lunch and a bottle of wine. Put a bear trap on the joggers' path, sit back and enjoy. You deserve it. So do they. While you're there, Get Naked! Go and get back to nature, the way you were born. But remember Nude Beach Etiquette: It's not polite to point. Down periscope, guys.

• Get Mobile. Buy some Rollerblades or a skateboard and have a head-on collision with a bike courier on the sidewalk of your choice. It's such a nice way to meet new people.

• People Watch. There's no better way to pass a sultry summer day than to find an outdoor café and simply guzzle frosties and watch the human parade pass by. The risk of a random drive-by shooting only adds to the excitement.

• Fall in Love by Making friends with Your Local Biker Gang. This may take some doing but I, personally, have the luxury of passing my very own biker gang every time I walk up the street (they'd be the ones with the dirt front-yard and the Harleys and the babe who always wears nothing but a bikini and a lot of tattoos. Every time I pass she yells out, "You look like a fucking idiot!" And I just smile and wave. This has been going on for weeks now. But I think I made a breakthrough. The other day as I was passing their house, and as their pitbull was diving at my throat (another neighbourly ritual) only to bounce off the fence, the bikini biker babe said — with a def-inite sweetness in her voice — "You still look like a fucking idiot, Darling." She called me "darling." Could this be ***love***?

• Kill Bugs. You can kill a lot of bugs in the summer but there are certain "Do's" and "Don'ts" to the bug-squashing ritual. It is morally OK to kill blackflies, deerflies, houseflies and mosquitoes, but do NOT kill spiders. Spiders are you friends. Just yesterday I went to the can and there was a spider floating in the water. Did I flush him away? Did I piss on him/her? I did nothing of the kind. I used the toilet brush to lift the spider out and set it free. This is only right. And will also bring you good luck. Also don't kill bats. They eat their weight in mosquitoes, thus saving you a lot of swatting time.

• Bird Watch. I have a feeder in my backyard, which allows me to spend many fascinating hours watching sparrows and pigeons make pigs of themselves (They don't call them pig-eons for nothing, ya know).

Occasionally I get a red-winged blackbird or a cardinal or a blue jay, although the blue jay always misses the cut-off man.

• Above All, Stay Alive. Don't drink and drive. You might spill your beer when you roll over in the ditch. Have a good summer everyone. Over. And Out.

Dog Day Afternoons

The coolest thing to do in the Big City during the summer is to get the hell out of it and head somewhere Up North. (Just as, in winter, the hottest thing to do in the Big City is to get the hell out of it and head south.) But, of course, this is not always possible, due to annoying inconveniences like work. The two uncoolest things to do in the dog days of summer are to swim in the lake (which you can't do anyway because summer is the time of year when the sewers love to back up and they close every beach in town since the water is roughly a 50-50 mixture of H_2O and poop) or to jog.

I view swimming and jogging in roughly the same way: I can do both, but only in case of the most dire emergency. For example, if I fall out of a boat or off the end of a dock (and I have done both more than once), then I will swim. Running is something you should only do by sheer necessity — like, say, if the cops arrive just as you are knocking over a bank or variety store. But one key tip: be sure to run in a zigzag pattern because it makes it harder for the cops to shoot you to death and that really pisses them off. (They hate to waste taxpayer-funded ammo.)

There are plenty of great places to walk in Toronto: Toronto Island, Kew Beach, the Leslie Spit, the Don Valley park system, High Park (but be careful in High Park — if you go for a leak in the bushes you might never resurface). Walking has its hazards, but it beats jogging because it looks cool if you do it right (not in that dumb elbow-swinging, bum-wiggling, speed-walking manner — that is most uncool). The trick is to saunter or swagger or amble or loaf along — whatever. Did you ever see James Dean, Humphrey Bogart or Marlon Brando jogging?

Joggers piss me off because they think they've cornered the entire world market on smugness. I hate the ones who keep jogging in place when they're at a red light. If I kept walking in place at a red light, they'd haul me off to the Puzzle Factory in a rubber truck (again). And anyway, who stops for red lights in this city?

The other reason that jogging is uncool is that it is unhealthy. I used to work for the environment ministry and I remember reading one report that said that the deep breathing invoked by jogging in a smoggy, car-fumed city is equivalent to smoking two decks of butts a day, giving health-seeking runners a set of lungs that would have made the Marlboro Man himself cringe with envy. Why not just sit at a nice outdoor café with a frosty mug and smoke the two packs without moving? That would not only save time but also reduce the risk of ankle sprains and impact-induced knee injury.

But jog if you must. We'll be glad to wave if you land on the pavement anywhere near the table we're under.

Crawl in for a beer. It's nice and shady under there.

As for my first suggestion — getting the hell out of the city — it helps if you have a cottage or cabin, but it is not essential. For a really cool time, drive to a provincial park, rent a canoe from an outfitter and get waaaay out there. All you need is a tent and Algonquin Park or some other northern wilderness paradise. You get out there a few portages from anywhere and it's only you and nature.

There is nothing more peaceful than to sit by the fire at night and listen to the cry of the loons and the rustling of the rattlesnakes and the snuffling of rogue bears as they stalk you in the dark.

One tip: Buy a map from the outfitter and avoid camping on sites with names like Berserk Grizzly Massacre Isle.

Unless, of course, you want to get some jogging in. And possibly some swimming.

But remember, Berserk Bears can jog and swim faster than you can. So if you must go camping, please don't feed the bears. You could really upset their digestive system. And that would be most uncool.

Roughing It in the Bush

NORTH TEA LAKE, ALGONQUIN PARK — Our forefathers and foremothers were hardworking Puritan types whose idea of a good time was to take off their collective pants and sleep in a snowbank. They came to Canada, looked around, and said, "This looks like a great place to discover in the hope that, many centuries from now, our descendants will freeze their asses off eight months of the year! Ha! That'll teach the little bastards! Why should they have it soft?"

It's part of the legacy of being a Canadian.

Life is pretty soft in Canada during the summer months. That's why Labour Day is such a depressing holiday.

It means summer is over and fall is coming and another long winter is just around the corner and soon we'll be fighting our way through the snow and slush, wondering why the hell our forefathers and foremothers hadn't decided to discover Costa Rica or Mexico or Tahiti or, shit, even Fort Lauderdale.

I've found over the years that the best way to prepare for another hard winter is to take off to the wilds of Algonquin Park for five days or so in the waning weeks of summer. The idea is to paddle for hours, portage, paddle some more, portage some more, paddle some more, make camp, forage for wood, make a roaring fire and then spend the night as our ancestors used to do: shitting your pants every time you think you hear a bear.

Of course, you won't always find bears in your campsite. Sometimes you will find rattlesnakes or maybe a moose who mistakes you for a female moosette. Ouch!

But it is good for your soul to stand by the fire late at night, miles from any other human being, completely isolated from civilization, and think to yourself, "Boy, if anything happens to me out here, I'm really fucked!"

It is how our forefathers and foremothers would have wanted it.

Camping in the wild gives you a rare chance to walk around half naked, armed to the teeth with Rambo survival knives, axes, saws and other primitive weapons that, nowadays, you would find only at your typical high school dance.

Well, okay. I know that's a ridiculous generalization and totally unfair. Very few, if any, of our modern high school students bother to bring saws to a dance party.

But there is something about camping that brings out the primal wild man or woman in all of us — especially when you run out of toilet paper and have to scour the woods for those really big frond leaves.

Actually, there's a trick to dealing with bears. If you follow these handy wilderness tips, you'll do fine (or at least won't suffer too long).

Tip #1. Never startle a bear. You have to warn him that you're around. If, say, you are heading out in the middle of the night to have a nice, forefatherly dump in the woods, you should always bring two pots with you and bang them together as you are staggering around in the dark with your pants around your ankles. If a bear should chance upon you in this state, it will take one look at you and die from laughter.

Especially if it catches you wiping your bum with one of those frond leaves.

Tip #2. If you're camping with a friend who is in a separate tent, sneak over after dark and lay strips of raw steak on the top of his or her tent. In case of a bear attack, the horrible shrieking from the next tent provides a perfect, natural alarm that warns you it's time to get in the canoe and paddle like hell.

Tip #3. If you are camping alone, or in a single tent, play it smart at night. Pack all your food into your cooler, lash it with rope, and hang it twenty feet or so from the ground. The reasoning behind this, as all expert woodsmen know, is that if a bear comes into the campsite, he will not be able to reach the food in your cooler and so will have to settle for slashing open your tent and eating you instead.

It's just one of the basic rules of camping: Human life is cheap but you must defend the beans 'n' wieners to the very death!

Tip #4. Try to look and smell as unappetizing as possible. This shouldn't be difficult after four or five days of camping, but the most important rule of thumb is to always stay downwind of a bear, never wash, and — this is vital — never change your underwear. Bears are easily disgusted.

Tip #5. Take pepper spray with you. If a bear decides to eat you, simply spray a big gust of pepper at him. The wind, of course, will blow it right back in your face but at least you will die knowing that you are nicely seasoned.

Algonquin Park is that beautifully rugged and ominous land that was the muse of the famous group of Canadian artists known as the Group of Eighteen (sadly renamed the "Group of Seven" after a painting trip to deepest Algonquin in 1916 ended in disaster. Following that extremely messy tragedy, the surviving members resolved to stop painting angry grizzlies and concentrate on jack pines and barren rocks and stuff).

Tom Thomson, perhaps the best known of the Group of Seven, was famous for painting while standing upright in a canoe. This technique created many works of stunning, austere beauty, but ended tragically one day in the middle of Canoe Lake when Thomson drowned after he finally created his masterpiece and, overwhelmed, took a few steps back to admire his work.

As I write these words the wind is blowing in hard from the north and a storm is brewing on the horizon. The giant pine trees bow in homage to the coming foul weather. They whisper to each other that winter is on the way. The giant pines welcome the coming frost, for they know it will kill off the fronds of summer, and, when the fronds are gone, the assholes with the clanging pots and pans will pull up their pants and make the long trek back to the cities and leave the wilderness in peace.

And as the last campers make that final portage and paddle to the far shore, they know that the ritual of the past week has prepared them to face another cruel winter in the city. They begin to look to the bright side of winter: the beautiful, clean white snow, the Christmas lights, the crisp night air, the logs burning in the fireplace, the warm whisky in the glass.

And the soft, two-ply Delsey in the bathroom.

Have a Horrible Halloween

OOOOoooooOOOOOooooo.

BOO!!!

Scare ya?

Didn't think so.

I don't get the whole concept of Halloween. If you're only going to get spooked and horrified one day of the year, what planet are you living on? And if you only put on a mask, invade private houses and demand "treats" at the ominous risk of unspecified "tricks," you're running with the wrong street gang.

Tricks can be had at any time of the year. I've seen some of the tricks downtown and I can tell you they ain't no treat. Although you may get a trifle "spooked" when your dick falls off a week later.

The good thing I remember about Halloween night when I was a young punk was that it was Payback Time for all the nasty old bastards in the neighbourhood. Our favourite trick — one that is still used by the mob — is the Flaming Bag of Shit.

Here's the recipe:

A. Fill up a paper bag with shit (human, animal, doesn't matter).

B. Place said bag on Mr. Grumpy's door step. (Important Note: If his front porch is not made of concrete or stone, place the bag on the front walk. In all cases, keep the bag o' shit at a safe distance from anything flammable. It's payback time, yes. But we are not out to torch the place. Believe it or not, the law has no sense of humor when it comes to arson. There. I think the preceding warning should cover my ass in case you try to blame any three-alarm sky-scorchers on me.)

C. Save a not-so-small amount of fecal matter to spread on the outside doorknob of Mr. Grumpy's front portal.

D. Knock on the door. Of course he won't answer, knowing it is Halloween, so persistent pounding and ringing may be required before he comes storming out through the front door.

E. Set paper bag on fire and run like hell (he may be armed).

F. From a safe distance, concealed by shrubbery, watch in delight as Mr. Grumpy angrily stomps out the flaming bag — only to find he has shit all over his shoe!

G. Get that "extra laff-riot" when Mr. Grumpy — after the blaze — reaches for the door knob to go back inside and — yes! — gets shit on his hand!

HAHHAHHAHAHHAAHHmaAHAHA.

I know, I know: I shouldn't pass on such wicked wisdom to the younger generation, but there are traditions that must be passed down from generation to generation or Grumpy Old Bastards with shit on their feet and hands will become extinct.

Another Halloween gag I and my gang of thugs (I mean, my fun-loving chums) used to enjoy was the Invisible Rope Trick. Here's how it works:

A. You get three cheap punks on each side of the road (for those who failed math, that's six in all).

B. Wait until a car approaches.

C. At the last minute, the crews on either side of the road pretend they are pulling and straining for all they're worth (roughly $5 if sold for parts) on a rope or wire across the road. Of course there is no rope. But the driver doesn't know that.

D. Have a great laugh as the surprised driver puts the brake to the floor to avoid the ghostly rope.

E. Run like hell.

F. Repeat process until you see flashing red lights. Then repeat Step E.

(NOTE: Hardly any drivers were killed while reacting to this tricky treat.)

Yeah. When you think about it, we had our good times.

Halloween isn't all that bad.

But forget Halloween. If you're looking to be horrified, you don't need a special day. A guy like me is absolutely horrified by what I see, hear, watch, smell, read and step in 365 days of the year.

Here is just a random list of everyday things that horrify me:

• Global Warming and Giant Meteorites From Space will wipe out the Earth and you and I could be dead in five billion years. So what's the point? We might as well pack it in and party. I wonder why I'm even bothering to finish this column.

• Wayne Newton makes waaaaay more money than me. So does Rita McNeil. Can anyone explain this chilling mystery? It has me spooked.

• I'm starting to like soccer.

• Here's a spine-tingling, haunting feeling I can't get over, which is just perfect for a day like this: I can't help thinking: Maybe O.J. did do it.

• The most horrifying thought of all: Winter is coming. Six long months of slopping through slush and freezing your balls (if any) off.

To end on an upbeat note, I can only quote an old Native saying: "May you prosper and have a good day, even though you are about to get flaming shit all over your feet."

Do the Right Thing

I've been in a charitable mood lately and it's time to stop thinking and start acting. It is up to you and me to make this a better city, a better country and, dare I say, a better world to live in.

I know many of you already are working for some Good Cause or other, but I read in the paper that it is the people with the lowest incomes who give the most to charity. It's time some of you who have been a little more fortunate in life got off your hands and did your part. That's why Marlon Brando and I have always steadfastly refused to accept our Oscars (I've even refused to host the event) because Marlon and I know that it's just rich folks patting other rich folks on the ass.

You know all the Serious Causes. If you can't find time for them, here are a few less serious (but still vital) ways you can Do the Right Thing for the less fortunate in this city:

• Insane Babbler Aid. There are two kinds of citizens who walk down the street holding animated conversations with themselves: rich business guys with cell phones and crazed babblers and religious nuts. Now if only the rich yuppie types would donate their burned-out cell phones to the street babblers, they (the babblers) could walk down the street with the cell phone to their ear and say whatever they liked and no one would place a hurtful stigma on them as weirdos. Like I said, it's for a good cause.

• Helping-the-Old-Lady-Across-the-Street Aid. I think grossly overpaid baseball players should donate their time to community service to teach old ladies (and old gents and young hammerheads) how to cross the street, especially those really wide streets. Wily, fleet-footed fielders could hold seminars for the Little Old Person on how to lead off the curb, how to dive back safely in case a bus or crazed taxi driver tries to pick them off, how to know when they have the green light, how to know when it's a "hit and run" and how to slide safely (even face-first) onto the opposite curb.

• Malls at Christmas Aid. Football players might be able to give seminars in how to Get Through the Mall Crowd at Christmastime.

• Bike Courier Hurrier Aid. A recent stat showed that, out of seventy bicycle rider deaths, only one — count 'em, ONE — was one of those "crazed" bike couriers everyone bitches about. I know these guys aren't rich but they know one thing: you can never get hit by a car when you ride exclusively on the sidewalk. No — well, not many — cars surf the sidewalks of this fair town, as the bike messengers well know. If they would only take the time to teach the Sidewalk Slalom to everyday, ordinary bike riders, just think of the lives that could be saved! Full speed ahead and damn the old ladies. They've had their time on this hill 'o beans we call our overcrowded Earth.

• Homeless Feeder Aid. We well-off types spend hundreds of bucks putting out seed in feeders for the birds (and squirrels). Why not put out feeders in the parks for human types who don't have enough to eat? You could try sitting on a park bench and Feeding the Homeless the way people feed pigeons. But these people are human. They have pride. Just discreetly leave an offering and go away. If you have to watch, use binoculars.

The Investment of a Lifetime

The following idea is patented and copyrighted by the Chez Burrill^{tm} empire — so please, no calls or letters unless you're a serious investor. If you are serious, however, now's the time to get a piece of the action, so don't spare the ink on that chequebook.

Here's the basic plan: We have to start small, with an original Chez Burrill restaurant location, but so did McDonald's and I don't have to tell you what happened to them.

I'm thinking someplace downtown that has the funky decor of a college student's frat house. (Note to frat houses: The Chez Burrill Corp. Inc. is interested in any portions of your carpeting that have particularly interesting stains. Each carpet patch must, of course, come with a Letter of Authenticity and a provenance that explains the no-doubt-hilarious story of how that stain got there. Competitive prices offered.)

Now for the heart of the matter — the menu: The beauty of a Chez Burrill franchise is that everything on the menu will be extremely inexpensive but also the sort of food you (and of course I) love to eat. Here is a rough working list, but suggestions are welcome:

• Kraft Dinner. Say no more about this classic. You come in out of the cold and sit down to a steaming whack of KD. Specialty dishes, such as KD à la Canned Tuna, are slightly extra. Ketchup is free.

• Beer. Best prices in town for the suds of your choice.

• Beans 'n' Weenies. Who can say no to this classic taste treat? Servings will be limited to six per person to preserve the ozone layer.

• Puritan Meatballs. This is as close to dog food as a human can get, but, at a buck a plate, I see lineups around the block.

• Soup Du Jour. You have Chez Burrill's promise that no soup will be served that does not come directly out of a can.

• Cheez Whiz. On celery, on Wonder Bread, you make the call. House Rule: No eating directly out of the jar unless you purchase the whole package.

• Jello à la the Occasional Interesting Foreign Object and/or Species. Every bowl of Jello at Chez Burrill's is a new adventure in epicurean delight!

• The Chez Burrill Special. Peanut-butter sandwiches on white bread.

Available with jam, honey, cut-up bananas or — Monsieur Burrill's personal favourite — peanut butter and iceberg lettuce. (Note: One of the early investors has suggested — nay, insisted — on serving peanut butter and molasses sandwiches. But she comes from Hull, Quebec, so… We'll deal with this delicate issue at the first stockholders' meeting.)

• Haggis. I know it's disgusting — it's the belly of a sheep, for Christ's sake — but it will only be served on nights when my close personal friends, bagpipe king Craig Downie and Enter the Haggis, drop by to jam. Motto: "We'll eat anything as long as it makes you want to hurl." Hurling is apparently a national sport in Scotland and they actually — I'm not making this up — hold tournaments to see who can hurl the farthest. Bangers and mash and Grease 'n' Grease will also be available that night as a tribute to this fine group of musicians.

• Specialty Sandwiches. Certain well-known patrons will have their own favourite sandwich added to the menu. Burrill's "Ham on Rye," Donna Lypchuk's "Baloney in a Dark Sauce that You Don't Want to Know About," and so on.

• SPAM. Served straight out of the tin (Warning: Chez Burrill takes no responsibility if you cut your finger while trying to work that little winding key that is supposed to open the damn thing. Cost me six stitches on the left Toby Tall one time).

• Catch of the Day. Do not ask how the Sea Bass got fur, ears and a long bald tail and we won't tell you. Deal?

• The "I've Been Smokin' Weed" Salad Bar. Load up on chips, jujubes, penny candy, pizza, Twinkies, shrivelled pepperettes, popcorn, Cheesies and everything else that makes a great post-ganja repast. One low price.

• "Hot Dogs." For the vegetarian this is a good choose because the Chez Burrill Hot Dog is guaranteed to contain no part of any animal that you would eat if you were smart.

• Burgers. See above.

• The Coked-Up Special. It's nothing but an empty plate, but you can stay as long as you want, provided you consult Chez Burrill Himself in the washroom.

All this and more can be yours when you drop by the informal and surprisingly affordable confines of Chez Burrill. Of course, the place will be packed with celebrities, and this brings up the only other House Rule: No bothering Brad Pitt or Johnny Depp or Winona Ryder when they're eating their Kraft Dinner. This is, after all, basic courtesy.

Chez Burrill: Once again — serious investors only.

Read This if You Have No Class

Hey you! You college frosh. Get down off that roof. Don't jump. Things may look bad. But help is on the way.

I know the first few weeks of the school year can be a bewildering time for university and college freshpersons. Many of you frosh types are away from home and turned loose in the big city for the first time in your life. You don't know your way around town. You're lost. You're lonely. You have no friends. You're homesick. You're feeling overwhelmed by the challenge of entering university life. You're shitfaced.

What's worse, far from being helpful, the snotty senior students treat you like shit. They make you parade around in green garbage bags. They give you wedgies. They play "Sea Hunt" with you in the washroom. You have no shoulder to lean on in these tough times.

Well, I was in university once. The University of Guelph. An institution whose top scholars spend most of their research hours with their arms thrust elbow-high up the asshole of a cow. (Due to government cutbacks, they can only afford one cow, and it is getting justifiably indignant these days.)

Anyway, coming from such a prestigious college, maybe I can give you a little advice, offer a helping hand in getting you oriented into the ways of university life.

First of all: the workload. It may seem insurmountable now just because most high school grads are functionally illiterate, but — listen! — don't worry too much about things like spelling and grammar in the post-secondary ranks. My university major was in English, which meant I had to read books by guys like Chaucer and Spenser, and I'm telling you, these assholes were as dumb as a box of rocks. They couldn't spell their way out of a wet paper bag. You want proof? Spenser's most famous snore-fest is a book called *The Faerie Queene*. You'll notice that, even in the title, Spenser only spelled one of three words right (and the one he got correct was "The," which is sort of a gimmie).

Another English-major standard is *Beowulf* — a 32,000-line eye-glazer written in the eighth century. The spelling in this whack of shit is so atrocious that the author was too ashamed to even sign his name to it for fear of being hunted down and boiled alive by medieval English students.

What I'm saying is: correct spelling is highly overrated. Spenser and Chaucer couldn't spell, and they're still famous centuries after they kicked the bucket. Even in modern times, poor spelling has not held many people back. Look at former Blue Jay manager Jimy Williams. He couldn't even spell his own first name and he got to manage in the Bigs!

In general, I'd advise you to stay away from CanLit courses, because if you take one, they'll make you read *Roughing It in the Bush* by Susanna Moodie. This book has been blamed for more student suicides than any other factor. If you're assigned this piece of literary cyanide, throw it away at once! Don't even open it. If you're asked a question about it in class, simply say it's a book about a woman named Susanna who came to Canada from England in 1832 and just bitched and whined about everything (having to dump in the woods, getting blackfly bites on her white ass, having to deal with disgusting, smelly Native people who acted like they were there first, as if they owned the place or something). Bag it, Suzie.

We won't even talk about the W.O. Mitchell classic *Who Has Broken The Wind?*, which is an entire novel about a dozen people arguing in a stalled elevator.

No matter what you choose to major in, the first thing to do is to find a really smart student whose notes and essays you can borrow and copy. Plagiarism is risky, so the safest way not to get caught is never to return the original notes and essays to the brown-nosing little keener. Just copy 'em and burn 'em.

Of course the most important part of your university orientation is to find out where the best and closest student pub is. Once you're in, take careful note of where the door is, because it may be difficult to locate after the first dozen frosties.

But if you simply can't find the door, don't sweat it. A friendly, helpful bouncer will be only too happy to airlift you teeth-first into the night shortly after that point in the evening when you decide that wearing your pants and underwear on your head is a neat idea. (Tip: It is helpful to pin a note with your name and address onto your shirt to ensure safe delivery back to your dorm or apartment. No postage is necessary.)

Most of your college days will be spent in the pub but you might , at some point, actually consider attending a class or lecture. WARNING: This is extremely risky. If the professor sees your face once, he or she may notice that you are not there for the rest of his or her classes. It is better simply to use your "browner" contacts to find out after the fact what the prof was droning on and on and on about. Your borrowed notes and essays, supplemented with Coles Notes, should be sufficient to get you through the course without actually having to show up in person.

I mean, some of these classes are actually held before noon! I kid you not. Some — so I've been told, although I would not know from first-hand experience — are scheduled as early as 8 o'clock. In the morning! I am not making this up.

One trick, if you must attend a class, is to wear dark sunglasses and sit as far to the rear of the lecture hall as possible. Place your head thoughtfully on the desktop. And try not to snore. Unless of course the lecture is on *Roughing It in the Bush*. Because then the entire hall will sound like a roomful of chainsaws and the prof will have difficulty singling you out (especially since he or she will also be wearing dark glasses and snoring up a storm).

After all is said and done, if you carefully follow my advice, I guarantee that you will one day be the proud holder of your very own diploma.

Sally Struthers may even sign it personally.

Fifteen Easy Steps to Proper Student Nutrition

This is the time of year when many young college freshpersons are turned loose on the big city for the first time. Living on your own — or sharing a dorm or apartment with a bunch of other shitfaced animals — can be an exciting but bewildering experience during your first college semester.

But it is a startling fact that some freshman students simply do not know how to prepare a nutritious meal, having eaten nothing but mom's home cooking all their lives. A proper diet is essential. You can't withstand the strenuous pace of university life if you don't eat right. You've got to keep up your strength if you hope to endure the strict regimen of staying up all night and drinking beer seven days a week. So I'm only too happy to pass on some cooking tips I learned while I was in college.

It is vital to stock up on food that does not require refrigeration, as there will be no room in the fridge after you have laid in the correct amount of beer. ("Correct" being defined as "as much beer as you can cram into that sucker.") All you really need is a couple of cases of Kraft Dinner (or generic equivalent, which is even cheaper if you buy in bulk). "But," I hear you say, "I have never learned to cook for myself. I'll starve to death!" Not to fret: although preparation of KD is tricky, it is a dish you can eventually master without too many calls to the fire department — if you carefully follow this simple recipe.

1. Locate your stove. It's a square appliance, with knobs and "burners" and probably white and usually found somewhere in the kitchen. (As well as four burners, the stove also contains a door that opens into something called an "oven," but you won't be needing that. The "oven" is only for

highly advanced recipes and besides, there is probably a family of mice living in it.)

2. Find a pot. (A metal cooking device that is usually blackened and scorched, with something really disgusting stuck to its inner receptacle. It usually has a "handle," sort of like Davy Crockett's hat, only harder.)

3. Hold pot under tap, fill halfway with water (if no water comes out of tap, try turning "cold" or "hot" water knob). Important note: If the water is not easily filling the pot, but instead is splashing all over, you are probably holding the pot upside down. Try turning it over, with the handle thingie up.

4. Use stove "knob" to turn a burner on about halfway. If you can't figure out which knob controls which burner, turn them all on, but first remove any borrowed notes and essays from stove-top surface. (Unless you've already copied them. In that case, let 'em fry.)

5. Have a couple of beers and then go and look at the water. If there is steam rising and bubbles forming, this means the water is, in the arcane jargon of gourmet cooks and chefs, "boiling."

6. Open Kraft Dinner box and pour contents into boiling water. You will notice some dry noodles in the pot and also a sealed package of cheese powder. With tweezers or pliers — NOT with your bare fingers!!! — carefully remove sealed cheese packet from boiling water. Its use will be explained later.

7. Stir.

8. Let boil for seven minutes. If you have no timer, have seven beers, taking roughly one minute per bottle or can.

9. Go look at pot. If on fire, carefully douse flames. Remove pot from stove (crowbar may be needed).

10. Drain remaining water (if any).

11. Open sealed packet of dried-up cheese crap and pour into pot. Add a lump of butter and a dash of milk (or beer, if you have no milk).

12. Optional for gourmets: Add a can of tuna. It is wise to open the can first. Another advanced recipe — "KD à la Bobbitt" — calls for the addition of cut-up weenies. (Boil the weenies first, following the "boiling water" procedure explained above.)

13. Stir and blend. (A fork usually works better than your bare fingers, but what the hell. It's your dinner, not mine.)

14. Optional: You might want to chip the finished results onto a plate but this is messy because, after a few months, the plate will have to be "washed."

15. Voilà! Repeat every night and enjoy!

As for lunches, you can always eat the occasional meal in the school cafeteria, but let me warn you — and I am not making this up — in high school science class we took scrapings from the school cafeteria table tops and also from the toilet seats. We analyzed the samples under a microscope and there were way more bacteria and germs and other festering little microscopic meanies on the table top sample than on the toilet seat samples.

In other words, if you must eat at school, it is much healthier to eat off the toilet seat. Bon appetit!

Eating out can be a financial drain after a while and can really cut into your beer money. So you might want to "brown bag" your own lunch as often as possible. Try this simple yet sumptuous recipe.

Burrill's Peanut Butter And Jam Sandwich Surprise:
1. Buy or scoff a loaf of Wonder Bread, a jar of peanut butter, a jar of jam and a head of lettuce at store.
2. Take out two slices of bread. (We'll label them slice "A" and slice "B.")
3. Open peanut butter jar. Slap a generous amount on Slice A. (Using a knife is optional.)
4. Open jam jar and slap big whack on Slice B.
5. Here's the "surprise." Cut a thick chunk of lettuce and place it on Slice A.
6. Place Slice B on Slice A (with the "jam" side down). Presto! A sandwich that tastes great and (thanks to the lettuce) does not stick to your mouth.

Sometimes students with a busy schedule don't have time to do all this fancy cooking.

For a quick and inexpensive snack when you're on the run to the pub, locate one of those downtown sidewalk "Smog Dog" vendors who will cheerfully sell you a nutritious and delicious hot dog for only two bucks. It is essential to eat a balanced diet and Smog Dogs have it all (being made of a mixture of ground-up cow and pig ears, noses, tails, hooves and assholes, with a generous dollop of rat shit).

Add some relish, pickles, tomatoes, onions, mustard and ketchup and there you have it — all the major food groups wrapped into one taste treat.

If you follow all of these inexpensive eating tips, you'll have plenty of student loan money left over for several kegs of Molson Export Ale. And a case of Preparation H.

You'll need it.

The International Draft Beer Conspiracy

I know a lot of you college kids out there are starting a new year and that usually means a lot of parties while you get to know your new school "chums."

I went to college once myself and it is from experience that I issue this warning: BEWARE OF CHEAP DRAFT BEER!

You know, the kind of draft beer they sell by the jug in places with tables covered by elasticized terrycloth and where the only available food is pickled eggs and pepperettes? Students love to drink in places like this because the draft beer is so surprisingly affordable.

But be warned: This sort of beer has a secret ingredient that can't be found in most bottled or premium beers, which ensures that the finished product tastes and smells like the bat piss that students know and love so well.

The secret ingredient remains a mystery. But the side effects, the least of which is a sudden tendency to forget where one left one's pants, are known all too well.

It can also induce a sort of mass amnesia. Many even forget their own names.

Draft beer has other side effects that don't show up until the next day, including the eerie sensation that someone has snuck into your room at night and driven a red-hot rail spike through your skull.

You may also notice — if your dog sleeps on your bed — that in the morning it will take a keen interest in trying to roll in your breath.

But the worst side effect is far too delicate to mention.

Let's just put it this way: I'm pretty sure that Johnny Cash drank a couple of kegs of draft beer the night before he wrote "Ring of Fire."

As I say, I speak from experience. When I went to school at the University of Guelph, I majored in two activities: 1) drinking cheap draft beer by the keg in a place cleverly named The Keg; and 2) writing extremely bullshitty columns for the free weekly student newspaper.

Once in a while a prof would pull me aside and stress the importance of taking the other things offered at the university — such as classes — more seriously.

"It's all very fine to drink draft beer and write extremely bullshitty columns for a free weekly newspaper while in college," he would counsel, "but that's not the sort of thing you can make a career of out there in the real world."

These college professors. What do they know?

Cheap draft beer can make you feel invincible, but the higher the high, the harder the fall the next day.

Just look at the people of Germany.

For centuries Germans have guzzled mass quantities of draft beer and then tried to take over the world. They try this every few decades or so.

They get the shit kicked out of them every time.

And then they wake up in the grips of a serious depression.

But you can learn one thing from the Germans: the way they go to the beer halls wearing those "lederhosen" — funny leather shorts strapped on with huge heavy duty suspenders on them.

That way, no matter how much cheap draft beer the Germans drink, they will never, ever, ever misplace their pants.

Cuba's Hemingway Trail

HAVANA — Halfway through the flight — and half in the bag — I leapt from my seat and shouted, "I DEMAND YOU TAKE THIS PLANE TO CUBA!!!"

The stewardess brought me another beer and offered no resistance. "Of course we will take you to Cuba, Señor. That is where this flight is going. To Havana. Which is in Cuba."

"WELL... UM... TAKE ME THERE, ANYWAY."

So they did.

Which is, I guess, how I got here.

When I make demands, people listen.

I am in Cuba working on a book, which requires me to retrace the footsteps of writer Ernest Hemingway, who lived on this Caribbean island for about twenty years on a ranch overlooking Havana and the sea. It is no easy deal following the footsteps of Ernest Hemingway, especially after he had his usual daily three bottles of rum — or maybe gin for a change — because you spend a lot of time bumping into things and you had better hope that there is a public washroom nearby wherever you go — or, failing that, a bush.

But retracing the footsteps of Ernest Hemingway is not as unhealthy as one might think because you do not walk in a straight line; you sort of weave from side to side. So if you retrace the footsteps of Ernest Hemingway for three miles as the crow flies you actually cover more like ten or twelve miles, what with all the lateral movement.

I started out by renting a room in a hotel in Havana that Hemingway actually stayed at (although he doesn't remember much of it). It was a nice breezy Spanish colonial room with sixteen-foot-high ceilings and the kind of balcony that is only big enough to make speeches to the masses from — which I did, although the masses for the most part ignored me, probably because I was on the ninth floor and I tend to mumble.

There is something magical about staying in the same place as someone you consider a hero. You look at the bed and say Hemingway slept in this very same bed. You look at the toilet and say Hemingway puked in this very toilet, which is a very romantic thought, although you kind of wish he had flushed afterwards.

Of course, you cannot retrace the footsteps of Hemingway without spending a lot of time in bars. In La Floridita in Havana I slugged back a drink that Hemingway invented and which they still serve — a "Papa Doble," which is a daiquiri made with four ounces of seven kinds of rum over crushed ice (no sugar). Hemingway still holds the house record for putting away the most glasses of this drink even though (or maybe because) he is dead. One night he drank seventeen. Which works out to sixty-eight ounces of rum, or 2.615384615385 bottles of rum. If he had taken one sip more, he would have felt like a bag of shit the next day.

I visited other favourite Hemingway haunts which for some reason all seemed to be bars. I think the barkeepers, not knowing that Hemingway was a notoriously poor speller, got him to translate the menu from Spanish to English. Thus, to this very day, you can enjoy such delicious translated entrees as "Prickles of Skrimps" or — my personal favourite — "Lobster Is Used Plunger." That's how they get that secret sauce.

I rented a cab for the day and went to Hemingway's old home, La Finca Vigia, which translates to the Old Farm — or , if you let Hemingway translate it, The Tractor In The Septic Tank. I asked the taxi driver, through my translator Renata (who was posing as my wife but is really a spy), what the Cuban people thought of Hemingway. He shrugged. In Spanish he said, "People always ask us that. Sometimes we say he was a great writer. Sometimes we say he was a great fisherman. Sometimes we say he was a drunk. But we don't know his personality, what he was really like. When someone asks, we make something up."

Hemingway's "farm" is really a huge old colonial house with a lot of side buildings, a lookout tower and a swimming pool. His boat, *La Pilar*, is also there in dry dock and is very well preserved thanks to all the rum and gin and whisky that was spilled on her.

Hemingway's house is very nice. His desk has a stapler, a letter opener made out of a dead thing and a lot of shotgun shells. In short, all you need. (Real writers will understand.) The old Royal portable typewriter he used is on a bookshelf, since he typed standing up. Everything is carefully watched over by the stuffed and mounted heads of other dead things. There are books everywhere — more than 9,000 in the house, including more than fifty in a bookshelf beside the toilet.

Hemingway liked to hunt, but he was a sucker for pets. He had more than thirty cats and you can still see the carefully tended plots, complete with inscribed gravestones, of his four pet dogs. Sentimental, maybe. But he was handy with a shotgun when the going got tough.

Had a drink in the little fishing village which Hemingway used as the setting for *The Old Man and the Sea*, then rented a little farm of my own ($25 a day) from a Cuban family. This is better than staying in hotels. It had a kitchen, a toilet, a bedroom, a garden, a patio, two pigs, a kitten and assorted lizards. From up there you could sit in the sun and read or write or just look out over the sea.

The rum costs three bucks a bottle.

The little tienda — the store — didn't have much in the way of food. You could buy ham and cheese and bread or, if you preferred, cheese and bread and ham. I fed some bread to the pigs. I almost fed them some ham but that would have been morbid and there are things you should not think about.

Into the Liver of Darkness

I'm reading *Pursued by Furies*, this new biography of Malcolm Lowry, and it occurs to me that it was just over fifteen years ago that I found myself living in Mexico. I say "found myself" because, when I quit my job at *The Toronto Star* and headed south back in October 1983, I actually thought I was going to live in San Francisco with a woman from New York (who was really from Detroit) whom I met in Key West. HAHAHAHAHAHA!!!

I actually did go to San Francisco — for about two days. But then things blew to hell with such atomic intensity that I found myself doing one of those Bogartesque beelines for the airport with no idea in hell where I was going to go.

It was time to improvise a little.

Since I happened to be reading Malcolm Lowry's *Under the Volcano* at the time — which really should have been called *Under The Table* — I asked myself, "What would good old Malcolm Lowry have done if he were in my shoes?"

Of course! He would have done the only sensible thing. He would have taken off to Mexico, found a cheesy place to live and spent the next year writing a Famous Novel while drinking himself silly.

So I did. Well, all except for the part about the Famous Novel. I did write a novel, but it's not all that Famous. Probably because it hasn't actually technically been, you know, published yet. But it has received some glowing rejection slips!

I wasn't even the first William Burrill to take refuge in Mexico under emergency circumstances. My Uncle Bill, for whom I'm named, spent his last days in Cuernavaca, under the same volcano that Lowry made famous in his mescal-soaked novel.

Now Uncle Bill — always dapper in his Clark Gable moustache and ascot — was a guy who loved a good time. Not that he ever called it a "good time," because he had a speech impediment that caused him to stutter if he sounded words beginning with the letter G. So Uncle Bill invented his own language to get around the problem. Instead of saying, "having a g-g-g-good time," he'd say, "having a Hey-Hey time!"

And did he ever.

My grandfather owned a cotton mill in Hamilton and Uncle Bill "worked" for him, supposedly as a cotton crop inspector in Mexico, South America and the Caribbean. It's doubtful if, in all his years in the Tropics, Uncle Bill ever filed a single crop report. Instead, he would send my grandfather postcards or telegrams that read, "Having a Hey-Hey time in Brazil [or wherever]. Send cash!" And my grandfather would! But once Grandfather died, the new owner of the mill's first astute business move was to fire Uncle Bill.

Bill, who happened to be in Cuernavaca when news of his dismissal reached him, made the best of the situation by using his remaining funds in the most sensible way he could devise: he got a cheap room above a cantina that was also a brothel.

Uncle Bill stayed there for years, having the Hey-Hey time to end all Hey-Hey times. Then one day my family received a tin can, plastered with Mexican postal stickers, mailed C.O.D. from Cuernavaca. It was Uncle Bill. Or what was left of him. He'd Hey-Heyed himself to death. The Mexican government — unable at first to locate a next-of-kin — had had him cremated. But once they found someone who knew Bill's home address, the Mexicans thoughtfully popped Bill in the mail, C.O.D.

At his funeral another of my uncles cracked everybody up by saying, "It's just like Bill to go to Mexico and make an ash of himself."

I ended up in the colonial town of San Miguel de Allende, 7,000 feet up in the mountains north of Mexico City. My hotel room was close to the jardin — a bargain at 500 pesos a night, or one peso per roach. The room was ancient, with high-beamed ceilings, and the señora claimed that Cortez himself had once stayed there (which was fine with me but I wish she'd at least changed the sheets since).

San Miguel and Lowry's Cuernavaca have a lot in common. Both are overrun with expatriate gringo artists and writers, many of whom are more or less professionally drunk. The cantinas are open all night long (closing only for an hour or so around dawn to sweep out the bodies). Some of the more, shall we say, pleasantly affordable cantinas even have a handy trough right there at the bar so you can go to the washroom without actually having to go to the washroom.

Soon I found a house with high walls around it and a gardener named José who, true to his name, did nothing but stand around all day with a hose drowning plants. By day I would work on my novel, which, as we all know, is thirsty work. By night, I'd make the rounds of the bars and parties. I'm not saying I had a Hey-Hey time of Uncle Billian proportions, but I did enjoy the occasional cool beverage. One of my neighbours, who became a good friend, was the *Toronto Sun* columnist Paul Rimstead. Paul was renting the house of a Hungarian count who had left the place fully furnished with rare and extremely breakable antiques. There was a huge arched doorway between the living room and dining room that had a sort of porthole window at the apex of the arch — just the right size, Rimstead soon figured out, to shoot basketballs through. On more than one night we sipped a few cocktails and played a little one-on-one. Miraculously, hardly any antiques got seriously broken.

I met a lot of would-be writers down there and almost everyone was reading (or had read) *Under The Volcano*, the rather depressing and highly autobiographical account of one man's descent into booze-fuelled hell. Its very depressing nature, I soon figured out, was what made it so popular among the boho expatriate crowd. No matter how badly you'd behaved yourself in the cantina the night before, you could merely open *Under The Volcano* randomly to any page and read about someone who was acting much worse!

And now we have another book that's even better for that purpose. It's *Pursued by Furies: A Life of Malcolm Lowry*, by Gordon Bowker. If you ever start feeling like you're screwed up, just skim anywhere in this 672-page baby and you'll instantly feel extremely normal — boring, even. Reading Bowker's biography confirms in hair-raising detail that Lowry was every bit the binging, mescal-maddened menace of the Consul who is the protagonist of *Under The Volcano*. But Bowker further proves that Lowry was like that long before he had his first tipple of tequila. Lowry's wife left him in Mexico, as did the wife in the novel, and Bowker shows how Lowry used his wife's letters and other real-life material to fashion his now-infamous novel.

Anyway, I left Mexico in one piece and even met my future wife down there. We've returned three times since we were married and will go again.

I mean, where else can you go for a truly Hey-Hey time?

You're a Poet, but You Don't Know it

Writing and drinking have always gone together like flies and a turd. They just sort of naturally fit. I'm not sure if writers drink because they write or write because they're hammered. But there's no denying the connection.

Let's look at the hard facts. Pretty well every U.S. writer to win the Nobel Prize for literature — from Sinclair Lewis to William Faulkner to Eugene O'Neill to Ernest Hemingway — was a total piss-tank (Scott Fitzgerald deserved a Nobel but unfortunately drank himself to death before he could accept it).

Let's take my specialty, Hemingway, as an example. As author Jeffrey Meyers points out in his book *Hemingway: A Biography*, old Hem spent at least half of his life in an alcoholic fog. According to a close Hemingway friend quoted in Meyers' book: "His drinking would have killed a less tough man. Two or three bottles of hard liquor a day. Wine with meals, etc. Gin a favourite drink. I suppose he was drunk the whole time but he never showed it."

And you wonder why he blew his brains out in 1961? Probably just to get rid of the headache.

Of course, one of Canada's most famous writers, Mordecai Richler, doesn't exactly drink cream soda. I know. I've drunk with him. And we won't even mention Malcolm Lowry, author of the classic *Under the Table Under the Volcano*...

You can trace this literary occupational hazard all the way back to the authors of the U. S. Constitution. My handy washroom reading guide, *Uncle John's Bathroom Reader* (Bathroom Reader's Press, $24.95) quotes from historical material discovered by researchers at the U.S. National Constitution Center in 1992: "And how did the Founding Fathers unwind during this pivotal moment in [U.S.] history?" the book asks. "By getting drunk as skunks. One document that survived is the booze bill for the celebration party thrown two days before the U.S. Constitution was signed on Sept. 17, 1787. According to the bill, the fifty-five people at the party drank fifty-four bottles of Madeira, sixty bottles of claret, eight bottles of whisky, twenty-two bottles of port, eight bottles of cider, twelve bottles of beer and seven large bowls of alcoholic punch.

"'These were really huge punch bowls that ducks could swim in,' reported researcher Terry Brent. 'They signed the Constitution on the 17th, but on the 16th they were probably lying somewhere in the streets of Philadelphia.'"

This may explain why only thirty-nine of the fifty-five American

Founding Fathers actually got around to putting their trembling scribble on the document. And why only one signature — John Hancock — is legible. And also why the famed parchment is covered in barf.

The competition for being a writer is tough. But drink enough beer, and I just know you can do it. I mean, how do you think they wrote the U.S. Constitution?

Gone With the Broken Wind

Many great artists have farted their careers away, but today I want to tell you about a man — a new hero — who, a century ago, farted his way to within a whiff of immortality.

This is a high-brow sort of book, as anyone can see, and it is my mandate to promote the arts of every kind. But I personally am more of an archaeologist of art. I dig into the past, discover lost art forms and restore them to their proper place in history.

And so it was like a clarion call to action when I got wind of a long-lost art form called petomania.

Although I am often accused of making things up, I swear that — this time, at least — the story is true. The facts of the case are contained in a copy of an article by reporter Peter Lennon that appeared over a quarter of a century ago in the British paper The Guardian. It was the story of Joseph Pujol, better known 100 years ago in Paris as "Le Petomane," which translates as "The Fart Maniac."

(The article was passed to me by my friend Iain The Gas Pipe Weasel, who, fittingly enough, makes his living at TransCanada PipeLines, passing gas across this great nation.)

Le Petomane was a Marseilles baker who had a unique talent: he was the world's most artistic farter.

The artistic farting business is a hard field to crack, and Pujol remained a virtual unknown until he was thirty. But after years of working family parties and weddings, he finally got his big break at the swankiest Paris club of them all, the Moulin Rouge.

At the height of his fame in the 1890s, Le Petomane earned an average of 20,000 francs per show (to put this in perspective, the other star of the Moulin Rouge, Sarah Bernhardt, was only pulling in 8,000 francs per performance).

Le Petomane was a talented virtuoso who took his art seriously. He was a handsome and impassive man who took the stage dressed elegantly in a short-tailed red coat and black satin breeches. With the sort of gravity that such a performance demands, he solemnly announced, "Mesdames,

Mesdemoiselles, Messieurs, I have the honour to present to you a perform-ance of petomania."

His show was well paced. He would bend over in a dignified fashion and begin with a girlish, tender fart ("le petit pet timide de la jeune fille") and then a loud aggressive blast ("le pet rond de macon"). He would then imitate the farting mannerisms of a nun, a butcher, a priest, a general.

He would then work through a series of impressions and sound effects, mimicking with startling accuracy a creaking door, ripping cloth, a hooting owl, an amorous bullfrog, the rapid sound of machine-gun fire and the blast of a cannon.

Next he would move on to the musical portion of the show, playing a scale to warm up. Then, with perfect pitch, he would play a musical score, complete with such varied instruments as the violin, the bass and, of course, the trombone. As a finale, he would play a sort of rapid-fire medley of his entire repertoire and then dramatically blow out a candle.

To avoid a bum rap that he was faking his talent, Le Petomane offered demonstrations and submitted to countless probings and proddings by doctors, who not only confirmed that his act was legit but published lengthy medical reports on his phenomenal talent.

Although Le Petomane remained absolutely deadpan throughout his hour-and-a-half long performance, he was almost literally slaying his audi-ence. Said an eyewitness of his Moulin Rouge shows "At first the audience would remain astounded. Then someone would be stricken with a crazy laugh. In a moment people would be howling and staggering with laugh-ter. Some would stand paralyzed, tears pouring down their cheeks, while others beat their heads and fell on the floor. Ladies would begin to suffocate in their tight corsets, and for this reason there were always a number of white-coated nurses in attendance."

Said another witness: "It was at the Moulin Rouge that I heard the longest spasms of laughter, the most hysterical cries of hilarity that I have ever heard in my life."

Like any sensation, Le Petomane soon had imitators. The artistic world was rocked with scandal when a female rival petomane was discovered to have hidden a whistle up her ass.

Soon Le Petomane was summoned for command performances. The King of Brussels even travelled to Paris for a private audience. A star was born. When Le Petomane left the Moulin Rouge to go solo, the club owners tried everything, including lawsuits, to keep their star attraction. But he was free, and soon stooped to conquer new audiences throughout France and North Africa.

He continued performing until the outbreak of World War I, when the people of France did not need a guy with gas to create the sounds of machine guns and cannon fire. He died in 1945, at eighty-eight, and is now all but forgotten, never again to be seen, heard or smelled.

But I know Le Petomane is still up there somewhere, a Blue Angel who is looking out for all of us, lighting up our very lives. When you hear the thunder and see the lightning, that is he, my friends.

Le Petomane — a genius who is now as free as the broken wind. Let's all light a candle in his memory.

And then drop our pants and — solemnly, solemnly — blow it out.

Insomnia Alert!

It's 7 a.m. Do you know where your neighbourhood jackhammer operator is?

I certainly know where mine is.

He's right outside my bedroom window, earnestly pursuing his noble profession of Making Holes in the Road at an Obscenely Early Hour so Other Guys with Hard-Hats Can Fill Them Back Up.

BRRRRRRAAAAACCCCCKKKKKK!!!!

I've heard that guys who operate jackhammers end up jiggling their guts so much that, after a while, they go for a dump and their heart pops out their ass.

This is only fair.

It's 7 a.m. The world is not kind to chronic insomniacs.

You know why I can't sleep at night? Why I toss and turn until the break of dawn?

I can't sleep because I'm troubled every night by that haunting and seemingly unanswerable question. A question that has me obsessed. A question that hits me and slams me wide awake at four in the morning. A question that, if I am not very wrong, some of you may be spending your very own sleepless nights asking yourself: Whatever happened to Thor?

You know... THOR!!!!

Big dumb-looking muscle-guy who used to have a rock band and sang songs like, I dunno, "Whipping the Dogs from Hell".

That guy.

Where is he? It drives me crazy. Into thin air ...

When I was a kid I got kicked out of high school for, of all things, Getting Smart. "Don't get smart with ME, young man."

Shit. I thought that was the whole point of school. You learn something every day.

I ended up taking a job, straight midnight-to-7 shift, in an electronics factory.

It sucked donkeys. I hated the smell of the chemicals and melting plastic that hit you the second you walked through the door. I hated the heat — about 400 degrees — that spewed out of the moulding machine I had to operate. I hated the little widgets (called "comb brackets") I had to spew out by the trayful.

I hated the old bastard who worked at the next machine. He was always sneaking over to peek at my widget counter, to see if I was producing more comb brackets than he was. If, by some fluke of nature, I actually was, the old bastard at the next machine would work right through his lunch hour to try to get ahead of me.

Like I really cared who made the most widgets.

I finally fixed the old peckerhead by taping a piece of cardboard over my counter. Then, no matter how much he skulked around, he was never quite sure if I might just outproduce him on the widget production forms we had to fill out at the end of each shift.

He started working through his lunch hour all the time. Sad, really.

HA HA HA HA HA.

Once — this would be years ago — I saw Thor perform in the Choo-Choo Lounge in Guelph, where I went to university (got in as a "mature" student — which is, oddly enough, what they call people who got kicked out of high school).

I saw Thor bend a solid bar of steel with his bare hands. I saw Thor blow up a hot-water bottle until it burst. He had these tear-away gold lamé pants he would rip off halfway through the set. He had goth boots you would die for. And a whip.

We are talking about a Major Canadian Talent here.

At least, he might have been. Dammit, would have been. If not for his highly suspicious disappearance.

My last week on the job, some other kid got his long hair caught in the machine and got pulled right through before you could hit the emergency stop button. There was nothing left of him to speak of. They blasted high-powered fire hoses through the thing to clean him out.

The old bastard next to me kept right on working through it all. He (the old bastard) always had a butt in his mouth, like Andy Capp. He'd been there like thirty years and was still afraid he might lose his job if he stopped work for anything.

I walked out that morning into the sun, feeling stunned. I went home and drank a few beers on my front step. People going to work or school looked at me funny.

It was 7 a.m.

Thor, if you're out there somewhere, if they're holding you in some dark dungeon cell, if somehow, by fate, you chance to read these words: TRY TO GET A MESSAGE TO US!

It will have to be in code, of course — Pig Latin at the very least — for your captors are obviously both very cruel and extremely cunning. But just send the word, any way you can.

We'll whip up a posse. We'll find you. We'll come and save you. We'll pull you out. You have my solemn word on that.

Once we spring Thor, his comeback tour can begin. I've taken the liberty of penning his Comeback Hit Single. Imagine a really heavy Goth Rock beat. Cue the howling dogs. Cue the babes in leather. Cue the hammers and anvils! Cue the lightning! Cue the dry ice! Cue ... "Thor!!!!/Valhalla's great Lord!/Odin's fabled son!/Mighty God of War!/Hammer of the Sun!/THOR! [whiplash!] Making evil reel!/THOR! [whiplash!] Bending solid steel!/THOR! [whiplash!] Taking on the worst!/THOR! [whiplash] Hot water bottles burst!/THHHOOORRRR!!!"

The all-night job as a molding machine guy paid $4.45 an hour, which was Big Money in those days.

That was the first job I had after getting kicked out of high school. If you don't count the time I was a Fuller Brush Man.

Never slept very well since. Can't count the times I've seen the dawn from the wrong side. They say the sun is actually the All-Seeing Eye of Odin. Watching over us. Protecting us from evil thoughts.

Here he comes again. Over the trees. Winking at me. Now at last I know I can sleep.

It's 7 a.m.

Here Comes Your 19th Nervous Migraine

The window is open to let in some fresh air — or as fresh as it gets here in the city.

The old lady across the street is out front, loudly sweeping her path. The old lady across the street is always out front, sweeping her path. It is only when squeezed in the vice of migraine pain that you realize just how loudly this old lady sweeps. She doesn't sweep her path because it is dirty.

No path in existence could be that dirty. She sweeps her path as an excuse to be out front and keep an eye on things. And so she can be ready to talk to anyone who passes by. She can talk for an incredibly long time about things you or I would not think worthy of much serious discussion. And just when you think it's over, it continues for another forty-five minutes.

Sort of like a CBC Radio interview.

I knew the migraine was coming when the aura kicked in.

The aura — as any classic migraine sufferer knows — is a little aurora borealis all your own. It starts slowly, with just a few little fitzs and fizzles of dancing light before your eyes, like when someone pops a flashbulb right in your face.

But soon, sparks fly, lights shimmer, lightning zigs and zags, hellfires dance, images blur and distort like a melting movie frame. The first time this happens, it scares the shit out of you. You think, what is this? Am I going blind?

Then the pain hits.

The first time the pain hits, you worry that you might die. Then, after a few hours, you worry that you might not. It's technically known as acute pain. But believe me, there's nothing cute about it.

My first migraine didn't hit me until I was thirty, but it can start any time. It can be triggered by anything from changes in the weather to harsh light to cheese to chocolate to red wine to whatever. Maybe some of you out there have had this happen lately — the dazzling lights, the head pain — and think you're going crazy or suffering a brain tumor.

You're not, you know.

You're only getting a migraine. Welcome to the club. Have fun.

Even as I'm scribbling this, I can hear the old lady with the broom through my window, talking in that half-shouted manner of hers with another old lady from down the street. They are discussing — and have been for twenty minutes now — the relative merits of buttermilk.

The old lady with the broom is pro buttermilk, but the lady down the street is con. The lady down the street speaks more softly than the lady with the broom, but for some reason, she always raises her voice an octave and a few hundred decibels every time she says the word buttermilk, which she pronounces "buddermilk."

So her side of the conversation comes through my window like so: "(Inaudible) BUDDERMILK! (mumble-mumble) BUDDERMILK! (unintelligible) BUDDERMILK!"

I begin wondering if Dr. Kevorkian is in the Yellow Pages...

When you have a migraine, the pain doesn't fill your whole skull, like a normal headache. Instead it hits one small area on one side of your head —

in my case, a silver dollar-sized patch on the right side, at the base of the skull, below the ear. The word "migraine" derives from the Greek for "half a head," due not only to the uniquely lopsided pain, but because, after a few hours, most migraine sufferers feel like taking a shotgun and blowing half their head clear off.

The afflicted area is small and localized, but the pain, the pain is like — what? A red-hot railroad spike driven into your skull? Nah, duller than that. Like a blunt jackhammer inside your skull, trying to drill its way out. No, it's more like — the phone rings.

I'm waiting for an important call so I answer.

"This is the CIBC VISA Centre for a Mr. William Burrill."

"He's ... ah ... not here."

But the bank lady is insistent. Her high-pitched nasal shrill pierces your skull like a berserk Nazi dentist. You take down a number, agree to pass it on to the deadbeat Burrill if he ever shows his "face."

Click.

Now the dog wants out. The dog lets you know this by saying, as follows: "Yip! Yip! Yip! Yip! Yip!

"Yip! YIP! YIP! YIP! YIP! YIP! YIP!"

Seven more phone calls: MasterCard. The Liberal candidate's campaign office. *Toronto Sun*, flogging subscriptions! The — HA! — Tory candidate's office! Rogers Cable TV bill collectors. Someone selling burial plots. Then a call from a computer from the bank that wants YOU to hold while it locates the weasel who will pester you for cash.

Click.

You wish you had something cold to press to your head.

Like, I dunno, maybe, a Colt .45.

Maybe I'll lie back against the pillow, turn it over to the cool side, bury my head. Maybe try some transcendental meditation. Breathe in. Breathe out slowly. Repeat the secret mantra. Beeeer. Beeeeeer. Beeeeeeeer ...

A breeze comes in through the window.

And a sound.

"(garble-garble) BUDDERMILK!!!"

The phone rings. Need a new tactic here. Something twisted and desperate.

"Holà?"

"This is American Express for Mr. William Burrill."

"Lo siento! Senor Burrill no està en casa!"

"Pardon me?"

"No hablo inglès!"

"IS ... MR. ... BURRILL -?"

"Que? Que? No burros ici!"

"CAN ... YOU ... GET ... MR. ... BURRILL ... TO -?"

"Burritos? No sé! Solemente cervezas! Adios!"

Click.

They bought it. Morons.

I mean, is it just me? My head is splitting, splitting... Is it just me...?

My apologies. You see, I've got this migraine. There will be no column this week.

Through the window it is still going on:

"(babble-babble) BUDDERMILK!!!!!!!"

Seinfeld Prompts Rash of Home Invasions!

I'm at home, sipping a scotch and soda and trying to write some of my usual deathless crap. But I have to type very, very quietly because people keep coming to the door and ringing the doorbell. Some of them are very persistent. When I don't respond to the doorbell, they start hammering on the door with the door-knocker I very foolishly installed.

I mean, they *know* I'm in here. They can hear the TV and they're probably peeking at me through the mail slot as we speak. But the thing is, I will never, ever answer the door if I am not expecting somebody.

I've learned from hard experience that the only people who show up unannounced and pound on your door are one of the following:

a) A pair of Jehovah's Witness weasels

b) A bill collector

c) A summons server

d) A survey taker

e) A Fuller Brush Person (or equivalent door-to-door sales pest)

f) A campaigning political jokebag

g) A swarm of Home Invaders

h) The Moonies

i) A charity drive pitch-thingie

j) All of the above

In other words, nobody I want to see.

My home is my castle and the clear message is "Do Not Disturb." In medieval times, they knew how to build their castles right. They built a moat around it full of water and alligators. They had a drawbridge and armed sentries. They had a pot of boiling oil they could pour on your head if you fit into any of the above categories. In other words, they knew how to keep unwanted intruders away from the front door.

They had, in short, the right idea. A man has a right to his privacy. Go away.

I point the finger at TV sitcoms like Seinfeld and Friends for this current notion that blatant invasion of privacy is acceptable.

I was watching a Seinfeld episode the other day and was shocked to learn that Jerry was surprised that someone had broken into his apartment and ripped off his TV, stereo, VCR and all kinds of other stuff. He blamed it on the fact that someone (that would be Kramer) had forgotten to lock the apartment door. Seinfeld whined that he had no insurance to cover the loss because he had spent all of his money installing fancy locks on the door.

Who's kidding whom here, Jerry? Have you ever seen an episode of any sitcom where the front door is actually locked? Worse yet, have you ever seen a sitcom character actually *knock* before making an entrance? Take Kramer of Seinfeld fame. How does he make his signature entrance during every show? Does he knock? Does he ring the bell? Does Jerry ever go over and look through the peephole to see who's at the door? Never. What always happens is Kramer just barges right in, unannounced, through an obviously unlocked door, and stands there staring with that patented look that puts one in mind of a man who has just had a 50,000-volt cattle prod shoved up his ass.

Same with Friends or any of the other "Seinfriends" clones. Nobody ever knocks. They just barge right in. And nobody seems surprised.

I mean, what if Jerry was sitting on the couch, choking the ol' chicken while watching a porno flick? Or having sex with George? Or what if he was doing something really embarrassing, like country line-dancing?

Maybe Kramer has barged in unannounced and seen these very acts. That would at least explain the way his hair is always standing on end.

Still, I've never once heard Jerry say, "Hey, Kramer. For fuck's sake, use the goddamn doorbell!!!"

That's TV for you. It's all a fantasy world. If you barged in Kramer-style to any real apartment in New York City, you'd find yourself with a .357 Magnum slug right between the eyes. And no jury in the land would find the killer guilty.

Justifiable homicide.

Maybe all this barging-in business is starting to get to Seinfeld. Maybe that's why, although it's a monster hit, this will be the last season for the show.

Of course, if a show like Seinfeld is going to call it a wrap, they'll have to come up with a killer plot for the finale episode. Maybe Kramer will barge in, see Jerry doing something unspeakable to a gerbil and then take a gun to his own head. A sort of Kramer-vs.-Kramer finale.

Or better still, maybe Jerry will go berserk, get a semi-automatic rifle and take out each and every cast member who comes through the door without knocking. Then he could appear as a guest-star door barger on Friends and blow the cheesy grins off their all-too-smug mugs.

"Knock-knock."

"Who's there?"

"Seinfeld."

"Seinfeld who?"

"Sein who felt it was time for you and your 'friends' to eat tasty death!!"

RAT-A-TAT-TAT-TAT

"AHAHAAHAHA!!!!"

That would not only make a great ending to the series, but also teach the people of North America a valuable lesson: always keep your door locked. And never, ever answer the doorbell. At least not until you've got the M-16 primed and cocked.

And make sure you don't leave any Witnesses. But you've got to work fast. They always travel in pairs.

Ask not for whom the doorbell tolls. It tolls for THEE! Go ahead. Ring my bell. Make my day.

A (Barely) Living Medical Miracle

Maybe it's that time of year when all kinds of weird bugs and flus are going around, but I was feeling like a regular sack of burning shit last weekend. I mean, when you drink a lot of beer for a living you are used to feeling slightly queasy, but this was something else altogether.

It was bad enough that it sent me to my bed for a couple of days to "recuperate." When you combine some very realistic, basic symptoms with someone who is a certificate-holding hypochondriac, you end up with a period of recuperation that is scheduled sort of like this:

1. Rest in bed.

2. Drink plenty of fluids.

3. Prod yourself all over looking for weird things you didn't remember being there.

4. Read a lot of "Home Medical Adviser" type books.

5. Drink plenty more fluids.

6. Make your will.

My last worldly advice to you is to never, ever read those doctor books that let you look up symptoms and see what is really wrong with you so you will know how to "treat" it. These are the type of books that have those handy cross-referenced indexes that invariably read like so:

• Hacking cough (see Lung o' Death, p. 456)
• Headache (see Massive Brain Tumour the Size of a Grapefruit, p. 876)
• Heartburn (see Inoperable Stomach Cancer, p. 564)
• Heart Palpitations (see Poppin' the Big Aorta, p. 897)
• Heaves (see Exploding-on-the-Spot Syndrome, p. 654)
• Hiccups (see Black Plague, p. 984)
• High Fever (see Spontaneous Combustion, especially if you are a rock 'n' roll drummer, p. 265).

As you can see, we are not at all well here. And we have only barely worked our way through the H's.

As I lay there on my deathbed I was able to determine, with the help of such medical books, that I was a (barely) living medical miracle. I had been able to narrow down the nature of my affliction to not one, not two, but some 492 separate illnesses.

The good news is that none of them was contagious. The bad news is that all of them were instantly fatal.

So, by the time you read this, all I can say is: Weep not! Think of me in the happy times, the times you remember me traipsing through the copse as a merry young lad. Do not dwell on my demise, heed not even my extremely brave and profound last words.

Weep not as I read with rasping breath the last lines from my tattered volumes of Keats and Shelley.

For I am gone to a Better Place.

As I go, so shall you follow.

And when you follow, I shall be there.

Waiting with open arms.

And a case of beer.

For mine time on Earth is nigh.

...either that or I just have a really wicked case of the shits...

I guess if you really feel sick you should go to a doctor. I have resisted this idea for years because it is my theory that if you feel sick and go to a doctor, he or she might actually find out that something is Really Wrong with You. And what fun would that be?

Plus, when you get to be my age, they have these rubber gloves. And they are not wearing them to do the dishes. Can you say Cadbury Cockpit? I knew you could.

My fear is that not only might they find something seriously wrong with my prostate gland, but they might also find some coke I was innocently smuggling back from Colombia many, many years ago and had simply forgotten about.

Can you imagine the scene in the doctor's office?

"Mr. Burrill, I have some bad news. You have six months to live. And you're busted!"

My method is much better. I simply curl into the fetal position and whine.

Or sometimes I consult my friends. This is pretty dumb, I suppose, but I do it all the time.

"Hey," I say, as I enter the old eye newsroom, "Has anybody else around here found a weird-looking gargoyle-shaped thingie growing on their shoulder? That sings filthy songs? Is that going around??? Or what???"

Oddly enough, most of them have it, too!

Consulting your friends is not nearly as dangerous as consulting your relatives. I speak from experience. Once, twenty years ago, when I was a kid living for six months in Vancouver, I came down with some kind of throat thing: I could not talk, breathe, swallow or move much, since I also had a temperature of 104. Did I go to the doctor?

I did not. I went to my sister's place, just down the street in Kitsilano. She took one look at me and — judging my the way I was crawling through the door on my belly, using my bleeding fingernails for traction — figured I must not be feeling well.

"I have just the thing to fix you up," Vicky said.

As a historical note, I must add that this was at the very height of the hippie period in Vancouver, when (and this is true) a junkie once gave me shit for eating white bread while he was hitting up at the kitchen table.

"Do you know what that white bread shit does to you?" he said.

He was probably right. But why preach? Anyway, my sister had all these herbal teas — each one good for this or that — and after reviewing my symptoms, simply mixed them all together into one brew from Hell!!!!

I lay on a mattress in the guest room, shivering, sweating, talking gibberish. Every few hours she'd bring in a new cup of B.F.H. and I would try to force it down my rapidly closing throat.

I lay there for three days, reading *The Lord of the Rings* in my moments of consciousness and dreaming weird, Orc-infested, *Under the Mountain* dreams in my delirious snatches of sleep. To this day I do not know how much of *The Lord of the Rings* I actually read and how much I dreamed.

I might have died there if — faced with another dose of Brew — I had not dragged myself to the door and weaved to the hospital on the fourth day.

The doctor said it was acute tonsillitis. He said that if I had come in sooner, he would have immediately removed my tonsils. But now the infection had made an operation too dangerous. The only hope was antibiotics. He gave me lots 'n' lots o' drugs and I lived.

But I still have my tonsils, sort of.

Doctors. Ha!

What do they know?

As we go to press I am still quite ill. If I live, I will raise a glass to you all and say "Salud," as the Mexicans put it.

To your health. And, believe me, the Mexicans know a thing or two about the gastrointestinal tract.

If not, my last words:

Adios amigos.

Y dos cerveza...

Toronto Hopeless

I could never figure out why all these hospital dramas like *Chicago Hope* and *ER* are so popular these days. Perhaps it's because I'd never spent a night in a hospital bed in my life. Maybe I was missing something.

Sooooo, in the interests of investigative journalism, I cleverly became extremely ill last weekend and wound up in the emergency ward of St. Michael's Hospital.

It all started Thursday night with a sharp gnawing pain in the middle of my guts. By Friday the pain was worse and had spread to my entire abdomen, aided and abetted by some symptoms that have a lot to do with the washroom.

I toughed it out all day Saturday but the pain got worse and worse and, by the time the Leafs were down two goals in the first period of Saturday night's hockey game, I decided I had better rush myself to the emergency ward of the nearest hospital.

There I fell into a chair, doubled over in pain, clutching my guts, while the admitting nurse played "Twenty-one Questions" with me. Being a practising hypochondriac, I had pretty much already diagnosed myself.

"What seems to be the problem?" the nurse asked.

"I think it's an acute gastritis attack," I rasped. "I've ruled out intestinal blockage because things are flowing very well at both ends. Could be an ulcer but I doubt that because the pain is too sharp and widespread. It goes from my ilium straight up the ascending colon, hangs a left at the gallbladder, crosses over the pancreas then goes south at the spleen down the descending colon to... "

"So," the nurse stopped me, "what you're trying to say is your tummy hurts. Please wait there and a doctor will see you."

To paraphrase the sage words of Samuel Johnson, or Ben Franklin, or maybe it was Ben Johnson, "Any patient who diagnoses himself has a fool for a doctor."

So I waited.

And waited. After about an hour they took me to a little room, dressed me up in a blue gown with no ass coverage, drew blood for tests, then put me on a stretcher and wheeled me into the Emergency Ward Itself! Yet another nurse jabbed an I.V. thingy into my arm and strapped pasties on my chest which caused a monitor to make jagged lines, indicating I was not dead yet. (I had a scare when the monitor line suddenly went flat until I realized that, in all my writhing around, I had unhooked my pasties.)

"Nurse, I need something for the pain."

"We can't give you anything yet," she said. "We need the pain so we can tell where it hurts."

"I KNOW where it hurts. Want me to draw a map?"

She smiled a nursey smile. "Don't worry. The doctor will be along shortly."

Shortly, in E.R. talk, means two hours.

The emergency room is a zoo on Saturday night. You've never heard so much wimpy moaning and whining — and that was just from my bed.

In the bed next to me was an old guy who had been rushed into the ward after wandering off in a confused state. The old-timer was seventy-eight, the son said.

A very professional doctor, played by a real doctor, asked the patient a series of questions.

"Do you know where you are?" the doc asked.

"France," the man said.

"When were you born?"

"Nineteen thirty-eight."

"What year is it now?"

"Nineteen forty-one."

"What month is it?"

"Ahhh... July?"

"What day of the week is it?"

There was a long silence, broken by the patient's son, who said, "He's not very good at days of the week."

The professional, actual doctor looked serious and then made his diagnosis.

"It seems," he told the son, "that your father is in a confused state."

That's why doctors make the big bucks.

I had to wait even longer when two dudes came in who had been injured in a knife fight.

One had two bad slices to the back and the other a small slice to the hand.

"OOOAAWWWW," the double-sliced guy kept yelling as the doc stitched him up. "You hurtin' me. Why you gotta hurt me? Las' time I got carved up the doctor at Toronto General, he don't hurt me none. You an amateur."

The doctor finally ordered the patient tied down so he could sew him up. Then he put two stitches in the hand of the other guy. "You can go now," the doctor told the only-slightly-carved guy. "See your family doctor in a few days to get those stitches out."

"I don't got no fambly doctor."

The doctor looked at him, then at the badly cut guy: "Are you good friends with that guy?"

"Yeah man, we hang."

"And you don't have a doctor?"

"No."

"Then," the M.D. advised, "find one. I think you're going to need him."

Like I said, you could hear everything the doctor said to the other patients: "When you wet the bed, do you do it in your sleep or do you know you're wetting the bed?" Or: "Ma'am, you have a boil on your anus we have to drain. You see there are fissures in your anal region that..." And so on.

About three hours later a nurse finally gave me a painkiller. "Go to sleep," she said. I tried, but the Colombian to my left kept kicking and pounding the metal rails of his stretcher, moaning and uttering Spanish blasphemies. The big baby. I would have said something to him if I weren't curled in the fetal position with my thumb in my mouth (or somewhere).

The stretcher was about as comfortable as sleeping on an ironing board. A bright fluorescent light directly above my bed was adding to my joy by giving me a migraine. I put the puke bucket over my head to block the light.

At 8 a.m. the doc came back to my bed with the diagnosis. "OK, William, you can go. I checked the test results. Your condition will be painful for a couple of days but it isn't serious. It's a thing called 'acute gastritis.'"

Gastritis is a common ailment of people who drink and smoke too much and don't eat properly.

But be warned: it can just as easily strike someone like me.

A Handbook for the Casket

Author's note: This story is about death but has funny bits. If stories about death make you dwell on your own mortality, think positively: just because everyone else in history has died, that doesn't mean you will. There's always a first time.

So I just had a complete physical and they ran an extra special battery of enzyme tests, etc., on my liver (twice to be sure), and to the doctor's frustration, she couldn't find a damn thing wrong with me. Even my liver, which I imagined would look not unlike a hockey puck, is doing fine, thanks. I figured, as a writer, I would at least have consumption. All writers worth their ink have consumption. But nooooooo. Oh well. There's always spontaneous combustion and flying truck tires...

One thing that does need a little work is my back, which, in medical terms, "hurts like shit" once in a while. So I went to a chiropractor. First thing he did was take a series of X-rays and then patch them together so I could see what my skeleton actually looks like. He was showing me my skeleton and I said, "Great! Now I know how I'll look if I die." It was meant as what is called "a joke" in literary jargon, but the chiro merely looked at me and said, "That's a strange way of looking at it. Nobody's ever said that before."

When he told me I had trouble with my Third Thoracic Vertebrae, I said, "I know. You should call this place Thoracic Park." He gave me a look chiropractors give you when you tell them a joke they've heard a million times. "That, as you can well imagine, is a common joke at chiropractors' conventions," he said. Damn. The upshot is: My chiropractor can crack me up all he wants — and those old bones of mine really do crack nicely — but I can't return the favour.

I'll have to bone up for next time... get it? Get it? No? Well fuck it then. I give up.

Speaking of bones, there was a story in the paper a while back about a company that sells coffins for $2,000 by mail order to "keep down the high cost of funerals." Apparently this is half what you'd normally pay. But two grand still seems a bit steep for a box that will be burned or buried. I was talking this over with my ma last week and she was adamant: "When I go, don't spend any money on me. Rent a coffin. Or put me out in a green garbage bag, for all I care." Of course I'd never do this. It lacks dignity and would require at least two Hefty Bags, and they ain't cheap. I have some better ideas:

1. I read an article about a master fireworks artist who, as his last request, had his ashes mixed with the powder that went into his favourite

firework creation. They had a little service and then — BOOM! — there goes Arnold rocketing up into the sky and — OOOOooooooHHH. AAAhhhh!!! — look at Arnold's ashes scatter in an explosion of spectacular beauty. This would be a great way for anyone to go. Arching heavenward and lighting up the night sky with searing, booming reds and golds and silvers and blues. Out with a bang... and after a high-body-count disaster like a plane crash or a Holiday Weekend, you could put on a whole half-hour program!

2. Whatever happened to the Relic Business? When I was travelling the Middle East a few years ago, you couldn't go 100 yards without tripping over Holy Relics of this or that Saint, Martyr or Prophet. In various places I saw the bones of Old Saint Nick, John the Baptist and a bunch of other Holy Guys. And EVERY city had at least one relic of the Prophet Mohammed. They even had his beard in Istanbul and people lined up to put there noses against a crack in the glass and snort some Mohammed for luck. Mohammed was everywhere. I figure that if you took all the relics of Mohammed I have personally seen, you'd have enough bits to build at least twenty Mohammeds and still have plenty of spare emergency replacement parts left over. This is a viable option for the Here and Now: Instead of a funeral, simply will your various bits to friends and relatives. "Aunt Esther gets my tailbone because that's where she always gave me a pain. My son gets my head because he never used his..." Collect the whole set. Trade with your friends. Fun? Wow!

3. There's always mummification or preservation and you don't have to be mummified or preserved all in one piece, like King Tut or Michael Jackson (who is the first known human being to be mummified BEFORE death). Take Emperor Napoleon of France, for example. As per his last request, when he died in 1821 his head was shaved and his hair passed out to hundreds as souvenirs; his wisdom tooth was given to a doctor who sold it for seven guineas; his stomach and guts were saved in a silver pepper pot; his heart was placed in a silver vase, preserved in wine and spirits and given to his true love (ahhh!). In short, no part of Nappy went to waste.

Speaking of short, in 1972 Napoleon's one-inch penis was auctioned at Christie's, described in the catalogue as "a small dried-up object [that looked] like a seahorse." Trouble is, no one bid on it. "Napoleon's bone apart" failed even to reach Christie's reserve price. This has to be a trifle embarrassing, even for a dead guy.

4. When (if) I go, I want to do some good for my city. I read recently that by the turn of the century a tower will be completed in Jakarta that will be ten metres taller than our CN Tower. All I want is to be entombed in a golden ten-metre statue Krazy-glued to the top of the CN Tower, then we could glue Napoleon's dick on top of my tomb, thus beating the Jakarta tower's

record by an inch (a quarter inch in cold weather). And every visitor to Toronto could gaze in awe at the tourist landmark atop the tower known as A Couple of Real Dicks.

Christmas Party Etiquette for the Hopeful Survivor

Christmas is only two weeks away and that signals the beginning of the holiday party season.

While Christmas parties may be lots of fun, they can also be extremely damaging to your reputation if you go out and act like a really big asshole.

Sometimes we get caught up in the giddy social whirl of the festive season and don't realize until it is too late that we've committed an embarrassing social faux pas.

That's why it is vitally important for both guests and hosts alike to know these few basic "Do" and "Don't" rules for safe holiday party fun.

To be a genial host, DO try to speak to everybody, if only briefly.

If you see two obvious losers sitting in the corner with nobody to talk to, DON'T just leave them there to fester.

DO introduce them to each other so they will have at least one friend. This can be done by simply saying, "Oh, Mr. Mayor — have you met Al Waxman?"

As a polite guest, DON'T try to take over control of the stereo. Some hosts are very fussy about their stereo equipment and CDs. If you have a request, simply ask the host nicely, by saying something like, "Hey fuckface! Get a Thor record on or this dump is coming to the ground!"

Here's a handy tip for hosts: DO fill your medicine cabinet full of marbles and carefully shut the door. Then, when a guest opens the cabinet to steal your prescription downers, all the marbles will fall out with a hellishly loud clatter for all the party to hear. The guest's red-faced expression on emerging from the bathroom is simply priceless!

Remember, DO strive for an interesting mix of guests. For example, invite striking auto workers and the scabs who have been hired to replace them. Lively conversation is sure to ensue!

DO have fun but DON'T drink too much. You are your own liquor control board and it's up to you to know when you've "had one too many." Heed those almost imperceptible tell-tale signs. If, for example, you wake up on the bathroom floor, hugging the toilet while lying in a pool of your own bile with your pants inexplicably around your ankles, it is probably time to say "when."

Subtle body language is also a useful way of attracting the opposite sex. You can communicate your attraction to a woman across the room by such subliminal signals as taking off your pants and sitting with your legs spread while winking, clearing your throat and pointing alternately to you, her and *it*.

However, as a general rule of etiquette, DON'T take your pants off at a party unless the host does so first. (This is only a guideline.)

As a good host, DO plan fun party games to involve all your guests. One of my personal favourites is a game I made up myself called "Curse of the Mummy." Simply wait until some pantywaist passes out on the couch, then fill his pockets with raw eggs. Next, wrap the sleeping beauty in toilet paper from head to toe (three rolls should do it). Now simply tie his shoelaces together, toss a bucket of water on him and hear the "mummy curse" as he lurches around and does a highly amusing header down the cellar stairs. Fun? Wow!

Guests, DO try to mingle. DON'T hang around together in cliques. It is imperative to make personal contact with new people. This is, after all, what parties are for.

If you're the shy sort, here are a few sure-fire "ice-breakers" to get that conversation going:

• "So, when do we get to don our gay apparel?"
• "Hey, have you ever noticed that there's not one person named Hitler listed in the phone book?"
• "Wanna see my North Pole?"
• "Fat greasy slobs like you really make me puke."
• "Did you know that you have red hair dye all over your neck, ears and forehead?"
• "Is Burrill allowed to piss in the potted palm?"
• "Hey, you can go down my chimney any time you like."
• "Isn't Sally Struthers just fabulous in those International Correspondence School commercials?"
• "Do you know anything about lancing boils?"

For simplicity's sake, if you want to be a gracious host, DO try to ensure that people who don't drink are included in the conversation. Designate an interpreter who is neither completely snockered nor completely sober to explain to the teetotallers what all the shit-faced people are laughing about.

It can be so embarrassing when you've over-imbibed and suddenly realize you have to be sick to your stomach. To avoid being observed committing this social faux pas, DO try to find a discreet place to spew, like, for example, in the bowl of chili. DO stir it afterwards.

If you're the sort who has trouble meeting new people in party situations, DO bring an extra carton of smokes with you (even if you don't smoke yourself). Simply hang the carton around your neck like a St. Bernard, and then wait until about midnight. You'll be surprised how many instant friends you'll make.

DON'T pass out on the couch, whatever you do. (See "Curse of the Mummy," above.)

Guests, make sure you DON'T search the medicine cabinet for Valium (it's full of marbles!).

Remember, hosts, please DON'T run out of booze halfway through the party or things could get ugly and someone might get hurt. Always DO hide a couple of extra cases in the closet, to be shared with your valued guests once you've gotten rid of the usual collection of wombat's assholes.

Hosts, when you want to get rid of those last few stragglers who are kissing the carpet, DON'T play Karen Carpenter records in a continuous loop. Although this is a highly effective room-clearer, it is not only bad form but also banned under the Geneva Convention.

Remember: It's all right to have a good time, but it's also important that you get home safely after the party. DON'T drink and drive. You might spill some.

DO take a cab and make sure you DO affix a self-addressed adhesive label to your forehead so the driver can figure out where you live.

Above all, DO have fun and try to get through the holidays without any rug-burns on your forehead.

Stop the Insanity of New Year's Resolutions

We spend most of our time bullshitting other people as we try to get by in life.

But once every year there comes a day on which we traditionally look inward and try to bullshit ourselves.

We're talking about New Year's Eve, a time to take stock of all the things you've done in the past year. It's an occasion to mentally dredge up all your faults, follies and foibles, to identify your weaknesses and failings and write them down on a piece of paper (or, in my case, several pieces of paper).

Then it is traditional to concoct a list of New Year's Resolutions that are designed to turn you instantly into a perfect little angel.

You know the drill: "This year I resolve to go on a strict diet, quit smoking, quit drinking, quit using speedballs, lay off the China White, get in shape, get organized, stop knocking over variety stores, find true love, get promoted, be really nice, stop worrying, write a best-selling book and an Oscar-winning screenplay, travel the world, become famous and handsome and incredibly happy and just completely, disgustingly, stinkingly rich."

Then, once your list is complete, it's time to go out and "ring in the new" by getting absolutely shit-faced.

(People have been getting ritually shit-faced on New Year's Eve for 2,500 years. The Druids started the tradition and it was during one New Year's bender that they built Stonehenge "just for a laugh.")

The reason it is important to get hammered on New Year's Eve is to ensure that you will start the New Year with a crushing hangover, waking up in a strange bed with your arm around a naked circus geek.

As you're looking for your pants you'll swear to never drink, smoke, do dope, wear lampshades, or consort with strange, half-human, worm-eating, scab-festering freaks whose names you can't even remember. Ever!

And THIS time you really mean it!

Ah, but that feeling of resolve usually lasts, oh, about two days.

That's because most people make resolutions that are simply too sweeping and unrealistic. In doing so, you're only setting yourself up for failure: you'll find it impossible to create a perfect "new you" overnight, and will only end up feeling that much worse about the old you.

It's much better for your peace of mind if you simply learn to bullshit yourself into believing that you're already as perfect as you can be, despite a few minor but lovable flaws and shortcomings.

So to hell with the New Year's Resolutions.

What you really need is an annual list of New Year's Rationalizations.

Compare the resolution method to the rationalization method, and see how much simpler your life will be.

• RESOLUTION: I'll get in shape by swimming.

RATIONALIZATION: Swimming? No way! I could end up as a floater, like that crazed dog-paddler, Brian Jones of the Stones. Or Dennis Wilson, the Beach Boy who became a beached boy!

• RESOLUTION: I will begin a weight-lifting program.

RATIONALIZATION: Hey, wait a minute. Didn't the western novelist, Zane Grey, pop the big aorta while lifting weights? And besides, who the hell wants to look like some steroid-puffed pig-fucker like Fabio? Or, worse yet, that Susan Powter bimbo. Now SHE is one scary nubble-head.

• RESOLUTION: I'll get in shape by riding a bike.

RATIONALIZATION: Bike riding? Are you crazy? That's what killed Nico from the Velvet Underground.

• RESOLUTION: I'll take up a nice safe sport like golf.

RATIONALIZATION: Golf? Bing Crosby was playing golf and — whammo! — bing went the strings of his heart! Nope. It's much healthier to sit right here and work out the arm by lifting a few frosties.

• RESOLUTION: I will join an aerobics class!

RATIONALIZATION: What if Richard Simmons shows up? What if he tries to hug me? Yeeech!

• RESOLUTION: I will quit drinking.

RATIONALIZATION: I will keep a scrapbook of those frequent newspaper articles that report studies showing that moderate drinkers live longer than teetotallers. And of course, as a firm rule, I will only drink alone or with someone else.

• RESOLUTION: I will strive to create works of lasting importance.

RATIONALIZATION: There's a giant asteroid heading right for Earth and it's got my name on it, and the sun is getting hotter every day and, in a few million years, the world will be toast anyway so, what the hell, might as well sleep in.

• RESOLUTION: I will change my ways.

RATIONALIZATION: I will learn to accept myself, because, as the great existentialist Jean-Paul Sartre once quipped, "Life sucks, so why bother?" In the sage words of that famed philosopher, Popeye the Sailor Man, "I yam what I yam and that's all that I yam."

• RESOLUTION: I will quit smoking.

RATIONALIZATION: I will buy only packs that carry the warning: "Smoking during pregnancy can harm the baby."

• RESOLUTION: I will work hard and become famous.

RATIONALIZATION: Who wants to be famous? Mikey Jackson, Pauly Shore, Barney the Dinosaur, Oprah Winfrey and John Wayne Bobbitt are what passes for famous these days.

• RESOLUTION: I will go on a strict diet.

RATIONALIZATION: By eating sensibly, I will keep my weight below 400 pounds.

• RESOLUTION: I will get organized.

RATIONALIZATION: I will set aside a day every single month to do the dishes.

• RESOLUTION: I will stop procrastinating and finish everything I start.

RATIONALIZATION: I will…

Which Way Ya Goin', Billy?

It's kind of too bad that the Eagles reformed and recorded an album called *Hell Freezes Over* because, before that, I was not so much dreading the prospect of going to hell.

Not that I necessarily think of myself as hell bait. I've done some bad things in my day and I'm probably not through yet.

But I've also done good things a few times too.

I'd give you an example, if I could think of one. There... must be... something that... Hmmm. I fed the birds today. There. I filled both the feeders for the usual collection of sparrows and pigeons and they had a good meal and then went and sat in my backyard tree and contentedly shit all over my car.

That should count for something at the Pearly Gates.

But if not, it's a drag. Because the only good thing I could think of about hell is that it would at least be warm. Now, it will not only be freezing but will also feature the song "Hotel California" played in a continuous loop.

Can you imagine the song selection on hell's jukebox?

1. "Seasons in the Sun" by Terry Jacks
2. "Honey" by Bobby Goldsboro
3. "Knock Three Times" by Tony Orlando
4. "Have You Never Been Mellow?" by Olivia Newton-John
5. "I Write The Songs" by Barry Manilow
6. "Brandy" by Looking Glass
7. "You Light Up My Life" by Debbie Boone
8. "MacArthur Park" by Richard Harris
9. "Muskrat Love" by the Captain & Tennille
10. "One Tin Soldier" by whoever the hell inflicted that piece of shit on the human race
11. [YOUR PERSONAL SONG-FROM-HELL CHOICE HERE]

Heaven or Hell?

"Which Way Are Ya Goin', Billy?"

Arrrgghhhh! Nooooo. Not the POPPY FAMILY, too!

It's enough to scare the shit out of you.

I better clean up my act fast.

I got a soul to save here.

"Bless me, Father, for I have sinned. It has been ... umm .. like... forty years since my last confession.

"You'd better sit down, Father. This may take a while ..."

Actually, who knows? Maybe I might get used to the music in hell.

Maybe I could even learn to like it. Maybe, after a couple of stints in Eternal Damnation, I'll suddenly find that "You're Havin' My Baby" by Paul Anka is not such a bad little toe-tapper after all.

But I can never, never, ever get used to freezing my ass off.

Everybody I've talked to lately — including myself, although I never listen — is feeling sick and/or depressed.

It's an epidemic.

And it's no fucking wonder.

It's the WEATHER.

IT'S TOO DAMN COLD!

When it comes to Canada's freezing cold winter temperatures — like the brass monkey, ball-freezing, minus-100 weather — there are only two kinds of people.

a) Those who will readily admit that they do NOT enjoy freezing their fucking asses off.

b) Liars.

I have to type fast because my pipes are freezing and bursting all around me and if I don't remember to let the dog back inside, I am going to end up with a very dog-like lawn ornament.

Here in Toronto you meet people — for some odd reason they always seem to come from either Calgary or Calgary — who brag about how we Ontarians wouldn't know cold if it frost-bit us right on the ass.

These people are actually proud of the fact that, where they come from, you cannot go outside from September until June without dying of what doctors technically refer to as Frozen SnotLocker Syndrome.

Is this something to be proud of?

"People from Calgary tend to be extremely full of shit," a Noted Psychologist told *eye* in an interview. "They don't like freezing their asses off any more than people from Toronto or anywhere else, but what else are they going to brag about but their city's extremely frigid conditions? It's simply a means of overcompensating for a sense of inferiority. It is a phenomenon that we Noted Experts refer to as Phallic Tower Envy. Our tower is bigger than their tower. Waaaay bigger. I mean, Toronto has the Johnny Holmes of Towers and what does Calgary have? A lot of ice and snow and a Pee Wee Herman tower. It's sad, really. Some Calgarians will try to tell you that their tower is just as long as our tower but that towers tend to shrink a little in the extreme cold. But this is sheer, pathetic desperation. No wonder they're all full of Export Ale before noon and freezing in the ditch with their pants around their ankles by sundown. Hahahahahaa. Their brains are literally frozen like a Hungry Man Dinner. It has been clinically proven through highly scientific experiments that they [Calgarians] deserve to freeze in the dark."

Conversely, we, in Toronto, have done nothing to warrant this shit. I HATE IT!!!!

It bums me out.

It depresses me.

It makes me want to go to bed and sleep until April.

It makes me wonder just how hammered our ancestors were when they decided to settle here. "Thay. Thish looks like a nith frozen hellhole! Let's SETTLE here and freeze ta death ..."

We, the Children, are the ones who must suffer.

It's a cold world out there ... if you're dumb enough to actually GO out there.

My advice: Stay inside, keep your taps dripping so your pipes don't burst, make a nice roaring fire (it helps if you actually have a fireplace but if not, improvise), drink lots of Canadian Club.

Pray for spring and an end to this Frozen Hell.

It also might not hurt to go to Confession.

You know, just in case...

You've got two choices, my amigos: Get ready for heaven.

Or get Helen Reddy.

Forever and ever.

(Amen!)

Let's try to break the negative thought patterns and look on the bright side of Canadian winter. When you're living in a constant, ball-numbing blizzard:

• No one can tell if you have dandruff.

• The dog shit in the street doesn't stink.

• There's always a chance your school or office may be closed due to foul weather.

• If you sleep until 4 in the afternoon, nobody can accuse you of "wasting a beautiful day."

• Thanks to the new provincial cutbacks on snow and ice removal, you can skate to work (try not to trip over the frozen guys).

• If you don't shovel your sidewalk, the Jehovah's Witness tag-team will have to ask the Lord why they were chosen to fall on their asses.

• There's professional curling on TV. YES!!!

• It's just the winter blahs. The winter blah blah blah...

• If you're feeling SAD, hang in. I'm with you. You've got a friend. Who is freezing his ass off. We just have to chill out for a while.

• Spring is coming and before you know it the frozen dog turds will be thawing.

• Just stay cool... as if ya got a choice.

The Agonies of Victory

[Cue the stirring sappy background muzak and the horrible wipeout footage and... action!] VOICE-OVER: "No matter how high the world's finest athletes soar in their bid to touch the stars above, there is always the potential within each and every one that what goes up must come down. Nagano '98. Where you can watch the stars fall. Right on their asses. Good old-fashioned keester-plants. The Winter Olympians. If they're lucky, they'll live."

During the Nagano games you may have noticed that some Olympic winter sports are far more popular than others. The fans love any sport that combines high-speed action with the ever-present possibility of a spectacular wipeout that could cause serious and highly entertaining injuries and/or death. We want TV optics that could be used to illustrate the Agony of Defeat.

On the flip side, some winter sports are, to put it politely, considered a big yawn. These include long-distance skating, cross-country skiing, non-contact women's hockey and the dreaded biathlon, which can't spark fan interest even though it involves cross-country skiers toting rifles and ski masks and looking ready to knock over a bank. The rifles could boost the popularity of this event if only the biathletes would shoot at each other.

At the top of this list of eye-glazers is the newest official Winter Olympic sport — curling. If you want thrills and spills, curling doesn't cut it. You can watch all night but you'll never see a curler fall down, unless he's had too many beers. And even then they fall down veeerrryyy s-l-o-w-l-y — ploop! — right on their plump, fleshy bums like sun-stroked Pandas. Watching a curler fall is sort of like watching a glacier recede. You know there's movement, but it can't be detected by the human eye. If curling is recognized as a Winter Olympic sport, how long can it be before the summer games recognize 10-pin bowling?

And televised Olympic bingo.

It is sad but true that, although it cost him his life, Michael Kennedy may have accidentally invented the perfect winter sport for a Japanese audience — a high-impact mixture of breakneck downhill skiing and American football that is played while simultaneously using a video camera and slamming face-first into a large tree. It's got it ALL! And what great TV! The athletes would provide their own first-person TV blooper video coverage of their own gruesome doom. Wham! In your face. You are *there*, man!

Beer companies would love to sponsor Kennedy Ski Blooper Ball, since your typical beer ad already shows athletic, good-looking men and women happily riding mountain bikes off sheer 300-foot cliffs or committing other equally stupid stunts that only start to seem like a good idea after generous use of the brewer's product. I AM... DEAD MEAT!

But let's not stop there. *The Toronto Star* has called for an end to the deadly "Snowmobile madness" that has seen 29 Ontario snowmobilers die in tragic accidents so far this winter. Maybe this is a signal that snowmobile racing might just be ready to debut as an official Winter Olympic sport, especially if the snowmobilers are allowed to carry rifles, like the biathletes.

The Winter Olympic format needs work, but then so does our very own favourite Canadian winter sport, NHL hockey.

Lately there has been a lot of whining from the likes of star puckster Brett Hull, who says the current brand of NHL hockey, and I quote, "sucks." What Hull and countless others are whimpering about is lack of artistry and talent being demonstrated in the new, close-checking, clutch-and-grab, hack 'n' whack, neutral-zone-trapping NHL game. This season the collective NHL braintrust is deperately trying to come up with rule changes to open up the game and make it a fast-moving and exciting talent showcase once again.

As usual, I have the perfect solution. Under existing NHL rules, one point is awarded for a goal, whether it's a top-corner-picking bullet scored on a dazzling end-to-end individual rush or a "garbage goal" deflected in off a goon's jockstrap. My simple rule change would enlist a panel of international judges to decide how much each goal should be worth — anywhere from one to six points — based on degree of difficulty, artistry, talent, grace, presentation, poise and how nice the player's buns look in baggy shorts. No more garbage goals. Once again highly skilled hockey players would be rewarded for their innovation and skill. You'd see goals scored on clear-cut breakaways complete with mid-ice sit spins and perfectly landed quadruple-axels.

Play-by-play announcer: "Gretzky's got a breakaway! He crosses center ice with a triple-triple axel-lutz combination. Over the blue line and into a sit-spin as he shoots and SCORES!"

Colour man: "Wow, that would have been a perfect 6.0 for Gretzky if he hadn't two-footed the landing on his triple lutz!"

Announcer: "Still, Gretzky will no doubt — wait! — the opposing coach is calling for a pee test! This goal could be disallowed if Wayne tests positive for Being in the Same Room as Pot-Sucking Shredder Ross Rebagliati."

The Winter Olympics. Pull up a joint and tune it in. Warning: If you find yourself simply fascinated and transfixed by three hours of televised curling, you are smoking some *killer shit*.

The World of High Finance

I was wandering along the beach on a spring-like day last week, pondering my future (if any), looking for some kind of Sign, an Omen. You know, in the Bible or in classical mythology you couldn't walk ten feet without a Sign or Omen whacking you right in the head and maybe even knocking out a few teeth.

But me — nothing. No Burning Bush. No Sirens' Song. No Golden Fleece. Omen-wise, I've seen dick-all lately.

The water was remarkably clear and free of the usual floating Oh Henry bars you see every summer when the sewers back up. And as I peered in, I saw something — a flash of metallic blue a few feet offshore.

I waded in, fished around in the icy water and pulled out... a Porsche 928.

Granted, it was one of those Matchbox Dinky Toy Porsche 928s, but it was a Porsche 928 nonetheless. There could be no denying that fact.

It was a 1978 model and a little worse for wear, but the doors still opened and, hey, with a little touch-up on the paint job, the thing would be in near-mint condition.

It's not every day a Porsche of any description just washes right up out of the sea. It had to be a Sign. An Omen. A Message from God or some other Higher Being.

And the message was this: you're flat broke, asswipe, and a sand-filled Dinky Toy Porsche 928 is the only type you'll ever own.

The Gods have kind of a warped sense of humor.

Or maybe I'm reading this thing all wrong. Maybe They were trying to tell me that I could one day afford things like ridiculously expensive sports cars if only I learned to manage my finances a little better.

There's no point in keeping your money in a savings account in a bank. I've come to understand how the expression "sock away your money in the bank" came to be. Banks are like washing machines. You know, you put two socks in the washing machine and, when you go to withdraw the socks, one of them has magically disappeared. You can't figure out where the other sock went but it is definitely gone forever.

There's no explaining it. Don't try to figure it out. You'll only suffer a potentially serious brain-pull.

But facts are facts are facts: your sock investment has somehow lost 50 per cent of its original value. Same thing when you go to withdraw your money from the bank. Where did it go? You can't remember buying anything but half of what you socked away has vanished.

Hence the expression "money laundering."

Your first lesson in High Finance is usually your Student Loan. This is when a nice, friendly, smiling person gives you money and then immediately turns your file over to a pack of collection-agency Nazis who hound you to the ends of the earth until you pay them back twice what you've borrowed, due to accumulated interest.

Interest is a very interesting subject indeed. It's funny how banks can charge you, like, 26 per cent in interest on money you owe them on your credit card, but when you go to invest your money with them, they offer you the financial equivalent of a swift kick in the balls.

The other day I got an advance cheque from a publisher and I took it to my bank and told them I wanted to open a separate savings account so the money would grow and grow and soon I'd be just stinking rich.

This seemed like a good plan until the bank clerk told me what the bank's interest rate was for their savings account: 0.1 per cent.

I am not making this up.

They would pay me one-tenth of one per cent in interest on each and every dollar I socked away. That would just about cover the bank charges they tack on to every transaction.

With a payout like that, you'd be rolling in it no time. But the substance you'd be rolling in is the same thing that dogs inexplicably like to roll in.

Groundhog shit.

I've tried other means of striking it rich. Like the stock market. I am still the proud owner of 600 shares of a company called Omnibus. The shares were worth six bucks each when I took a trip to Greece and Turkey a few years back and when I returned, they were worth... oh, in round figures... absolutely nothing.

The company had gone belly up.

Luckily the 500 shares I had paid $15 a pop for in another company called Noma had rocketed to a current rate of $4.90 a share.

Now you know why they call the guys who sell you stocks "brokers." You invest your money, and soon you're broker — if not busted flat on your ass altogether.

After a few stock market experiences like this I got smart. I bought shares in — what else — the Big Banks. They've doubled in value and it's no fucking wonder.

Now if only the washing machine would give me back my other sock.

When you invest in stocks you have to learn to read the financial pages. Each company has a symbol or short form for its stock and, if you're a true masochist, you can watch your stocks plummet on a special cable TV channel. I think maybe they were hinting around a little when they made up some of these short-form stock symbols. Here are some real, not-even-made-up short forms I copied out of last week's financial pages: MAD, GON, UGG, SIC, SAG, REK, BONAR, ICY, BRR, DOM, AW, EAT, FOE, MOB, LAM, LOW, NA, HOC, WAK, APE and NOB.

You could look it up.

Conclusion: brokers have an even more warped sense of humour than the Gods.

But why shouldn't they be laughing? They charge a commission when you buy a stock and they charge a fee when you desperately dump it. Either way they win. Unless you outwit them by cleverly investing in a recommended company that goes out of business altogether. Then they lose their "Sell" commission.

You can't sell worthless stock. So, you see, they suffer too, sometimes. It could break your heart if you bothered to think about it.

High finance. It's a cruel world, babies. We're all hurting in these tough times.

But at least I've still got my Porsche.

Four Legs, Hairy Tail, the Whole Bit

Well you can tell by the way I use my walk/I'm a wanted man, no time to talk/Something something blah-blah-blah/Something something nah nah nah/Ah-ah-ah-ah Stayin' Alive! Stayin' Alive!

That annoying piece of disco drivel from the Brothers Gibb was the theme music as my pal Andrew "Andrew" Clark and I strutted toward the newly refurbished Woodbine Race Track one bright and sunny afternoon last week.

The continuous aural loop inside my skull had nothing to do with thoroughbred horse racing, but it did sort of capture the Travolta-esque cool that was clearly emanating from our every pore as we dropped the nine-buck clubhouse entrance fee and another five bills for a racing program and a Daily Racing Form.

"Come on, 'Bill'," Andrew said, calling me by my street name. "Let's head over to the paddock and check out the horses."

We sat on a bench and checked out the horses as they were led around by jockeys who were all decked out in pink and yellow silk outfits that could get you beaten up in bars where Export Ale is the favourite brew.

Andrew, who comes to the track a lot, explained that you can often just tell a winner by taking a close look at it in the flesh. I took a close look, studying them with a keen eye. They were horses, all right. I could almost swear to that. You know: four legs, hairy tail, big snouty head, hooves, the whole bit. These were highly strung, beautiful beasts, not the sort of nag that winds up as a major ingredient in Alpo. There were some jackasses nearby, too, but they were sitting in the stands.

Andrew studied the Racing Form, closely reading the indecipherable agate-type boxscore thingies. These give you a synopsis of each nag's past performance and odds under varying track conditions in recent races, who they raced against, what they did (or didn't) do, plus everything from their bloodlines and pedigree to their weight and even what drugs they were taking.

This was only my second time at the track. Last year, I'd come out with Andrew and he had tried to explain how he employed his expert analysis of the Form. Before the first race, he explained why an 18-to-1 longshot would win. The trouble was, he explained it so well and thoroughly that the wicket closed before he could get his bet down. The 18-to-1 shot won by a mile.

For the rest of that first time out, Andrew employed his sensible handicapping methods while I relied on a sure fire system that consisted of betting on horses that had weird names or who wore my lucky numbers 4 and 5.

I smoked him. He lost every single race while I won repeatedly. You know you're a real man — a man just bulging with cojones — when you can swagger out of the track knowing you're up twelve bucks on the day!

Stayin' Alive! Stayin' Alive!

But that was then and this is now. A whole new, fresh and bright day at the track. And Andrew was out to prove his system really worked.

We moved through the clubhouse and out to the stands. Woodbine is now running TV ads to try to attract a young, hip crowd, but one look around can tell you it ain't working. At least not yet. The crowd was colourful and diverse, but decidedly on the crocky side. I mean I'm a bit of a sabretooth myself, but not quite as fossilized as the regulars here. Generation X-Lax.

Nice trousers, though. I love lime green.

Andrew placed only one bet on each race and only bet to win. I, as usual, went all over the map, betting on three, four, even five horses at a time. And for the first six races, Andrew's system seemed to be almost working. I say "almost" because, without fail, the horse he picked to win thundered along the rail and over the finish line ahead of the pack, only to be nosed out at the wire.

After six races, Andrew's horses had placed second an incredible six times.

The only time he strayed from his pattern was when I picked a horse called Final Edition — because, as a news hack, I like the name. It was a 50-to-1 shot, given no chance by the touts. We both bet on it to win.

It damn near did, too. Losing by a length in a dead heat, placing a close third.

After seven races, I'd managed two wins, a "place" and a "show" and had won $32.

Which almost made up for the $40 I'd laid out, but I was Stayin' Alive (Stayin' Alive).

The eighth race was interesting. While most had nine or ten entries, this one had only five horses in the running. Two clear favourites, one strong contender, one long shot and one really long shot, at 22-to-1.

My nagging horse sense told me that this was the time to make some hay.

Or maybe it was just the Beef 'n' Grease sandwich I was having a bad reaction to. But I had a bubbling gut feeling that was very hard to ignore. I'd also broken out in a rash.

Using a system that Andrew explained, I placed an exactor bet on four of the five horses, boxing them with a $12 bet. Don't ask me to explain this. The guy who took my money didn't understand what I was talking about, either, so why should you? But basically, an "exactor" is when you correctly guess the first and second winners in a race, and by boxing four horses, you greatly increase your odds.

It was only after I studied my ticket that I realized I had somehow included the loser nag — Canada First was his name, but he might as well have been called Dr. Ballard — in my four-horse set.

Too late now because: They're at the post. They're off.

The horses blasted out of the gate in a tight knot of thundering hooves. By the time they came around the clubhouse turn, it was still anybody's race. I knew this because the track announcer said, as follows, "It's still anybody's race."

As they pounded down the stretch — look at that! — old Canada First was making a move! Past the favourite, past the other favourite, past the strong contender.

As it came down to the wire, Andrew was up and howling, "C'mon Canada First! C'mon Canada First!"

The guy had actually bet on this horse.

On the nose. To win. And it did, too.

After some jumping around, we strutted to the pay window to cash our tickets.

You could tell by the way we used our walks we were wanted men.

No time to talk.

I collected fifty bucks on that eighth race, bringing my daily gross to $82. Andrew, who had bet $2 on the nose, collected $44.

We went out for shrimp cocktails and frosty mugs of beer and Andrew explained how he knew — just knew — that longshot was gonna romp. Something to do with it never having raced this circuit before. And he owed it all to some uncle or somebody who had taught him the ropes.

It had been a nice way to spend a hot, spring afternoon. We were both up about thirty bucks. Not a lot of dough, but enough to stay alive. With maybe even enough left over for some of them lime green trousers. For next time.

Let's see: Next time, I'm gonna figure out what horse Andrew likes to win. And bet it to place second...

Did I mention he looks a lot like Andy Gibb?

[Author's note: After this story was originally published dozens of indignant BeeGees fans wrote me to complain that these are not the 100 per cent correct lyrics to Stayin' Alive. *So if you were going to write and tell me that, send money instead.]*

Beer & Loafing in Las Vegas

LAS VEGAS — I am sitting at the roulette table in the Sands, flashing a wad of singles that could choke a hamster. The croupier stares at me sort of bug-eyed — probably pure admiration — as I put two bucks, straight up, on red.

And we're talking American dollars here. That's like $2.60 Canadian!

The dealer spins the wheel, tosses in the white marble. Around and around and around she goes. And stops on red 32!

I hit!

The dealer grumpily stacks two more coins beside my original bet. But rather than rake them in, I "let them ride."

I hit again!

I am on a roll.

After only half an hour, I am "up" well over ten bucks on the night. The cocktail waitress comes by and "comps" me a free scotch and soda. She knows who the players are in this hellhole.

I let it ride again.

This is Vegas, after all. And you only live once. What would Frankie do in my place? Or Dean? Even Jerry Lewis would have "gone for it" on a night like this. I haven't broken the bank yet, but at least I'm not losing my shirt, like the chubby Latino guy sitting across the table. He's dropped several hundred but keeps on making these insane bets.

It was shortly after midnight when the Latino lard-ass's luck began to change for the better. First he hit with fourteen coins on number nine. Almost $500 bucks at 35-to-1 odds. Only two spins later he hits with $25 on number 36! He lets it ride and — unbelievably — hits again on the very next spin.

Next thing you know, to my murderous envy, old Ricky Ricardo is raking in thousands and thousands of bucks' worth of these bright pink chips. He is grinning and slapping backs and tossing tips to the croupier and the cocktail waitress, who has deserted me for him.

After another healthy win, he starts looking at his watch, counting up his loot, making signs that he is ready to cash out, take his money and run.

The dealer shoots a look to the pit boss, who sort of oozes over and starts kissing the guy's ass. Gets him a fresh cocktail and some comp tickets for the Wayne Newton show at the Copa and some kind of plastic card that announces him as a V.I.P., a hotshot, a big spender, a high roller. The sort of high roller who would never, ever cash in his chips while he was up several thousand bucks on the house.

The slurp job works perfectly and, rather than quitting while ahead, the guy starts playing more aggressively than ever. He starts building bright pink towers of chips all over the table. Whoops — double zero! The croupier rakes in his hoard. Whoops! Thirty-two! Missed it. The dealer rakes in another bundle.

In less than an hour, the guy is broke. Tapped out. Busted. Scared chipless. A loser.

He gets up from the table, white-faced, stunned. He looks around for his pal the pit boss, but the pit boss has no time for him.

Nobody has time for a loser in Las Vegas.

He lurches off into the night. Wait till that sucker gets home, if he still owns one. "Lucy, I got some 'splaining to do ...!"

The wheel stops on red and the dealer fires me two more chips.

I am up $54.

The cocktail waitress brings me another scotch and soda — free!

I tip her a whole buck. An American buck.

I have made this pilgrimage to the Mecca of Bullshit to join the Rat Pack, to sniff Frank's butt, to clown around with Sammy Jr. (*What? You mean they haven't buried him yet?* — Ed.), to get lovably shit-faced with Dean, to take a swing at Wayne Newton and run off with Debbie Reynolds.

And, most importantly, to hit the Big Score and fulfill that long-elusive dream of becoming a stinking rich, impossibly smug waste of human skin.

Sort of like George Hamilton.

But it does not take long to figure out that the Sands has seen better days since it was thrown up in the middle of the Nevada desert back in 1952.

At this hour, the place is mostly packed with blue-rinse old babes, stuffing nickels into slot machines with both hands, working on the maternal instinct that, if you force-feed anything for long enough, it is eventually bound to spew up the entire contents of its belly.

The air smells of stale beer, rancid smoke and sour luck.

But you need only look as far as the next pair of eyes to see that everyone here is living under the delusion that today is their ****lucky day****. That he, she or it is on the verge of breaking the bank on that very next roll, spin, whirl, toss or hit.

I start playing number twenty-five — my birthday — on the roulette table, over and over, figuring it has to come up some time.

I play for thirty spins, forty spins, fifty spins.

Number twenty-five does not come up once.

The dealer looks at me as I burn my last chip.

As I'm getting up to leave he says, by way of explanation, "Number twenty-five was hot last month."

I cash more travellers cheques but blow the whole wad on slots, twenty-one, keno and — this was really pathetically desperately low — the Wheel of Fortune.

The cocktail waitress has by now officially declared me loser non grata.

Directly across the Strip from the Sands is Treasure Island, one of many monstrous new hotels in Vegas. The outside of the casino is modeled as a huge, fake 16th-century Caribbean port, complete with a mini-ocean and two full-sized, three-masted sailing ships — a British man-of-war and a galleon full of rum-sucking pirates.

Every ninety minutes, the British ship sails into position and engages the buccaneers in a fifteen-minute battle, complete with broadsides, blazing cannons, explosions, flames, fireworks, lights, action, hurtling bodies! A spectacular show! In the end, the thieving pirates win as the Brits take a bath and the captain goes bravely down with his sinking ship.

I understood the subliminal message much better two hours later when I left Treasure Island minus my booty and lucky to still own my pants.

The pirates win and keep the gold.

While everyone else goes down with the ship.

Next door to Treasure Island is a giant casino called the Mirage, a name that perfectly describes the reality behind the notion that every spinner is a winner in this town. To further hammer home the point, the Mirage features a pet volcano that — every hour or so — belches, spews and fumes before finally blowing its top.

Just another sore loser.

I know the feeling well.

Back in my hotel room, I broke into my stash of emergency cash and began plotting revenge. The casino had nearly all my money and it was time to mount a counter-attack against the greedy pig-fuckers.

I prepared myself for the mission by drinking duty-free Jack Daniels and flipping through the Gideon Bible and jabbing a finger to select passages at random. The first passage I hit was about a bunch of sons who begat more sons who begat even more sons. This begetting went on for three pages so I tried another random jab.

Psalm 100: "We are his people and the sheep of his pasture."

True enough, but I'm SICK of being a sheep. I am SICK of being led to the slaughter. I am SICK of being fleeced! I am PISSED OFF here.

I flip and jab again:

Ezekiel 24: 23: "And your tires shall be on your head and your shoes on your feet."

Why the hell would I put tires on my head? Was someone drinking when they wrote this? First they're begetting like a bunch of rabbits, now they've got tires on their heads. Is this an omen that there is a flying truck tire out there with *my* name on it?!? This is not the sermon I am looking to deliver here today.

Riffle. Flip. Jab.

Ezekiel 38: 22: "And I will plead against him with PESTILENCE and with BLOOD and I will RAIN UPON HIM and upon his bands, and upon the many people that are with him, an OVERFLOWING RAIN and GREAT HAILSTONES, FIRE and BRIMSTONE!!!"

Yeah! THIS is more like it. THIS is exactly the ruthless, vicious, weasel-skewering tone I had in mind! I poured more duty-free Jack D and tested the acoustics of the room. Not bad! Not bad at all. It's amazing how many different inflections and nuances you can get while screaming out a passage like this at 4 a.m.

But after a while I had to head back out onto the Strip.

Because the swine next door wouldn't stop pounding on the wall.

The new plan is simple. To hell with the games of chance. Let's stick to something we know.

And what does a Jack Daniels-crazed hoser from Toronto know more about than these festering jackals and parasites here in Vegas?

One word: Hockey.

I'd been to Vegas once before and the pattern had been eerily similar. I had lost my gauchies on every shyster-shucking shell game known to man, only to stage a late comeback by hitting four straight NHL hockey bets.

There was not much hockey action going down at the sports book at the Sands. I know because, when I stepped up and placed my bets, the guy actually looked at his partner and said, "Hey? All right. A *hockey player!*"

With my last couple of hundreds, I took Detroit to beat San Jose by two, the Leafs to beat Ottawa by a goal-and-a-half and the Mighty Ducks plus a puck-and-a-half against Chicago.

Detroit creamed San Jose. The Leafs puréed Ottawa. And — this was sweet — the Ducks not only stayed close but actually paddled Chicago 6-2! So: Now I had a stake. Some operating capital. The waitress was bringing me those watery scotch snow-cones again!

I rolled the whole pot into three more bets for the next night: the Leafs to beat Vancouver. The Mighty Ducks to stay within a goal and a half of St. Louis. And Detroit and the L.A. Kings to combine for an "over/under bet" of more than eight goals.

If I lost, I would be climbing out the window of my spacious Sands suite with tied-together bed-sheets.

Luckily for me, my suite was on the first floor.

At night the Strip is one never-ending blaze of neon that is so tacky you have to smile, if not actually cackle out loud. I deked my way through shills for Nevada's tastefully named legal establishments like Mabel's Whorehouse and the Cherry Patch Brothel and the Elvis Wedding Chapel. The old casinos, like the Dunes, are giving way to new mega-billion spots like the Luxor and the MGM Grand (he Dunes was not just torn down but — in true Vegas fashion — actually blown up with a cannon blast from Treasure Island, strictly for public amusement. Perhaps, in true Nevada tradition, they might consider toasting the Sands with a ten-megaton H-Bomb. That would "wow" them!).

To travel to the MGM Grand is to be literally transported to the Land of Oz. This place has to be seen to be believed. You enter through a huge lion's head gate and find yourself standing before a five-storey-high Emerald City, surrounded by smoke and glitz and glitter and the rumble of thunder and the flashing of laser lightning. Dorothy, the Tin Man, the Cowardly Lion and even Toto are right there to greet you, standing in a field of poppies. The Scarecrow is still looking for his brains (but then so are we all this late at night).

The Oz characters are stuffed dummies, robots — "animatronic figures," the bartender called them — but they're actually a lot more life-like than, say, Debbie Reynolds, who is still shucking and jiving in some cheezy hole over by the convention centre.

I sat at the bar beside a couple of twenty-foot-high mushrooms and poppies, looking at the shimmering, crystalline Emerald City. Through the window I could see the Excalibur, which is a full-sized medieval castle and, beyond that, the new Luxor, with its full-scale Egyptian pyramid and Sphinx. And next to that is the Tropicana — a disembodied tropical island. All around me, people were gambling away, their eyes dazzled by that tell-tale delusion of grandeur that can only seize you while in the midst of one very, very grand illusion.

Confronted with all this dazzle and lights and shimmer and glitz, you begin to understand what Hunter S. Thompson meant when he said of Las Vegas: "This is not a good town for psychedelic drugs. Reality itself is too twisted."

Across the lobby, over the booth where they give you rolls of quarters and dollars, was a sign that read, "CHANGE REDEMPTION."

But I'd already had enough cheap Biblical symbolism for one night.

The Leafs won! The Wings and Kings dented the drapes early and often! And I once again made some bills on The Ducks as they made St. Louis look like a bunch of watertight assholes!

I even dumped my last quarter in the slot machine and hit three sevens — 162 quarters came spewing out.

I collected my cash and was able to make the run for the airport without seeing any local vigilantes on my butt.

The plane made it back to Toronto without wiping out but, on attempting to re-enter the country, I realized I had somehow lost my passport and birth certificate. Not an easy thing to explain when you have a head full of three days' worth of complimentary beverages.

But luck was still with me. As I babbled my twisted gibberish to the customs guy, he looked at me and said, "I know you. You're William Burrill. I read your stuff all the time. I know you're a permanent resident."

Hey? Cool! My face is my passport!

Does this make me a player?

Does this make me sort of like Ol' Blue Eyes or Dean?

Does this mean I can get vanity plates that say "DRUNKY #1"?

Does this mean that when I walk into Ontario's new gambling palaces, that someone will show me to a table and comp me a scotch and light my smoke and give me unlimited credit at the dice table?

Oh yeah, how silly, I forgot.

In Ontario casinos, there is no smoking, no drinking.

And, of course, no dice.

Hack Like Me

The first sign of spring for me is when the journalism students start calling up and asking to interview me about what it takes to be a pro writer.

So, as a service to student journalism, the best I can do is present yet another in my series of lectures on How to Be a Hack Like Me.

Today I'd like to broaden the scope and discuss many of the basic elements of journalism that propelled me to a career of still writing for a free weekly paper twenty years after leaving university. We'll deal with each subject categorically.

Class, be seated.

HOW TO BE A FAMOUS WRITER

• The Five Ws. It is essential to get the famed "Five Ws" of journalism into the "lead" or opening paragraph of your article. We're talking "Who, What, Why, Where, When" and for added measure, even though it doesn't technically start with W, "How." Thus a perfect newspaper lead would be as follows:

HOLLYWOOD (AP) — "Who? Why? When? Where??? What!!? HOW???" the hooker asked actor Hugh Grant as she leaned into his car window one sultry night on Sunset Blvd.

• Use of the "I". It is important not to inject yourself directly into a story as this sullies the objectivity.

WRONG: "I would like to kick Saddam Hussein's fat ass."

RIGHT: "This reporter would like to kick Saddam Hussein's ass."

• The Use of Tense. There are several different tenses in journalism: jittery, a little tense, very tense, psycho and up on the bell tower with the AK-47. Try not to mix them up.

• Point of View. As with tense it is essential that I keep a consistent "point of view" when you are writing he or she's article or one will find their piece is confusing.

• Conflict. A good feature story — or any good story, period — is built on internal conflict. The main Conflict Categories are Man Beats Man, Man Beats Nature, Man Beats Himself in a Seedy Porno Theatre and the little used, but vital, Man Beats Saddam Hussein Like A Rented Mule. Memorize them. You'll need them in your professional career.

• Profanity. The use of profanity is occasionally justified in the proper context but should never be employed just for the fuck of it.

• Theme. "Theme" refers to the central idea or leitmotif of your column or feature. This writer, for example, finds that Beer is a useful theme, as is Pure Bullshit. Without a theme, your piece will lack focus.

• The Inverted Pyramid. It is vital to keep the sharp, pointy side of the pyramid face-down in any big city newsroom, as you will soon find that most of your colleagues already have enough things shoved up their ass without accidentally sitting down and jamming an entire pyramid up there. I mean, how would you get it out? Especially on deadline.

- Editors. Editors am a pane in the asss and think they no everything so dont let them get there hands on your your story or they willll messs it up.
- Deadlines. It is very important for a writer to meet deadlines. Whether you are given thirty days or thirty minutes to write a story, the trick is to start it five minutes before it is due. This is called professionalism.
- Active Versus Passive Voice. The "active voice" is always better than the "passive voice" in writing a story, so buy a lot of bennies.
- Developing Identity. It helps to carve out an identity for yourself as a columnist. For example, you could be a beer-soaked bullshit artist who — wait! that job's taken. Let's see… How about a puffy, know-it-all, condescending, right-wing British prig who — what? I'm told that vacancy is filled as well. Anyway. Work on it.
- Repetition. A writer should not repeat oneself in a story or it becomes tiresome and redundant if a writer repeats oneself in a story because repeating oneself in a story makes it redundant and did I mention tiresome? About repeating yourself, I mean.
Exception: After working hours, a writer is required to regale his or her cronies in the bar with the same boring story over and over again and it is only professional courtesy to act as though you have never heard it before.
- Adverbs and Adjectives. Nouns and verbs are your basic building blocks, and it bogs down a story to use superfluous modifiers — unless you are being paid by the word, in which case it is OK to lard your witty, tense, lean, taut, insightful, highly descriptive, well-thought-out, wry, sharp, cutting, coy but never cloying or purple verbiage with every colourful, action-packed modifier you can dig up in *Roget's Thesaurus*.
- Who/Whom/That. When referring to a person you should say "the man who" instead of "the man that" unless you are a British right-wing prig, in which case you will always use the phrase "the chap whom."
- Wombat's Asshole. Such overworked clichés are frowned upon, especially when describing Saddam Hussein.
- Graffiti/Graffito. "Graffiti" is the plural term for words you spray paint on the wall. "Graffito" is the singular. So if you simply spray "FUK" on the wall and a cop busts you for writing "graffiti," simply give him the death stare and say, "Yo, you wack, man. That ain't no graffiti. That *graffito*. Don' you know nothin'? Word to your mama." Such helpfulness may result in a somewhat lighter beating.

That's all the time we have for today.

Until next time, class dismissed.

The King of Heaven and Earth

Modern travel is amazing. I showed up at the Las Vegas airport at 4 a.m. on Monday morning and a mere twenty-four hours later I was in Toronto! I even managed to find my luggage, which had made the trip via Dallas while I eventually got home by way of Chicago. This is twice as fast as the last time I flew on American Airlines. That time it only took forty-eight hours to get from San José, Costa Rica, to Toronto. (There was a logical explanation that time: the plane had a very slight collision with a truck on the runway, causing only a minor hole in the fuselage, which apparently has some effect on whether or not the plane can sort of, you know, get off the ground without wiping out.)

The dinner sucked, too. It was sort of like a hockey puck with processed cheese sauce.

Once I got on board I ordered a double scotch and soda. They charged me eight bucks.

By the end of the ordeal I guess I had that kind of look in my eye that makes airport religious nuts hand you chap-books aimed at saving your soul.

Have a nice day.

Did I mention it was American Airlines?

Anyway, after being bumped from half a dozen flights out of Vegas, I finally did get home in less than one complete day.

On Tuesday, I called the friendly American Airlines consumer relations department to marvel aloud at this miracle of modern aviation and suggest that I might be better off taking a mule train next time. The friendly consumer relations weasel offered no apologies but, after listening to my opinion that maybe I had been treated like something you scrape off your shoe, he replied — and this is a very skillful phrase for all you aspiring consumer relations weasels — "I understand that that is your view."

You see how nicely this phrase works?

It means, in its purest essence, "I think you are full of shit but I will defend to the very death your right to be full of shit. This is, after all, a democratic society."

Did I mention it was American Airlines?

Then he sort of grudgingly offered me, as compensation, a $75 travel voucher.

Jeez. Seventy-five dollars. You can log a lot of time in the air when you've got $75 to throw around. Next time I need to fly from Toronto to Brampton, I'm laughing, pal.

I told him where he could stick his $75 voucher, and if you see an American Airlines consumer relations weasel who is walking sort of bow-legged, that'll be my man.

I'd tell you his name but — after a half-hour conversation — he informed me that he did not want to be quoted or named. Could I speak to his boss? No.

So I called the American Airlines media relations office. They were "in a meeting" and never did return my call.

Maybe I forgot to mention it was American Airlines…

Oh yeah, I'd gone to Vegas to try to find Elvis. It was, after all, his birthday last weekend and I was sure that, if he was going to come out of hiding, what better place to do it than Vegas?

I mean this is the sort of toddlin' tinsel town where people still pay real, actual cash money to see Wayne Newton "sing."

I waited for Elvis in the casino at the MGM Grand for three days but he never showed (probably got bumped from the Memphis flight).

But I did meet an extremely drunk, temporarily out-of-work NHL hockey player who (several times) showed me how easily his front teeth come out.

I also killed time at the sports book and the roulette tables. At the wheel I bought $100 worth of chips. The every-spinner's-a-winner guy gave me $50 in $1 chips and two $25 chips. I was up maybe $100 and was covering my usual favourite numbers when I realized one of my $25 chips was missing.

"Hey, did someone see a $25 chip?" I asked.

"You just put it on 16," the guy beside me said.

Being a cheap son of a bitch, I am not accustomed to placing $25 bets on one number. So I quickly snatched it back and replaced it with a purple chip — my usual lousy one-buck bet.

"Wouldn't it be funny," the guy next to me said as the little white marble clattered around the wheel, "if 16 comes up?"

Sixteen came up. At 35-to-1.

I — through my quick actions — had averted just in the very nick of time the bonehead move of winning, 35 times 25 bucks (You do the math. I don't have the heart to work it out).

Viva Las Vegas!

Elvis was not at the blackjack tables and he was not at the keno parlour and I'm pretty damn certain that wasn't him playing the nickel slot machines.

Nor was he at the sports book, where I made my usual paltry profits, although this time, with no hockey, I had to bet NFL football and even basketball (a sport I know less about than a certain airline knows about public relations).

I dropped $50 on the Packers and the Bears blew, well, bears, but luckily the Steelers won and the Lakers iced the Heat and the Dolphins covered the spread by one lousy, but crucial, point (with my $250 cash riding on their backs).

So, hell, maybe there is a God after all.

Jesus saith: "I am the way and the truth and the life. No one comes to the Father except through Me."

So maybe I do have a ticket to heaven. An angel with de-iced wings.

And, on that flight, it doesn't even matter if your fucking luggage ends up in Dallas. You can't take it with you anyway.

Elvis has left the building.

Weasels Ripped Our Flesh!

There are a lot of weasels in this world but most of them are just your everyday, garden variety, amateur weasels.

But once, in what was yet another twist in the knot of fate that makes up my life, I found myself serving quite unexpectedly with a hardened, mercenary, top-flight group of professional weasels.

Sort of like the Foreign Legion for bullshitters.

Officially, I was hired as a Senior Information Officer for the Communications Branch of the Ontario Environment Ministry. No one was more surprised by this turn of events than me. Here's how it happened:

It was 1985 and I was just back in town after a year or so in Mexico, working on a Famous Novel (not technically published as yet).

I briefly rejoined a paper called *The Toronto Star*, but — due to a power shift — immediately found myself relegated to the Broken Toaster beat and the all-night city desk.

It was a midnight call from the lamentably late Paul Rimstead that started my illustrious career as a government weasel.

The infamous, hard-drinking *Toronto Sun* columnist (who had been my neighbour and partner in crime in Mexico) had heard of my sorry job status and had taken it upon himself to arrange alternative employment.

"You should write for the government," Rimstead said. "It's a great job. You get your own office. You don't have to work much. And you can fuck off with only one week's notice."

He had arranged an interview for me the next morning.

I met with the director of the Environment Ministry Communications Branch, who turned out to be Rimstead's sister. But, knowing her brother well enough, she turned me over to a real newspaper vet for evaluation: assistant director Bob Reguly, a three-time National Newspaper Award winner. A great guy, it turned out, who also told the world's very worst jokes.

After talking for maybe half-an-hour about this and that, Reguly seemed to have made up his mind. But he still had to put me to the Official Test.

"Have you ever written a press release before?"

"Nope."

"You have to write one in order to get the job." He handed me a bunch of undecipherable scientific documents and left me in the office to churn out my first attempt at weasel words. It was something about PCBs. "And," Reguly said, sort of winking, "if I were you, I'd write it sort of like this."

He slipped me a pre-written, professional press release on — this must have been pure coincidence — THAT VERY SUBJECT.

I got the job.

I was given the rank of Senior Information Officer (Level 3) of the Communications Branch of the Ontario Environment Ministry.

I was given my own office, complete with a window that overlooked the corner of Avenue Road and St. Clair Avenue.

I was given a desk, swivel chair, bookshelves, coat rack, two chairs for visitors, a rug, and a very large credenza (I didn't even know what a credenza was until I joined the public service, but apparently you had to have one or you were weasel-non-grata).

The office even had a door!

That you could close!

I'm not making this up.

My job would be to write briefing reports, press releases, speeches and statements for the minister. The mornings were filled with making up "Proposed Responses" to any potentially dicey shit that had hit the fan overnight.

I was also technically open to calls from the press and the public, but this was where the fun started: The first step in being sworn in as an "Information Officer" was to SWEAR to God and the Queen that I would NOT EVER divulge ANY INFORMATION that I came across in the course of doing my job.

Something like this:

Caller: Are you an Information Officer?

Me: Yes.

Caller: Can you tell me about the dioxin spill in Wawa?

Me: No.

Caller: How about the PCB spill in Thunder Bay?

Me: Sorry.

Caller: What about the horrendous plume of leaking poisons that is working its way into Toronto's drinking water supply.

Me: Hey lay off, asshole. Just because I'm an Information Officer, do you

REALLY THINK you're gonna trick me into TELLING YOU stuff?

I refused to take the oath on the grounds that I was beholden neither to God nor the Queen.

Another officer, Ralph, now a good friend, also refused.

The people in the Communications Branch were pretty good about it. They were all refugees from journalism, just like me. Good people. The sixth floor we worked on was like an oasis of sanity in a desert of bullshit.

Our directors were supposed to sack us for refusing The Oath.

But, like so many things that happen in bureaucratic circles, they never actually got around to it.

It was my second day on the job when I was handed a thick pile of classified documents about some horrendous impending disaster that the public had not yet been told about.

Reporters were starting to sniff around the case and the minister needed some weasel words to throw them off the scent.

I read the file — most of it I couldn't even understand — and then dutifully wrote a Kennedyesque "Proposed Response" in case of media heat. But I knew it was all bullshit.

I had a few beers that night, thinking that I was a total failure as far as weasels go.

I got home, loosened the old tie (yes, I had to wear one) and switched on the Idiot Box. And there on the late night news was the Minister Himself, in the midst of a hostile scrum of reporters, repeating word for word the exact dismal piece of crap I had written that very afternoon.

It was my first shock. But not, by far, my last.

Things were only starting to get interesting, what with an election coming and all that stuff.

Bullshit would soon be at a premium. And I was just the man to dish it out.

This was back in March 1985, in the months leading up to the election that everyone was confident would see Frank Miller's Tories win another ball-crushing majority government.

The Tories had been in power in Ontario for the last forty-two years straight, and no one — not even the opposition — was guessing that things were about to take a savage swerve for the ditch.

When I arrived on the scene, Morley Kells had just been named Environment Minister, presumably on the basis of his experience as an old-timer hockey player. He was replacing Andy Brandt, who had served as Minister for twenty months, on the basis that, as the MPP for Sarnia, he had seen a lot of pollution.

We members of the sixth-floor Weasel Factory were still using a method invented by Brandt's team (Brandt was notorious for down-playing pollution, because, after all, his biggest backers were companies in his constituency that had turned the Sarnia area into a festering Chemical Valley cesspool).

If a reporter called, we were instructed to give the following stock answer: the spill or leak or emission was "of no environmental concern."

We were even issued a handy list of diminishing metaphors, to downplay any hard numbers offered by a persistent reporter.

Reporter: What about these 500 parts per million of dioxin in the drinking water?

Weasel: Oh, that's of no environmental concern. You see, 500 parts per million is like one inch in the distance from here to the moon, one grain of sand in the Sahara Desert, one drop of water in the Atlantic Ocean.

We began our day by showing up at 8:30 a.m. (Well, OK, I sometimes made it in by around 10, but that's pretty damn close to 8:30 in my book.)

Our "In Basket" held the morning assignments issued by a gruff but lovable, two-fisted, cigar-chomping, buzz-headed ex-newsman named Jim Hornick. Hornick's assignment memos were classics, and I reprint a few of them here, verbatim:

"Bill: Poor V____'s got another crocodile hanging off his ass over some spill near Thunder Bay. See if you can bash out a fast Issue Report."

"Bill: Some pompous young cocksucker from Canadian Press called up and demanded to know about this. Pls. handle."

"Bill: Torstar and Globe engage in second-day ball-scratching over toxic rain. Pls. strengthen yesterday's Issue Report."

"Bill: Pls. update Acid Rain Issue Report to reflect fact Myron Baloney [then Prime Minister Brian Mulroney] left his testes in Washington."

"Bill: Eight ducks in Hamilton Harbour have gone to meet their Maker. Pls. update boxscore."

"Bill. New alderman June Rowlands wants to pipe drinking water from Georgian Bay. Apropos of what? Star story doesn't say. Perhaps it's a quiet exercise in wang-pulling. Pls. dig into it for Issue Report."

One time, when the Deputy Minister was about to embark on some trip to Washington, Hornick's assignment note went like so:

"Bill: Pls. see if you can unearth some information on Washington mission of Deputy Doo-Daw."

The fact that his assignment memos had to be copied to the minister's office soon had Hornick in predictably deep doo-doo.

We, of course, being mature professionals, thought he was great.

Part of the job was simply to try to turn internal Ministry documents into some kind of English so the public might have half a chance of understanding the issue at hand.

Some of these public reports were first written by Ministry lifers, and then passed on to us for translation. The Ministry hacks really thought the public would be able to digest stuff like this bit of garblespeak:

"Several projects for particulate emission were completed in 1984 [at a Windsor casting plant]. These included the installation of a capture hood on the #3 mold line shakeout, the replacement of the water wash collector with a more efficient fabric filter installation and the installation of a fabric filter on the #2 molding line inoculation exhaust. A fabric filter on the last remaining significant source of particulate emissions, the Vanetta dryer, will be installed during the summer of 1985. These measures have and will significantly reduce the emissions of particulate matter into the air. Suspended particulates in the ambient air near the plant monitored by the Ministry have been reduced from 151 $\mu g/m^3$ in 1972 to 67 $\mu g/m^3$ in 1984."

There. Feel better?

With the election looming, Minister Kells started asking for speeches to deliver in areas that, rumour had it, were close to his old-timer hockey tournaments. But every time we came up with a speech, and a few million in funds to hand out, the Premier, Frank Miller (the Father of the Grunge look in his patented plaid suits), would grab the speech (and the glory) for himself.

Kells was soon angry with his Communications Branch, and began issuing memos that read like so: "Answer the questions asked [but] don't make any promises or volunteer further information. Words the Minister does not like and which should never be used in any document (news releases, etc.) are: concomitant, dieback, sewerage and whilst."

Whilst the election grew near, the concomitant media frenzy had not yet detected any signs of the dieback that was already into the roots of the party, nor of the sewerage that a certain Minister would soon be smelling of.

Kells, a shoot-from-the-lip maverick, had by now apparently decided he didn't need weasels to write his words for him. Whatever shit hit the fan, he was windy enough to blow it back on his own.

A few weeks before the voters went to the polls, there was a very nasty spill of PCBs along 100 kilometres or so of the Trans-Canada Highway near Kenora, Ontario. The toxic crud had splashed from a leaking waste removal truck and had not only contaminated the highway, but also soaked many cars. Cars with people in them.

The shit was clearly on the loose.

This was one mess that could definitely not be dismissed as being "of no environmental concern."

The Weasel Factory worked overtime, bashing out a bunch of concerned-but-taking-serious-action "Proposed Responses" for the minister, who was sure to be in the media hot seat that day.

But Kells decided to ignore his cue cards and ad-lib!!!

What Kells did (I'm not even making this up) was to dismiss the spill as of no environmental concern. PCBs had been proven to cause cancer in rats, but there was no direct proof that it caused cancer in human beings.

Was he actually saying the spill was not a health problem?

"If you're a rat eating PCBs on the Trans-Canada," Kells said, "you might have some problems."

The reporters were stunned.

But Kells wasn't worried.

Kells's riding was considered one of the safest Tory seats in the province.

The next day, the shit hit the fan. Every newspaper, radio and TV station in the province carried reports of Morley Kells's "rat quote."

Not a great thing to do with the election only weeks away. This only added to a public anger that had been stirred up by other issues.

But the Big Blue Machine had been in power in Ontario for forty-two straight years and people were positive that this would be another massive Tory landslide.

To his credit, Kells had ordered the Weasel Factory to work overtime (that is to say, more than two hours a day) churning out a big, glossy package of new anti-pollution programs to fight acid rain, clean up beaches and leaky landfill sites, improve air quality, stiffen penalties against polluters and a lot more.

The package was ready for release two weeks into the election campaign, but the Tory powers decided that pollution was very low on the list of voter concerns. The Premier's office decided to keep the anti-pollution package under wraps until after the Tories were swept back into power, and use it as a bone to be tossed to the public in the Speech from the Throne.

On May 2, 1985 — two weeks after Morley's rat quote — the Tories got stomped in a vicious voter backlash. The Tories didn't lose outright, squeezing out the Liberals by just two seats. But it was clear that this wobbly minority could (and would) be brought down by a non-confidence vote, with the Liberals and the NDP ganging up on the Tories.

Morley Kells lost his seat (and his pants) in what was thought to be a "safe" riding.

With Kells gone and the Tory Party on life support for a few months until the Liberals and the NDP mercifully yanked the plug, Susan Fish was brought in as the new Tory Environment Minister.

Fish — the third Tory Environment Minister in fourteen weeks — started earnestly announcing all the anti-pollution goodies that had been held back before the election. But by then everyone knew the Tories were doomed, and so this blizzard of new programs sounded like a bunch of empty promises, too little, too late.

Fish brought in her own team of aides who would prepare long, hilarious, step-by-step itineraries for all her public appearances.

Once, for example, Fish was scheduled to speak at the Black Historical Society. We whipped up a speech that covered four pages, triple-spaced, in large block leaders.

To this, Fish's own staff affixed seven tightly-crammed pages of itinerary that told her when to shower, what dress to wear ("the curtains are emerald so wear your Wayne Clark black dress"), when to get in the car, when to get out, when to mingle, when to stop mingling and seek out a list of important black people to talk to, and — to lend authority to her conversation — the itinerary even included the entire history of blacks in Ontario, boiled down to one paragraph.

It was all a charade, of course. This new staff. The renovations of the Minister's office. The weighty pronouncements. All theatre.

Nothing to do with reality.

With nothing to do until the axe fell, I sat in my office writing novels and staring at the ice cubes in magazine booze ads trying to see the subliminal naked bodies.

The rest of the day I spent perfecting the art of sleeping on the job. (Note to current bureaucrats: The trick is to wear dark sunglasses and snooze propped up in your chair behind your desk, like the corpse in *Weekend at Bernie's*. Then, if anyone actually comes into your office, they'll never notice anything odd about your behaviour, even if they actually carry on a lengthy conversation. You are, after all, a civil servant).

Two months after Fish arrived, she was gone. The Liberals and the NDP had brought down the government by joining forces in a loose coalition. David Peterson, with his trademark red tie, was now Premier and Jim Bradley was now Environment Minister. Ex-Premier Frank Miller returned to Bracebridge to become — what else? — a country bumpkin used-car salesman.

Suddenly all the bureaucrats in the building were tiptoeing around wearing red ties, looking as if their throats had already been cut. But we were assured that, even though we had been hired under a Tory regime, there would be no wholesale firings.

Instead, we were to be reindoctrinated into the Liberal way of thinking. The whole Weasel Factory staff was called into a meeting and told that, from now on, we were no longer to say that any form of pollution — even if measured in parts per kerjillion — was "of no environmental concern." Instead we had a new slogan for the press. "This is of grave environmental concern and just another Tory legacy of the forty-two years of shame."

This was much more fun to say. You could sort of get worked up and start raving like a Baptist preacher.

And the Minister's new personal Press Officer, an ex-*Sun* hack, told us we were not to give any good tidbits to reporters. That was his job. He could make or break an environmental reporter by ensuring that those "onside" got all the info they needed to meet deadlines and those viewed as enemies would be left with nothing (thus assuring that their editors would soon replace them).

"I'm the one," he told us, "who hands out the candy for the clowns."

The first thing you noticed about the new Minister, Bradley, was that the rather dweebish workaholic actually understood the issues. He had the personality of a lawn dwarf and wouldn't look you in the eye even if he was trapped with you in the same elevator. But I respected him because he began pushing hard for needed but costly environmental change (a move that would soon have him out of favour and in a losing power struggle with Liberal Treasurer Bob Nixon, who thought Bradley was too "pro-environment" and dangerous to Big Biz).

Anyway, despite the assurances, I knew we were all in for the chop. I quit and went to the Greek Islands and Turkey for a year.

I escaped just in time, abandoning a sinking ship like a PCB-crazed rat.

When I came back, every single member of the Weasel Factory I had served with had been fired.

Meanwhile, the Liberals were becoming more arrogant every day, doing flip-flops on this and that environmental promise.

They were gearing up to start a new dynasty, a new forty-two years of shame.

After all, they'd snicker, who was gonna stop them? N.D.P. leader Bob *Rae?!* Rae as *Premier* of *Ontario*? I mean, as if...

Career Opportunities

I'm going rapidly broke thanks to the good people at Nissan. My wife owns a Nissan Multi, which is a small van designed by the Japanese as a practical joke to get even with us for treating them badly during World War II.

Our Nissan (which is Japanese for "Worthless Piece of Shit Lemon") comes equipped with the world's first Kamikaze engine: every time you take off in the Nissan, the engine blows itself up on purpose. In the last six months we've had one engine self-destruct, which was replaced ($1,800) only to have the distributor blow up ($600), then the timing belt ($500), and now the whole engine again (another $1,800).

The upshot of all this shit is that I'm thinking I might have to moonlight in a second job to pay the repair bills. The only trouble is, when I stop to think about it, I've been a writer for over twenty years and I don't know how to do anything else. (Some may argue I also don't know how to write, but to you I say, I know where you live and if you're not careful I'll park our Nissan in front of your house. KABOOM! EAT TASTY DEATH!!!!)

So anyway, I found a magazine that has one of those aptitude tests that lets you find out what occupations you are best suited for. You simply answer a questionnaire about your talents (if any), your strengths and weaknesses, etc., etc., and then you find out what line of work is perfect for you.

After taking the test, I found out that the perfect job to fit my personality and traits is Mass Murderer. This gave me pause at first but, the more I thought about it, the more the idea grew (or should I say, festered) in my mind. Let's face it, there are a lot of advantages to being a Mass Murderer:

1. The hours are flexible.

2. You can work out of your own home.

3. You gain a lot of fame: TV and newspaper reporters will fall all over you and you get a nifty mug shot of yourself posted in every post office. Not to mention the quickie books and the made-for-TV movies.

4. You can think of a cool nickname for yourself, like Son of Sam, or Jack the Ripper, or Willie the Wacko.

5. There's job security: Once you're caught, you have guaranteed room and board and even free clothes for the rest of your life. Talk about an ironclad retirement plan!

6. You have instant I.D. when crossing borders or applying for loans. When they ask you what your profession is, you say "Mass Murderer" and show them your wanted poster and they'll treat you with respect.

7. Your AK-47 is tax deductible.

But of course there are drawbacks to the gig.

1. It's extremely hard to dig shallow graves in your backyard during the winter when the ground is frozen. So it's sort of seasonal work.

2. It can be really embarrassing when the dog drags in severed body parts while you're hosting a dinner party.

3. You might accidentally hijack a stranger who drives a Nissan and die a horrible death.

The next closest job I found I was suited for was Bike Gang Leader. At first I thought it might be sort of fun to be the leather-clad leader of the pack, with the cool denim vest with "Heck's Angels" emblazoned across the back. But then I started to think of the startup cost. I don't have any cool leathers. I don't have a Harley chopper. And I don't have a gang. All these things cost money. So the overhead is high. Also, the dental plan sucks.

So forget that one.

I put on the quiz that I liked to travel to exotic places, liked to work at a job where there is always a cart of hooch nearby and am also interested in a career that involves broadcasting, especially while wearing women's clothes.

The test results suggested I become an airline stewardess. I gave this some thought and my only concern is that, as far as I know, airline stewardesses don't make a big whack of cash. Plus people barf on you. The only way I could see making this job pay is to follow this plan:

1. Once the plane takes off, look extremely terrified and say things like, "What was that? I've never heard that noise before. Oh shit. We're GOING DOWN!!!"

2. When you're pushing the beverage cart around, you say as follows: "Coffee? Tea? Parachutes? Life insurance policies in asphalt-fire-and-bomb-resistant cases?" You could clean up.

I went to the interview but the airline folks said my legs were too hairy.

I just wish those pilots would stop calling for dates.

I also stressed on the questionnaire that I wanted a profession that would allow me to sleep on the job pretty well most of the time. But this turned out to be another dead end: Mattress testers don't make much, I'm too young to be elected to the Senate and the Toronto Transit Commission says it already has enough subway drivers.

It's cold out there in the ol' job market.

This is a true story: A friend of mine was having trouble getting along with some of his co-workers, so the company sent him to a psychologist to see if he was truly antisocial. The shrink handed my friend a list of jobs and asked which one he felt best suited for. The list included social worker, minister, doctor and other caring, socially-integrated professions.

He circled the last job on the list: Lighthouse keeper.

Anyway, I'm still looking for that moonlight job. Money is tight. One guy I know suggested that maybe I could save a few bucks if I quit drinking beer.

I listened very carefully to his wise advice. And then I killed him.

It turned out just as I thought.

Shallow graves are very hard to dig when your backyard is frozen solid. Maybe if I bought a freezer...?

Europe on $0 a Day

It was twenty years ago and I was a ragged-assed long-hair touring Europe with a guy I met in Amsterdam. His name was Butch and he had been in the army in Germany, a private assigned to the medical department of the base in Stuttgart. He got his discharge but not before helping himself to the medicine cabinet and making some travelling bucks by selling horseshit to the suckers in his platoon.

By the time I met him his hair and beard had grown long and he was a junkie trying to clean up — not the easiest thing to do in Amsterdam in the '70s. A bunch of us were living in a flophouse called the Fly Inn and we all made a general plan that we would head south to Athens, and later hit the isle of Crete.

We bought a car in a bar for $50. It was called a Dafmobile, a little green two-cylinder shitbox with a stickshift that was very easy to master: You push the stick forward, you go forward. You pull the stick back, you go backwards. You put it in the middle, you go nowhere. It had no brakes to speak of, but there were holes in the floor so you could drag your feet in case you needed to stop. Hey, what do you want for $50?

We drove with a guy named Don, whom I didn't trust because he had short hair. Funny how things change in twenty years. Now it's the guys with the short (or no) hair who are the rebels. Anyway: we drove through Holland, Germany, Italy. Clear sailing, even though we had no ownership papers or insurance on the Daf. It wasn't until we hit the border at Yugoslavia that a machine-gun-toting soldier finally pulled us over. I was driving and the soldier kept yelling at me in a language I couldn't hope to fathom:.

Soldier: [angrily] Unintelligible.

Me: [shaking my head no] Sorry. I don't understand.

Soldier: [turning red] Unintelligible. UNINTELLIGIBLE!!!

Me: [shaking my head no] Sorry. I don't speak Yugoslavian.

Soldier: [levelling his gun] Unintelligible. UNINTELLIGIBLE!!! @#$%&* UNINTELLIGIBLE!!!

Me: [shaking my head no] I don't know what the fuck you're talking about.

He was probably saying stuff like: "Do you promise never to pollute our country with your stinking filthy hippie presence again if I let you pass? Do you promise to obey our laws and get the hell out of here as soon as possible?" And I was, of course, saying "No" every time. This continued for a while until Butch elbowed me in the ribs and whispered "Next time, nod 'Yes.'"

I did, and it worked. The soldier continued howling and, as I began contritely nodding "yes", Machine Gun Ratko slowly calmed down and finally waved us through.

Somehow we skidded into Athens in one piece.

It was only then that we found out Don (the straight Yuppie Mr. Clean) had several kilos of hash stashed under the back seat.

If we'd been caught, Don would have shrugged and claimed innocence. And I would have had a nice long private course in Yugoslavian. Although I'm not sure the rats would have understood me all that well.

We dumped Don in Athens. (The reason Don had smuggled this hash horde to Athens was that he knew from experience that you were much less likely to get searched for drugs if you flew back to the States via Athens instead of Amsterdam.) Butch and I were almost broke. We both had guitars and made some money busking, but the song every homesick tourist wanted to hear was "Leaving on a Jet Plane," so it was brutal work. We hadn't eaten properly for days and so I finally went to the local Red Cross to sell my blood for money (something you can do in Athens). They took a blood test and said I was slightly anemic. "Have a few solid meals and then come back." Catch-22. Why did they think I was there in the first place? Then they looked at Butch, who was nodding off in the corner. "What about your friend?"

Butch had kicked junk but had discovered that in Athens you could buy Valium over the counter. He was going through a bottle of thirty-six a day, so he wasn't exactly what you would call jumpy. He was so constantly stoned that I had to tie a string to my belt and attach it to his belt to keep him from wandering into traffic. But when the Red Cross bloodsuckers tested Butch he passed. Catatonic, yes. Anemic, no. That night we bought some wine and bread and cheese and climbed the Acropolis and Butch fell off the ruins and hit his head.

Oddly enough, he didn't feel a thing.

Butch and I went to Crete (where the Daf finally died and I gave it to a Cretan farmer), and fell for two women who lived in France. We procured forged rail passes and did Southern Greece, Italy, the south of France (where we stayed for weeks in Avignon with our Crete girlfriends, living on nothing but leeks and wine). Then it was Spain. Finally we took the boat from the Rock of Gibraltar across to Morocco.

We still had no money other than what we could scrounge with our gui-

tars. If I ever hear "Leaving On A Jet Plane" again, I'll kill.
Casablanca is not the place to run out of money.
But we did.

Of all the gin joints in the world…
Why Casablanca? We weren't exactly thinking straight but we had a plan: I had a return plane ticket and figured I could fly from there. Butch, meanwhile, heard you could bribe Casablancan shipping authorities to get sailor's papers, then find work on a freighter sailing for the States. Simple. Almost home free.
What could go wrong?

Off the boat in Ceuta. Hiked to some windy-streeted joint called Tetouan. Sold my guitar for cash. (was tired of playing "Leaving on a Jet Plane" for money. Some things are beneath human dignity.) Roughly 124 guys named Mohammed or Abdul wanted to be our guide. One of them — I think an Abdul — showed us to a flophouse then asked the magic question: "You want Hashie-hashie? Keefie-keefie?"
Butch traded his silver high school ring for a big whack of black hash. "We can sell it to tourists in Casablanca," he reasoned. Of course, Butch was not above sampling his own product, just to make sure it was quality stuff. It was.
Butch stashed the hash in his guitar.
Next morning, walking to the bus station, some excitable boy stopped us and said Adbul had been busted last night and had informed on us and we'd better give him the hash right away or the police would get us, too.
"He's bluffing," Butch said. "Let's get the fuck out of here."
Bus station. Buy tickets for as far as the money would take us — Tangiers. Waiting for the bus, we went to the can. Some other excitable boy stops us outside the shit-smeared stalls. "Police!" he says. "I am police. You have hashie-hashie. You must give it to me now."
The guy didn't look like a cop but he also didn't look like he was about to go away. Butch and I exchanged looks and silently opted for the old "Patty-Cake" trick from the Hope and Crosby road buddy flicks. This manoeuvre involves simultaneously sucker-punching your oppressor and knocking him into a filthy toilet stall.
Then running like hell. He who fights and runs away lives to fight another day. And the day after that, as it turned out.
Once on the road, the cops searched the bus three times. We kept our heads down until they kicked us off just outside Tangiers.

Hitch-hiking on the road to Casablanca. Green bus skids to a halt. Loud rock music and hash smoke pours from windows. Painted on the bus: "Grateful Heads." Driver opens door, asks in a Cockney accent:

"Where ya goin', mates?"

"Casablanca."

"We're going to Marrakech, but — ya got any dope?"

"Who doesn't?"

"Get in."

Not your normal bus — full of hippies, no seats. Just mattresses on the floor. Four speakers blasting Hendrix. Plumes of smoke. Nobody Bogarting. A cop pulled us over every ten miles, but the driver had the routine down. He simply handed a deck of Camels out the window and the cop waved us on. One officer was more diligent. He held out for TWO packs of smokes before he let us go.

One man's life ain't worth a hill of beans in this crazy world if you have no money. Especially in Casablanca. Trouble started in one of the old twisting streets of the medina, or Old Town. Some guy with not one but two knives tried to make us buy some stuff in a narrow dead-end alley full of intentionally mutilated child beggars. We would have gladly bought his shit if we had any cash, but... so. Patty-cake, patty-cake WHAM!

Getting pretty good at this by now.

Trouble: Turns out my Air Canada airline ticket was no good in Casablanca. Nearest place I could fly from was Madrid. And Butch, after selling the rest of his stash, tried to buy sailor's papers only to get ripped off by a dishonest shipping authority. Some people have no scruples. BIFF! Found a hostel for the night that might have been a jail. Who knows? Who cares?

Wire home for money. American Express loses it. As we wait for cash, we sleep on the beach near a carnival. Meet a woman who keeps us in couscous and a place to sleep. Walking with her through the medina when scumbag grabs her crotch. Patty-cake, patty-cake. BAP! Only been in Morocco two weeks and already have more KO's than Tyson since he made parole. Yet another fight next day due to failure to afford dope. Play it again, Sam. Here's shwinging at YOU, kid.

It took three scary weeks before the missing Amex money wire was found. Took the train to Tangiers. As we were waiting for the boat back to Spain we met an American kid carrying a large Thermos. He nervously explained that the cooler was actually full of hash oil.

Boarding the ship, the dentally challenged customs guy treated it like a game show, picking three places to search on each hippie. "Hashie-hashie, keefie-keefie here? Here? HERE?" If he didn't find any in three tries he'd let you pass.

Our new American friend was in front of me in line. On the third try, the customs weasel grinned and pointed to the Thermos. "Hashie-hashie, keefie-keefie HERE!!!?"

I almost shit myself. But the kid played it cool, laughed and said. "OK, ya caught me. It's in there."

The customs guy stared at him — and us — for a ten-beat. Then waved us through to the boat.

I've never been happier to see a shoreline fade over the horizon in my life.

We got home safe. I never saw or heard from Butch again, despite trying to find or call him in California.

My guess is he's dead.

You must remember this: There's only so much shit you can get away with. But there are some things you never forget. As time goes by…

From Here to Paternity

Gotta fill you in about my old man. Walter Scott Burrill. That would be the same Burrill family descended from one Jesse Burrill, an Irish sailor who got hammered on shore leave in Yarmouth, Nova Scotia, and woke up to find his ship had sailed without him. Being an easy-going sort of guy, Jesse looked around and said, "Shit. I guess I live in Canada now." And he did, too.

This is in sharp contrast with my maternal side, the Trudeaus — yes, those Trudeaus — who sailed to Canada with purpose and ambition along with Cartier in 1641. (Give or take a decade. Look it up if you really care.)

Still, old Jesse did OK for himself once he sobered up. He founded a shipping line of nineteen frigates all named the Jesse Burrill, the Mary Burrill, even the William Burrill (one of the Burrill frigates is written up in shipping lore due to a particularly messy mutiny off Australia. Beer is the suspected contributing factor).

We once had paintings of all the ships, but my uncle and namesake, William Burrill, hocked them for a trip to Mexico. The paintings were never found. Hint: Never trust anyone named William Burrill. They're flighty, impulsive and prone to wandering.

So anyway I'm proud to say I'm directly descended from a true sea-farin' man. HARRRRR!!!!. Yo ho ho. And a bottle o' beer.

When sailing ships went out of style, my extremely proper and prudent grandparents moved to Hamilton and, using the sail-making expertise learned from the shipping line, founded a highly successful cotton mill. They lived in a mansion on Hamilton "Mountain." (It's really just a hill, but ya gotta give Hamilton every break you can. They tend to exaggerate over there. Wonder where I got that from? Now you know.)

And in 1919, Grandpa and Grandma Burrill unleashed my dad onto the world.

Forgive them, Lord, for they knew not what they did.

My old man could play seven instruments expertly, all by ear. In the late '30s he worked as a Toronto disc jockey back when a DJ actually played piano and sang on his own show. The war. The Air Force. The '40s. A stint as a newspaper reporter for a Toronto daily that still has no colour pictures. Then, due to pressure from his parents, he went back to school and became a lawyer. But his heart was never in it. He was, as Raymond Chandler said, the type of lawyer you hoped the other guy had.

He spent most of his time in the old Toronto Press Club, drinking with his cronies and playing the piano. Sometimes he'd bring his beer buddies back to our home on the Toronto Island. I grew up eye-high to the coffee table, draining the suds out of Carling Red Cap bottles left unfinished by writers.

On the day I was born — May 25, nineteen-something — my father was drinking in the Press Club with his usual suspects. When word was phoned in that a nine-pound, seven-ounce whopper had been successfully delivered, my dad and about eighteen beer-challenged friends went to Western Hospital and asked to view the Burrill baby. The head nurse said only the true father could see the baby. So, in a moment of inspiration, all nineteen of them claimed to be the real father. My mother was the talk of the ward for weeks to come, especially after, in the cold shivering light of dawn, all nineteen sent flowers to apologize.

The highlight of the Press Club in those days was the annual Fishing Trip, generously sponsored by a brewery (complete with more than enough free samples). Of all the Press Club gang who went fishing, there was only one who actually brought a fishing rod, which was considered very bad form. After three days my Dad phoned our Island home and had some good news and some bad. The good news was that he had dug up a rather large pine tree to plant in our front yard. The bad news was that he had somehow managed to fall into the bonfire and burned off his hair and eyebrows. The good news was that his guitar was safe. He was coming home to the Island by water taxi.

My mother waited and waited and — no Dad. She called the water taxi company and asked if they had delivered her husband.

Water Taxi Dispatcher: Lady, we deliver dozens of people. How would I know if we brought your husband?

Mom: Let me describe him — he's six feet tall, he's wearing a red lumber jacket, he's carrying a guitar and a large pine tree and, um, his hair and eyebrows are sort of burned off.

Water Taxi Dispatcher: [immediately] We brought him. We left him on your dock.

She found him on the dock. Sound asleep. Hugging his guitar. And his pine tree.

That was Dad.

The rest is sad. You don't want to know.

Burn the candle at both ends. Twice the light in half the time. Fall, glimmer, sparkle and fade. Anyway, Dad — hey — twenty-eight years ago this weekend. You died. "He's gone," is how they told me. Time flies like flies. By the time you were my age now, you were toast. I've learned some good things from you — wish I had half your talent — but I also learned something else. It's true what Jimmy Morrison said: "No one here gets out alive." And Jimmy should know. But here's the thing — that doesn't mean you have to go out with your hands up. This boy — this boy of yours — ain't goin' nowhere without a fight.

Just thought you should know.

Keep a cold one on ice for me (it might be a trifle hot where we're gonna meet again) and I'll see ya later.

But Dad. Don't wait up for me.

I'm planning on staying out a little late.

Miss ya.

How to Get Ahead in Newspapers

To this day I find myself waking up God-knows-where and asking myself: Just how did I get this job? And where are my pants?

The most important thing when you go in for a Big City newspaper job is to remember how to dress: A very short skirt, fishnet stockings, fuck-me pumps and a low-cut top are essential. This sometimes (but rarely) even works if you are a woman.

The first thing to do is show ambition: "I can make *The Star* the seventh-biggest paper in Canada." To which the editor might respond, "But we're already Number One." This is where you wink confidentially and say, "Not after you hire ME!"

JOURNALISM A to Z

A. When asked what job you want, say "Yours."

B. Compliment the editor's obligatory family photo: "Is that your wife? What breed is she? And THAT must be your daughter. I did her a couple of times in school, but then, who didn't? She's very attractive."

C. Be polite in case of a social faux pas: "WHEW! WHOOOA! Sorry! Guess I should have laid off the beans, beer 'n' cabbage for lunch."

D. Brag about your education: "Yes, I did four years in Kingston."

Interviewer: "Queen's?"

You: "The cell block was full of 'em."

E. Brag about extracurricular writing: "I've written a 400-page novel. It's nearly finished. I've got the title and already numbered all the pages. All I gotta do now is fill in the blanks."

F. If you get a tryout, prove you are a proficient typist but don't be a hot dog. Use only your right and left index fingers like everybody else. Nobody likes a rookie show-off.

G. Show ambition: Look around the newsroom for the sickest looking old hand and say, "If he dies, can I have his job?"

H. Show that you are adaptable. Say something like, "I can work with anyone, even a fat-assed, hairy-eared asshole like you."

I. Sometimes your editor will disagree with you over the content of a story. If this happens, don't go mouthing off. Just feint with your left and break his nose with a right hook. You must also perfect the art of the lead to survive in the newsroom and the rule of thumb is this: Never lead with your right.

J. After an initial interview and submission of a résumé or story idea, it is wise to follow up the submission by telephoning and faxing the editor every ten minutes from morning until night. Find out where he or she lives. Follow them home. Sleep on their doorstep. Editors really, really like such tenacity in a young reporter.

K. Pitch a firm idea immediately: "I want a three-times-a-week column."

Interviewer: "About what?"

You: "Oh... I've been reading William Burrill... I didn't realize it had to be ABOUT anything..."

L. Two words: Hooters.

M. Make sure you don't make an embarrassing grammatical error during the interview process:

WRONG: "I got me a gun, ya fat tub o' snot, and HOPEFULLY you ain't gonna give me no reason ta use it."

RIGHT: "I got me a gun, ya fat tub o' snot, and IT IS HOPED you ain't gonna give me no reason ta use it."

Interviewers hate improper use of the word "hopefully."

N. Show you've done your corporate homework:

YOU: "The Globe is a very viable and successful paper and I'd be proud to work for it."

INTERVIEWER: "This is the *Star*."

YOU: "Oh... ah... that's a good one, too!"

O. Show your knowledge of newspaper lingo. If the interviewer asks if you are a "two-way man," simply reply "You bet! Top, bottom, doggie style — been there, done that."

P. Try holding your breath until you turn purple. It's worth a shot, anyway.

Q. Bring Xena the Warrior Princess along to your interview as back-up. Nothing like a razor-sharp Frisbee to command a little respect. (Warning: Don't be surprised if Xena gets hired and you don't).

R. Here's a trick I learned when I was a cub reporter at the *Star*. Tie some fishing line to your hat — about ten feet of it — and then tack the line to your desk. When an editor barks at you to get out and cover a story your hat will fly off as you run out the door. This makes a very strong impression in the "hustle" and "enthusiasm" departments.

S. Two words: Knee pads.

T. Remember the motto of all successful journalists: "Suck up and kick down."

U. Once you are hired, hide in the coat closet for, oh, two years. No one will miss you. And by the time you come out of the closet, you'll have enough seniority that they can't lay you off.

V. If applying at eye, be wary if they offer to pay you not in straight salary but in a share of the profits from newsstand sales.

W. The first thing the interviewing editor will do is teach you "The Five Ws" of journalism, namely: "Who the fuck are you, what the fuck do you want, which rock did you crawl out from under, why are you holding me up when the bar just opened, and here's where you can shove your résumé." Your education has begun.

X. Whine that you are a "Generation X" victim and can't get a job. This will show your prospective employer that you have a keen sense of guessing correctly.

Y. As Timothy Leary said on his deathbed, "Why Not?"

Z. ZZZZZZZZZZZZZZZZZ! Is it noon yet?

Street Level

I am walking down the street on a warm summer night. Why am I walking down the street on a warm summer night? Because I am a Street Level Reporter and a Street Level Reporter has to get down to street level, to dig up at least one of the four million stories in the Naked City.

My editors have strongly suggested I ease off my usual confusing and pointless literary backflips and write the facts in simple declarative sentences. Like this one. And that one. Maybe even use not-even-made-up quotes. A tough gig for a rookie on the Street. Gotta keep walking, always on the lookout for facts, although I must confess I'm not even sure what a fact looks like. Gotta do the job, get the story. Why else would I be walking down the street on a warm summer night?

This is costly work: It has already cost me like five bucks in spare change and exactly — this is an actual, verified number — nine bummed smokes. Then there are the squeegee kids who try to squeegee my face, although I am not in fact driving an actual car. NO! SORRY! I made that up. The squeegee kids never tried to squeegee my face. I apologize to all squeegee kids for this obviously made-up statement.

I want to help the squeegee kids prosper. I want to — this is my plan — bring in some Indy-type pit crews to do Community Service and teach the squeegee crews how to not just smear your windshield with dirty water but also jack up the car, change the tires, fill up the gas tank, top up the oil, replace the damaged front end, fix the transmission, give you a cold drink from a squirt bottle and wipe the sweat from your face. Do all this and get you on your way again in exactly 9.23 seconds so you don't miss the light and lose your place in the traffic jam. Do this, my squeegee children, and motorists will happily give you two bits and drive off with a jaunty wave and a smile.

(*Wait a minute, Burrill. Such service would not be cost efficient as a transmission job alone would run you hundreds of dollars, more for a standard shift and it could never be done in 9.23 seconds. Stick to the fucking facts!* — Actual Factual Ed.)

Shit. Caught again.

Feets don't fail me now.

Walking down the street. Same summer night. Did I mention it was warm? "Hey, you're that *eye* guy," a young blonde girl says as she bums fifty cents off me. "I like *eye*. I read your column all the time." Nice try, but four bits is my limit. She is sitting on the sidewalk with a young guy who has Bo Derek braids. (In entertainment news, Bo Derek was a shitty movie star who was famous for showing her tits. I don't know what she's been doing lately. I haven't seen her tits for years, which is more than I can say for Farrah Fawcett's tits. THERE. I think that was just a fact. Just a minute ago. Didn't you see it? Shit. You gotta keep your eyes open, people.)

Anyway, the cute teenie blonde spare change girl asks me what I am doing and I said I am working on a fact-packed, not-even-made-up streetwise column which is due, like, tomorrow morning. "What's it about?" she asks. "I don't know yet," I say. "Got any ideas?" The cute teenie blonde spare-change girl does: "Why don't you write a column about us?" "Okay, what's your names?" "I'm Wendy and this is Paul. [It is at this point that Paul says, and this is an exact quote, "Hi."] I take out my real reporter's notebook. "Wendy.

And Paul. Is that P-A-U-L? With a P? Good. Okay. A column about Wendy and Paul. Now... ah... what should I say about you?" Wendy is ready for that one, too. "Just say we're, like, the coolest people in the whole city!" So here it is in "hard copy," as we street reporters say: Wendy and Paul are, like, the coolest people in the whole city. And that's a fact.

But somehow I feel I still am not getting the real feel of the street. So I take my boots and socks off. To really feel the warm cement and the hot-tarry asphalt. Immediately, relevant, newsworthy issues start spilling into my head and I record them in order of appearance:

1. Fucking street needs cleaning. That's bad.

2. Maybe I'll get murdered, walking the city streets late at night. Murder is bad. But we street reporters laugh in the fact of danger. Trouble is our middle name.

3. I think I'm getting a plantar's wart. Either that or I stepped on some gravel. Either way: bad.

4. And now for the weather: It is a warm night on the street. (*Too vague. Be specific* — Actual Factual Ed.) It is exactly 23° Celsius with a light wind off the lake at 12:24 a.m. on the street. The forecast calls for continued darkness this evening with scattered light beginning at 6:03 a.m. EST. (*Good.* — Actual Factual Ed.)

When in doubt, simply rip-off an old George Carlin gag...

The next morning the light arrives just as forecast. I still have no boots on. I am walking to the corner store, past the bikers drinking beer (as always) in the front yard up the street from my house. "Hey darling," my favourite biker babe/heckler says. "You forgot something. You got no shoes on."

I look down at my bare feet. "Oh shit," I said. "Thanks! I knew I forgot something!" Her gruff but somehow lovable old man comes out on the porch with a fresh beer in his hands. "Hey!" he yells after me, "You look funny. You got no feet on." Technically he was wrong. But judging from the pile of dead soldiers on the front yard picnic table, it had been a long, warm and extremely sudsy evening, night and morning in biker land. Besides, I knew what he meant, so I just grinned and waved and did not bother to correct his mistake. Turned out I didn't have to. My biker babe scolded him, saying, "I already said that. And it isn't that he doesn't have no feet. He has no boots."

Just the facts, ma'am. Maybe she should be my editor.

Greetings, You Ignorant Savages

BY JULIAN WALPOLE-SPENCER

EDITOR'S NOTE: We wish to welcome our new Naked eye *columnist, Julian Walpole-Spencer, who is an Oxford graduate and well-known social commentator in his native London. If anyone happens to see or hear from William Burrill, would you please contact this newspaper or the Missing Persons Bureau.*

It was with great amusement while wandering up your high street that I chanced upon something called the Toronto Historical Board.

How, I asked myself, can a Colonial city barely a century old have an historical board? Before you can have an historical board, you must first have some history. In my native London, any structure less than 400 years old is considered "new housing." The building in which I studied at Oxford was constructed in 1264, and it is one of the newer structures on campus. I daresay that in 1264 there was nothing on the site of Toronto but some wretched Indians and perhaps a drunken Viking who had lost his way from Newfoundland whilst looking for a place to piddle.

Perhaps the newness of your city is the root of your current social problems. One need only board one of your trams, those dreadful travelling communicable disease wards you at once redundantly and inaccurately refer to as a "street car," to see the desperate need for a social ranking system such as has been in place in England for thousands of years. Aboard one of your trollies it becomes obvious that the great unwashed do not recognize — and in fact dare to speak to — those who are clearly their social betters. May I suggest a separate seating section for the hoi polloi, preferably somewhere to the rear of the livestock car.

This is not to suggest that Toronto is a town completely devoid of culture. I believe that author chap with the unpronounceable name who wrote that unreadable book that won the Booker is from your town — or that is to say, now resides in your town, for no man of culture could actually be from Toronto. This is not to say that I am in any way prejudiced. Some of my best chums are right off the boat from God knows where.

Might I also suggest a dress code for this village, or at least some basic sartorial lessons for the common masses? For one, may I be the first to inform you that if you must insist on wearing a rounders cap — what you chaps here call baseball — that you at least understand that the peaked portion is designed to be worn frontwards as a sun visor. You need not keep the sun off your neck, for I am afraid it is already hopelessly red. One shouldn't think anything as simple as a ball cap would require written instructions for proper usage.

And may I also point out that the jerseys and blazers of basketball teams are not to be worn a dozen sizes too large, simply because the originals were designed for clownish mutant freaks of nature. A lad of five feet and eight stone looks nothing but ridiculous in the garb of a man who is eight foot and twenty stone. Just because you may worship the heroes of this idiotic game in which virtually every try is a successful score, that does not mean one should literally try to fill said hero's size-26 sneakers.

And one cannot imagine how the plebes of this town sit still for their "City" Hall's draconian and unilaterally instituted bylaws. If a British government attempted such a thing, the citizens would become almost so irate as to actually consider penning an angry letter to *The Times*. You would think that the fact we allowed you to help us give Jerry a licking in the Big One would have stiffened your upper lip ever so slightly, if only by osmosis.

Needless to say, the food in this outpost is indigestible, even in your so-called "British pubs." What an insult it is to a true Britisher to find imitation British ale and lager served straight out of the ice box, instead of at room temperature. May I suggest that you stick to the tasteless, watery, over-carbonated skunk piss that passes for Canadian beer and leave our native beverages alone. And if you see one of your betters in such a "pub," please do not address him as an equal, especially if all you have to prattle on about is some obvious and idiotic statement about the abysmal weather or the hapless doings of backwoods savages and Communists during the latest ice hockey match. Now, rugger. There's a man's game. And you don't see a rugger star insulated with paddings and helmet from head to toe like some sort of man on the moon. In England, if a player is decapitated, he simply rubs some dirt and spit on the wound and it's off you go, back into the fray, pretty as you please, Bob's your uncle.

As for watching telly, one can only snigger to find that a Canadian's idea of highbrow programming is Coronation Street. If the BBC were to base a series in Toronto, I daresay it would have to be entitled Downstairs, Downstairs, for there simply is no upstairs in Canada.

Who knows where to begin when attributing blame for this cultural mishmash you call Toronto? Someone clearly deserves a good thrashing, but there are so many ears to box and so few civilized hands.

One can only throw up said hands, book passage back to England, and hope that he is not killed by a flying lorry tyre on the way to the British Airways check-in desk.

Pip pip. Cheerio. And remember this: Bob may be my uncle, but never dare to presume that he is related to you lot.

A Writer's Life

If you want to get work as a writer in this town I suggest you fill a niche and put yourself in demand. Last week, just for a laugh, I pretended I was a pompous right-wing snotty British ponce named Julian Walpole-Spencer. (Yeah, that was me.) And the scary thing is I not only fooled a great number of readers, but "Julian" got several offers to lecture or speak at earnest gatherings of like-minded white groups who believe it's time everybody with a tan was sent back on the boat.

People agreed with Julian. I could have milked the gig for a while, but it was getting scary. And so, as is my prerogative as his creator, I hereby sentence Julian Walpole-Spencer to death by a medieval British execution technique called Banging and Mashing. He shall then be fried in grease and lightly battered. Bob's your uncle. See ya, Julian. Ya big twit.

Dismayed by the fact that I had unintentionally created a popular journalistic monster in the above mentioned Mr. Walpole-Spencer, I spent an aimless week poking around Toronto, maybe looking for a new career, maybe just looking, period.

My first move was to go to the beach with a mine sweeper and become a beachcomber.

I swept the beach all afternoon, which was great for the suntan but not so hot for the bank account. Here is an inventory of my findings:

1. Fifty-nine assorted beer caps (some antique).
2. Assorted used condoms and one hypo needle (with rubber gloves and a gardener's trowel, I removed and safely disposed of them to protect the public. We beachcombers are silent hero types).
3. One (1) Canadian one-cent coin (1982, muddy).

But I don't think I'm cut out for the beachcombing life: At fifty-nine bottle caps and one cent a day, even if I worked all 365 days of the year, my gross income would be 21,535 assorted beer bottle caps and exactly $3.65. That's more than I make at *eye* but the hours are shitty, especially on a sub-freezing Saturday in January.

"What is that man doing?" a German-accented child asked her mother as she watched me comb the beach.

"He is a poor man," mother explained. "He is looking for gold and diamonds in the sand."

Yeah. That's a pretty good way of looking at life.

Next, I tried to revive my long-lost career as a rock critic (I used to cover the rock beat in the early '80s). So I scraped up a behind-the-stage pass for last week's Beck concert at Varsity Arena. I even saw Beck's dressing room. (Which, using my hard-earned reportage skills, I sniffed out using the clue that there was a sign on the door which read as follows: "Beck's Dressing Room.")

The trouble with being backstage is you can't hear shit. The multi-tattooed roadie I talked to wasn't even bothering to watch the show. He was hunkered down, reading a book by flashlight until he was needed to run up and Move Something Heavy. I asked him what he was reading. He showed me. It was thriller writer Tom Clancy's latest.

"You heard all this a million times, eh?" I asked, in probing reporter style.

"Yeah," he confirmed.

Then he went back to his book.

Here's my review: I like Beck, but they have newer things than turntables. Get with the program, Beck buddy. Then maybe you can afford to buy a few vowels and get a first name.

Oh, yeah: security confiscated my engraved silver whisky flask at the door. I felt naked, like Mike Hammer without his piece under his arm. Why do you want my flask? You might throw it up on the stage. As I said, I like Beck. But not that much.

Went fishing last week. Didn't catch shit, even though I was right next to the sewage treatment plant. Don't tell Hemingway.

Another career move down the drain.

Farewell my Belly Rat

And now for something completely different. Excuse me while I quietly disappear from this spot for about a month. I've got to finish a couple of personal projects I started a few weeks ago.

Let's see? I cleaned up the basement. And, oh yeah, I quit drinking.

Since drinking has been my main profession for the last solid quarter century, I would rate deciding to kick cold turkey about a zero out of ten on the Fun scale. My body, you see, has grown used to a normal functioning level of blood in the alcohol stream that would do no worse than knock a normal person cold. And my body can be very whiny about this when denied — and how did my body get those annoying power drills and starving belly rats?

I stopped by using the novel method technically called Stopping. That was a few weeks ago. I lay in bed for three solid days having no more laughs than a torture victim during the Spanish Inquisition. This is strictly a Do-It-Yourself home project: I don't believe in higher powers or group snuggles. I believe in me. You can't do this unless you want to. No one can make you but yourself.

I read my old man's Big Book (he died at fifty, when I was a kid) and it makes some points, but I can't get behind the principal tenet that We Are All Powerless Worms with the Will of a Piece Of Gravel And Only God Can Save Us. Too cultist and herd-like. I'm fucked if I will turn my personal willpower over to a mass figment of the imagination.

I know, I know, some well-meaning reader will write to tell me I got it all wrong, that you can't do it alone. Thanks for the tip. But this is my project: And I always finish what I start, even if I am a little late at times. Just watch me. Anyway, enough about all that. Just got to relearn a few things.

I passed some friends on a patio the other day and they had the usual jugs and the usual empty seat. I stopped to chat but said I couldn't stay. I was going to McDonald's. They laughed. That Burrill really is a funny guy. Anyway, the lineup at McDonald's was too long — will you be fried with that, Sir? — so I went to another patio and drank Coca-Cola (straight up, on the rocks). It was just the same as always except completely different. But not different in a bad way. No big deal. The main problem now is what to do with all this weird speedy energy and all the extra hours someone snuck up and tacked on the day. But I need the time to lay low a while.

Anyway. I gotta go lie and stare at the ceiling for a while. (Just bought a new bed. Do you know that really good beds cost, like, two grand these days? But I digress.) Gotta sit on the back deck and finish those books and scripts I've been putting off. And maybe take a break to lie in my new bed (INDIVIDUAL COILS!) and sweat and shiver at the same time. This really IS fun. Anyway, right now the rat that lives in my guts is trying to chew his way out again. I know one way to make him quiet down. It always worked before. But this time...

Nah.

I've puked in every country from the Middle East to Africa to South America to Japan. It's sort of a Been There Done That kind of thing.

See ya in a while.

Zen and the Art of Nose-twisting

As I was saying before I was so rudely interrupted, the minute you decide to eliminate alcohol as your major (and, come to think of it, only) food group, everybody starts pushing religion on you, saying you can't do it any other way, you useless piece-of-shit worm. But I just don't believe in all this Higher-Power Put-Your-Hand-In-The-Hand-Of-The-Man eye-varnish.

And yet circumstances over the last few months have caused me to search for something — anything — to believe in, since I suddenly have lots of time on my hands now that I've given up lying in the ditch with my pants around my ankles. And, in the throes of a two-months-and-counting near-beer bender, I think I have at long last found It. Not quite a religion. A new way of seeing things.

It's Zen Buddhism and the reason I can so easily grasp the concept is that I quickly realized that this form of enlightenment is based on something dear to my heart: The Three Stooges.

I never would have guessed that the "Three Treasures" that form the basis of Zen are named Moeavishnu, Larryavishnu and Curlyavishnu. But after reading the literature, there can be no doubt.

If you don't believe me, check out this passage from my handy idiot-targeted volume, *Zen for Beginners* by Judith Blackstone and Zoran Josipovic (Writers and Readers Press, $15.75). They write as follows: "Ma-tsu was the inventor of Hard Zen. Punches, kicks, and even beatings and deafening shouts were his favourite methods. A monk asked Ma-tsu for the primary meaning of Zen. Ma-tsu knocked him to the ground, saying, 'If I don't strike you, the whole country will laugh at me.' ... Once, Master Ma-tsu was lying on the road with his legs outstretched. A monk came by pushing a cart and requested that Ma-tsu draw back his legs so he may pass. 'What is stretched out should not be drawn back again,' said Ma-tsu. 'What goes forward shall not retreat,' replied the monk and pushed the cart over the master's legs. Ma-tsu returned to the monastery hall, grabbed an axe and yelled, 'Let the one who injured me come forward.' Without hesitation, the monk came forward and exposed his neck..."

Not a good idea around a pissed-off ancient Zen master who happens to have an axe (and is widely credited as inventor of the now famous Ronco Neck-Whacker, available for a limited time only through this special TV offer).

Or sample this Stooge-esque story about how a famous Zen Master named Rinzai came in his youth to be enlightened by a master named Huang-Po. (No, I am NOT making this name up for the sake of a cheap scatological pun. That's really the guy's name. You could look it up in any Zen book. We're trying to be serious here. I can't help it if "Huang-po" makes me giggle and think of shit hanging from Banzai trees.)

Anyway, back to the real, not-even-made-up story: "Rinzai went to Huang-po and asked the standard question, 'What is the meaning of Bodhidkarma coming from the West?' Huang-po knocked him to the ground with his stick. Rinzai picked himself up in confusion, not knowing what to make of the answer. He tried twice more but twice more he was hit with the stick and knocked to the ground."

As the story goes, Rinzai returns to his monastery and reports this multiple shit-kicking to the head of his monastery, who tells him, and I quote: " 'How compassionate Huang-po is. He was just trying to relieve you of distress.' Hearing this, Rinzai suddenly had a deep awakening of his original nature. He jumped up and down exclaiming, 'Huang-po's Zen is very simple — there is nothing to it!' At this he punched his teacher three times in the ribs until the teacher said, 'You Scamp!' and kicked him out of the monastery."

So, anyway, Rinzai goes back to Huang-po and says: "It is because of your kindness that I returned so quickly." Then Rinzai tells Huang-po how he had knocked the snot out of his old teacher just for laughs. The text resumes as follows: "Huang-po said, 'What a big mouth your teacher has. The next time I see him, I'll give him a taste of my staff.' Rinzai yelled, 'Wait! I'll give you a taste right now,' and slapped the old master's face. The startled Huang-po said, 'This crazy monk is plucking the tiger's whiskers!' From here on, Rinzai and Huang-po had many sparkling encounters until Rinzai set out on his own, equipped with the Transmission and a repertory of punches and shouts that became his favourite teaching tools."

That is the way of Zen. You must look at things in a new way. You do not look at a face as ugly or beautiful or old or black or white or male or female. You simply see every face as something to be slapped and possibly bonged with a blunt instrument. That is why Zen has been linked to motorcycle maintenance — because just like Moeavishnu, you become very handy at wielding a pipe wrench. Eye-poking, double-face slapping, pie-throwing and, of course, ripping out hunks of Larryavishnu's hair are also important tenets of true Zen-ness.

And so I have found enlightenment. Of course I still have work to do before I can truly call myself a Zen Stooge-Master. I've got to perfect the Eye-Poke Defence, accomplished by holding your hand vertically across the bridge of your nose, thus blocking the thrust of veed fingers. And my nose twist could use work. Although I have perfected the tricky move where you shoulder a shovel and turn abruptly, striking Curlyavishnu in the face with a metallic clang and then spinning to the other side and doing a similar job on an unsuspecting Larryavishnu. It takes work, timing, precision, a straight face and above all, a very hard noggin. But it is worth it if your very soul is at stake.

Of course, I, Burrillavishnu, do not expect a lamebrain like you to understand unless you surrender yourself to Zen and come to me with a Stooge's Mind. And let me boink you with a crowbar. Ow! Nyuk-yuk-yuk. Why I oughta… *POKE*! Take that and that and THAT!

Zen. Like the man said: There's nothing to it. Why take Twelve Steps when Three Stooges will do?

That, my children, is the true path to Nirvana and to becoming a Wise Guy.

OOOOOOoooooommmm. (Soit-an-ly!)

PRINTED AND BOUND
IN BOUCHERVILLE, QUÉBEC, CANADA
BY MARC VEILLEUX IMPRIMEUR INC.
IN APRIL, 1998